LED BY SPIRIT

Led by Spirit

Published by Dolphin Media, LLC

For information, please contact:

Dolphin Media
6275 University Drive, Suite 37
Huntsville, AL 35806

www.dolphinmedia.com

Cover layout and design by Cliff Collier and Jim King.

ISBN: 0-9786664-8-8

Printed in the United States of America

DEDICATION

The book is dedicated to God, Jesus, Mother Mary, all the Saints, the Angelic Realm, the Guides, the Olden Gods and Goddesses, the Fairies, Mother Nature, all the realms of Light Beings, and all who took part in raising me as a child in the physical and the spiritual.

Thank You.

TABLE OF CONTENTS

FOREWORD

The first time I met Sha `La was at a meeting where a handful of psychics were having a little get-together. This has been some fourteen years ago.

We would meet at Dot's house for conversations and testing of our psychic abilities. We would play games in which we would hold up a sealed envelope and tell what was in it. Or sometimes one of us would go into another room, close the door and look through a book or magazine and focus on a picture. Then everyone in the other room would draw a picture of what we were focusing on. It seemed we were always good at games like these. But Sha `La always stood out to be better than most.

We've all had very good experiences from Sha `La but one event stands out above all the rest to me. Several years ago I was having trouble with some earthbound spirits keeping me awake at night. I asked Sha `La if she would drive up to the mountain where I lived and clear the spirits there. It had gotten to the point that a good night's sleep was hard to come by. I wasn't afraid of those spirits but by the same token, no one could sleep if something was banging on the walls at two in the morning or pulling the bed sheets off. Sometimes they would even grab my feet and pull on them trying to drag me out of bed.

Sha `La came up with two more psychic friends and they performed a clearing that lasted for several years. I've seen her do many other spiritual things over the years and I firmly believe she's one of the most gifted people I've ever met.

Bill McCowan, author
"Diary of a Psychic-Visionary"

PREFACE

This book is written for people who like to read, have spiritual gifts or connections with the unknown and for people who are seekers, wanting information on how to develop their own spiritual, or physic gifts.

I have written about much of my life to show people that there is hope in all levels and departments of your life. We can overcome life's lessons through prayer, meditation and listening to our higher selves, and guidance from God, Goddess, Source, or whatever you want to call the Divine that shares our identity of life.

God has said, "I will grant you pardon from past sins. Sin is harming yourself or others through thought, words, actions and deeds."

The first thing is to forgive yourself. Forgive yourself for allowing emotions to build and be stored that harm your body, mind and spirit. Once you let go of these emotions you can live a healthier, happier, wealthier and more productive life and lifestyle. You can feel, and be, the peace that everyone prays for. And therefore the vibration from you can spread throughout the Universe, putting things back in Divine Order.

You will then know through the experience why you are here and what to do about it. Divinity is in all of us; we just have to tap back into that vibration and frequency to become the greater I AM PRESENCE OF THE I AM.

As you will see in this book, I had to overcome a lot of things in my life to even come to this point to write about it. Through a lot of different clearings I had to learn to release not only things in this life but past lives and parallel lives, plus perpendicular lives, that connect into this dimension as a whole.

There will be much more information in my next book on how to perform energy clearings in greater detail to assist you on your journeys to grow and flourish with your desires and needs of today's world. So you can help in making the world a better place for you and your future and for others and their future.

Be good to yourselves and others. And things will work out for you.

Love, Peace, Blessings, and Divine Guidance to All,

~Sha`La

Acknowledgements

I would like to give thanks to the following people for helping me in my life and being there for me during life's struggles and adventures:

Alonzo Middleton and family, for being an uncle and helping my mom.

Antonio, Maria, Evelia Cordero and David Estrada for my beautiful jacket, their light and their many ways of helpfulness.

Attila Ferenczi, for being a friend.

Azalea Hislip, for being an aunt and being there to watch over me when I was a child.

Betty Adami, for being a friend and good listener.

Barbara Bennett, who prayed for me and made beautiful hand made silk and dried flower arrangements for us at Christmas and for her hand crafted items to help with many things we needed for different projects.

Beatrice Middleton, for being an aunt and teacher.

Betty Bottoff, for being a friend and creating ceremonial outfits for me.

Bill Gee, for being my step dad and helping in raising me and my siblings.

Bill Middleton, for helping me from the other side.

Billy Middleton, for being one of my uncles and helping me with Maggie.

Rev. Bill McCowan, for being a friend and helping me through a few things.

Brandon Gee, for being my nephew and helping me in many ways.

Cathy Hoskins Stivers, for being my friend.

Cindy Aycock, for being a friend and assisting me in some of the clearing work.

Collette Hardiman, for the pictures where spirit things manifested.

Charles Davis, for being my dad.

Charlie Davis, for being the grandfather that knew how to pass me through the chairs to keep me alive.

Rev. Deborah (Angel) Taylor, for helping me with the ministry work.

Deborah Hornbuckle, for allowing me to use her facilities to work on clients and taking phenomenal pictures of the channeling sessions.

Doris Sindelar, for being my mother and raising and taking care of me and my three siblings and our children.

Dot Harrison, for being the first person to bring me to Birmingham for work.

Ethan Cruze, for helping me with my animals when I was away.

Ethel Middleton, for being my grandma.

Evy Gewalt, for introducing me to people who needed clearings and readings.

Freda Middleton, for being the youngest aunt and hanging out together in school and assisting in some of the work we do.

George Ortiz, for helping establish the channeling sessions.

Ildiko Varga, for assisting in the clearings and ministry work.

Rev. Irene Simas, for being a friend and creating a space in her home to do the work.

Jackie Wadsworth, for being a friend and assisting me with some things I needed.

Janice Carver, for being a friend and Reiki master.

James and Reba King, for encouraging me to write my book and for publishing it for me.

Jason Druin, for being my wonderful son and teaching me things in our growth process.

Dr. Jerome Williams, in helping me keep my animals healthy.

Jessie James Middleton, for being an uncle and helping my mom.

Rev. Jessie Morgan, for encouraging me to stay with the church ministry.

Jim and Anna Wynn, for being my great-grandparents.

Jimmy Hoskins, for having the courage to keep screaming at me so I could come back from the dead.

Joe Terry, for being a friend and providing me with the van.

Joseph Gee and family, for being my nephew and helping me.

Kristy Gee and family, for being my niece and helping me.

Laurie Walker, for assisting in the ministry work and giving her van to me to travel in.

Rev. Louis Purdue, for being a friend and assisting me in the ministry work.

Louise Stanley and family, for helping my mom with us when we were kids.

Rev. Marie Trump, for helping me understand my gifts and ordaining me.

Nancy Flynn, for helping me in the learning process of the clearing work.

Rev. Martha Meadows, for letting me conduct my first church service at her home.

Mary Renshaw, for her continued support and contributions.

Micah Minor, for being a friend and helping me with paperwork when I needed help.

Patrick "Speaking Wind" Quirk, for being a guiding light.

Patsy Druin, for being my sweet daughter-in-law.

Parlee (Presley) Middleton, for being my wonderful great-grandmother and helping me understand some of the spirit world and believing in me.

Parnell Middleton and family, for being an uncle and teaching me to ride a bike.

Peter Rogers, for being my companion and helping me with many things in life.

Paula Gee, for being a sister in law that helped me through some crises in my life.

Rev. Patricia and Terrell Trott, for being good friends and helping me in many ways and being an assistant in the ministry work.

Randy Helton, for being a friend and doing my hair and giving me Mattie.

Rev. Rudiger Graf, for loaning us his house to hold services.

Ronald Gee, Sr., for being my brother and helping me in many ways.

Ronald Gee, Jr. for being my nephew and helping me in many ways.

Sandra Robbins, for being my sister and helping me in many ways.

Samantha Robbins, for being my niece and helping me in many ways.

Shirley Middleton and family, for being an uncle and helping out.

Theresa Bennett, for being there to do the energy work for me and giving me the laptop computer to write my books.

Theresa Rogers, for being a friend and helping me in various ways.

Thomas Druin, my late husband, my friend and companion, and the father of our son.

Tom Middleton and family, for being an uncle and helping my mom buy my first car.

Tracy Carpenter, for helping in different situations and assisting in angel wing art.

Walter Gee, for being my brother and helping me in many ways.

Walter Middleton, for being my grandfather and assisting me in both worlds.

William F. Robbins III, for being my nephew and helping me with different things while growing up.

William Gee and family, for being my nephew and helping out in many ways.

All cousins and other aunts and uncles who have been a part of my life.

And to everyone I ever knew in assisting me in my journey in life and helping me out. There are so many I can't list them all, including all the wonderful pets I had to love me and keep me going.

Thank You and God Bless.

~ Sha`La

INTRODUCTION

This book is about what God has revealed to me throughout my life. It's a story of me as a child who had no clue of what I was about to get into throughout life and life's adventures. The events in my life were real, but it should be noted that I have used a certain author's license in telling my story. While I have used actual names for some of my friends and relatives, I have used pseudonyms for most others. I have also taken certain liberties with the telling of my story, particularly with the precise sequence of events and who may have said what to whom. Nevertheless, my intention in allowing this narrative to stray from strict non-fiction was always to illuminate more brightly the truth.

CHAPTER 1
∞
THE AWAKENING

I was born September 26, 1954, in Harriman, Tennessee, and taken to my grandpa's, on my father's side, on Wind Rock Mountain.

The first week I was there, about twenty people came to see me; they each picked me up and held me. My mom thought my grandfather knew the people and he thought my mom knew the people. Neither one knew any of these people. One of my mom's brothers told the story one day and my mom told me too; it was the strangest thing. And she couldn't figure out why they would come and do this to me.

By the end of the week I had a lot wrong with me – jaundice, flu, hives, and colic. I was very sick and they could not find the doctor to treat me. So my grandfather took two chairs and put them back to back and put an old horse collar on them and passed me through it nine times and prayed. The next day I was better. I think that was the first time I was exposed to a spell that someone put on me.

When I was about a year old my mom, Doris, and my dad, Charles, disagreed on things and got a divorce. My mom took me to live with my great-grandmother on her side of the family. My first name is the same as hers. We stayed there until I was about four years old. I remembered walking around the house and under the log house because she had a big porch and a root cellar under it.

One day I saw a black snake on one of the chairs that sat on the porch. My grandma said that it came out of the attic to sun, that they were good to keep rats away. So for a long time I was not afraid of snakes, until my mom started telling me about rattle snakes. She told one story about her and her sisters and brothers picking blackberries on a mountain, and a rattlesnake stood up on its tail, straight up in the air, and hissed and danced and then started chasing them down the hill.

She said that they were poisonous. But I remember once I went to the creek down the hill and I saw a snake under the rock; it had a rattle on it, and of course, with kids not understanding much, I called to it like a cat or dog. It just looked at me. I'm glad it decided that I was dumb and didn't know any better. It stayed under the rock. It must have known I didn't know much about snakes. I heard my mom call me and so I just went to the house.

The ghost stories they told were wild; one was about a woman and her baby who were killed down the road and people would see her hitchhiking; and how one of our cousins picked her up thinking she was real and when he got across the bridge she would disappear out of the car.

Then there was the one about the time my mom and her aunt and some of the other kids were out playing on a hill when lighting struck and hit Lenora and she fell to the ground and turned black. One of the kids went and told the family and they came and picked her up and took her in the house and put wet cloths on her and prayed. And they said they looked up and saw a white square form in the ceiling and an angel or some sort of spirit came through and went to her and in a little while she was okay.

I don't remember it but my Aunt Lillian told me, when I was a baby at my great-grandma's, she and the other sister used to give me a lot of catnip tea to make me go to sleep. And then when they wanted my mom to come in the house they pinched me so I would cry and she would have to come in. They could be kind of mean to me.

I remember walking with my mom down the road to a little store, "Milt Jones' store" I think they called it, to buy groceries. In those days they called it trading. It felt like a long way to walk. I think they said it was little over a mile. But even as a child just walking down that road had a certain feel to it. It was good. When we went to visit afterwards I would walk down the road to the little store and wish I could live there again, saying "Hi" to the people that sat out on the porches as they rocked back and forth. Some of them were kin to us. The cool breezes in the air had a special scent and feel every time. It was really good. I always wished my mom had not left there with us.

At some point, when I was between two and three years old, my mom met a Cherokee man and dated him for a while and she had my sister Sandra. I guess they didn't work things out so she took us to Indiana where her mom and dad had moved to get a job at an Army ammunition plant. That was in 1957 in Charlestown, Indiana. There our mother met a man named William; she dated him for a while and married him in 1958.

At this little grey house I remember there only about three rooms, very small. I remember that there were some kids that came to play. I had some toys and a table, a stove, a refrigerator and a doll, a brown teddy bear and a big Panda bear. I loved bears and I would talk to them a lot.

My mom had a small garden; I would play in it sometimes and get in trouble. There was a girl that came to play too. Her name was Sally; she said she lived next door. One day she said to me, "Come to my house."

So I did, but we couldn't get in. She started crying and said her mom and dad were always leaving her. She said we should go through the window, so we did. In a little while she hid behind some clothes and a man and woman came in and looked at me and asked who I was.

I told them and said I came in here with your little girl, Sally.

They looked at each other and said, "We don't have a little girl."

"Yes, you do," I said, "over there."

But she disappeared. I really didn't think that she was a ghost; I thought she was playing a trick on me. But I got in trouble anyway.

A few days later I saw her again. I told her I was mad at her for leaving me standing there and tricking me. She said no one wanted her and she wanted to live with us. So I went to ask my mom if she could live with us.

Mom thought I was making this up. She said if you don't want a whipping you better quit talking about some girl that isn't there. So I was very confused. I could see her but no one else could.

So when I saw her mom and dad come home, I asked them why they didn't want her. They just looked at each other and said they didn't have a child. They didn't know what I was talking about. I was very frustrated. They moved soon after that. I saw the girl in the car when they left and she waved bye at me.

On my first Halloween outing by myself my mom gave me a tissue box. I went around the neighborhood. I remember getting some little candy and a chocolate bar. Then this dog came chasing after me. I was scared and I tried to shoo it away but it kept coming so I took my candy bar and threw the rest of the candy at the dog trying to get away. I was asked "Where's your candy?" so I told them. I don't think they believed me.

William went and found my candy box and brought it home. I think they were thinking I was making the dog up too. If these people and animals were ghosts they manifested to look real to me.

William and my mom would often get into arguments. Some were worse than others. I remember one of them ended in me getting a whipping. My bottom was black and blue when I came to. All I knew at the time was I thought I had caused their fight for some reason. Eventually, mom and William came to an agreement to stay together. I don't remember all the details.

I told my mom I wanted to go back to grandma's – that's what I called my great-grandmother that I was named after. I missed the road and the mountains.

My mom said, "No, I don't really like it there."

I really felt lost all the time. I thought if I get on the train it could take me to Harlan, Kentucky, to my grandma's house.

Ever since that day I was always going to the train track and standing, waiting for the train to take me away in some form. The train was next to Mrs.

Boggs' home which was beside ours. I remember my Aunt Anne grabbing me and pulling me off the track. She told my mom she should move from there or I would be killed.

We moved about a mile and a half away to Spring Street. There was a creek beside it and this house was a little bigger than the other.

In May, 1959, my brother Walter came into this world. He was born with spinal bifida. The doctors gave him up for dead. A lot of people prayed for him and one doctor told my mother to take him to Indianapolis. There was a hospital up there that accepted handicapped children. There were children there that didn't have arms or legs and some had two heads. It was strange. I went there one time. I did not know these type of children existed. After that I wasn't allowed in.

When they brought my brother home he had a cast on him from the waist down. I thought he look like a little doll when he was born. I would sit and look at him and touch his hand and tell him he would be okay.

I asked God to save my little brother. When he went to the hospital sometimes, I prayed for him to live.

I was about five years old, I guess, when I had to go stay with my grandpa and grandma and the other sisters and brothers of my mom. She had six brothers and five sisters, but my grandma said she (my grandmother) had triplets one time and lost them because they were born too soon and she couldn't get to the doctor back then because they lived up in the mountains.

My grandmother's oldest daughter died when she was a little girl with a fever; which left my mom and four younger sisters and six brothers.

One day my grandma was cooking and passing out the food and she told me she wasn't going to feed me. I asked her why. She said I needed to learn to tie my shoes. I told her I didn't know how. My grandpa sat down and tried to show me. My youngest uncle, who was two years older, and my aunt, who was nine months younger than me, walked by with food and laughed and teased me.

I started to tie my shoe but they still would not give me any food. My mom was coming back that night so I told her. But I think that my grandma was just mean; I was afraid of my grandma. I was even afraid to call her grandma, so I called her Freda's mommy. Freda was my youngest aunt. So we talked a lot, got in fights and then became friendly again. Weird.

At this house I met two new neighbors. My sister was walking by then, and she could play with us. Then there was another girl who came to play. There was also an older girl who did not like us and wanted to fight with us and we couldn't understand why.

I remember my Aunt Anne, getting in a fight with them. That's how big the girls were. She took up for us, mainly because we were too little to fight. I guess she was a teenager at that time. She was very pretty.

My Uncle Jesse would baby-sit for us too. I remember I did not want him to give us a bath. I was embarrassed and threw a wet diaper in his face and told him to leave.

He went to the creek and cried. He was about twelve or a little older. I went to tell him I was sorry and slipped on a rock and cut my foot. So he picked me up and carried me to the house where my mom bandaged me up.

I remember a flood that came up to the house and my puppies drowned. We were on the bed trying to reach for the one of them.

Somehow the water washed through the house and carried the puppy and stuff down the creek. It was awful. The water was up to the level of the bed all through the house. I cried for days and even months after that over those puppies. I think there were two.

It took a long while to clean up all the mud and stuff after the flood. We had to stay again with my grandma and grandpa, for a while.

There was a black girl that lived on the hill, but we weren't allowed to play together. They said she had some sort of disease. I guess my mom thought we would catch it. I am not sure what it was.

I met two boys, one named Tony and one named Kevin. Tony had black hair and Kevin was red. Kevin lived with this older couple that adopted him. Tony lived across the street on the hill. His grandfather was our landlord. They would come and hang out with my sister and me. The boys were around my age. At that time, I had been given a toy police car for Christmas; and that summer, a little blow up swimming pool. Tony didn't want me to let Kevin play one day because he said I was his girlfriend. He leaned over and kissed me, my first kiss.

I remember one day Tony told me to not let Kevin come and play and I told Kevin to go home. When I told him, he got upset. He grabbed a toy and tore it up, so I smacked him. My mom chased me around the house and whipped me. I told him I was sorry. He said he just wanted to play and my mom told him he could ride my little police car. Of course, Tony got mad and went home and didn't talk to me for a while.

One time it was storming and I was at the top of the hill next to Kevin's house, he told me to come inside, he said I was supposed to get inside because it was storming and he took me and my sister to the basement. He was afraid of storms.

I was too but I didn't understand a lot at that time. I was only five going on six. My mom was yelling at me and he had locked the basement door and we couldn't get out. I knew we were in trouble and we would get a whipping. My mom finally found us and of course started yelling at us and I got the blame.

But while we were in the basement, we had seen some little lights. I asked Kevin what those lights were. He did not know because there were not any lights in the place. (I think spirit lights were there because we were so scared).

I mentioned them to the woman and my mom. They just looked at each other and dismissed it and my mom took me and my sister home. I guess we lived there a couple of years and then moved to another street, right next to my grandpa and grandma and her brothers and sisters.

At night in this house, I would lie in the bed, my sister and I had to share a bed, and I would see dark shadows floating around the room. I did not think much of it. I thought everyone could see them and it wasn't a big deal. I told my mom. She said just go to sleep. So I just went to sleep.

One day, a terrible storm came and it rained for a long time. When it stopped, on the corner of my house and at my grandparent's house too, it looked like blood was coming up out of the ground.

One of my uncles said somebody was buried there. None of them saw any evidence of a grave. So the family chalked it up as an omen, or a warning. I did not know what either one meant at the time. The dark images still floated around the house. I guess I was the only one who could see them. Then my sister Sandra saw them too. I think we lived on a burial ground or where a war had been fought.

I told everyone again about what I had seen and at that time some of my uncles and my grandfather were there.

"You see the boogie man," one of my uncles said, "and he's going to get you."

Well, I got scared and always hid my head under the covers all the time after that.

We did not have running water. We had to haul water from the mill, and catch rainwater to wash our clothes. We heated pans of water on the stove to do our baths or wash up with. We had to go to an outhouse to use the restroom. We did not have much at all. We were very poor. We even had to stand in line once a month and get food called "commodities", it wasn't very much.

CHAPTER 2
∞
STARTING SCHOOL

My other brother Ronald was born about now (1960) and it was time for me to go to school.

When I was born I had black hair, but when I was one year old, my hair turned blonde and stayed blonde until I was about ten and then it changed colors throughout my life.

We would also go to church; people socialized more back then. There was one man that would come to the house and visit with my family and do some trading with my grandpa. They would trade knives or guns or something. But one day he started bringing pies or cakes to the house and a camera. He told my mom that he wanted to take pictures of me and see if the movie people would make me into another Shirley Temple.

I told her no.

And one day she said to let him take pictures of me.

I said, "Mommy, he is a bad man."

Well, I got into trouble for saying that. (At that time I said things in front of people).

He was shocked.

He said, "Little girl, I just want to take some pictures of your pretty face and beautiful hair."

I just stood there and pouted and cried and asked my mom, "Why didn't he take pictures of the others when they wanted theirs taken?"

I kept seeing a devils face over his face. I did not like him at all. One day I was by the fence and he pulled up and offered me some candy to go with him.

I said no and ran behind the house. I don't know why but I started screaming that he was going to kill me. After that he did not come back. My grandpa said something to my mother that he might try to take kids off and do something to them and not to make me go with him. She said she wouldn't. I don't know what was going on, but I knew inside he was not a good person even though he went to church.

We had to go to church a lot back then. One time my heart skipped a beat and I was sick a lot. I remember mom taking me up to the preacher and he took the Bible and prayed and this light and energy came through the Bible and I was cured. The preacher was amazed.

I remember one day my mom gave our boxer dog to a guy in Louisville, about forty or more miles away from us. The dog's name was Bouncer. I cried when she gave him away. She said we had too many. But I prayed for that dog to be okay because he looked so sad when they took him away.

Well, the next Sunday we went to church and he was sitting at the church door steps waiting on us. He had traveled over forty miles and crossed the Ohio River Bridge to get back to us. So I made mom keep him after that. Of course we had different pets growing up, a lot of dogs, possums, raccoons, groundhogs, cats, goats, a pony, rabbits, a few gold fish, geese, ducks and a few chickens.

I also had a pet pig named him Arnold, until one day I came home and he wasn't in the pin. They had killed him to eat. I cried and cried. I told my mom I was not going to eat any of him and I didn't. I went hungry for several days until she cooked some beans or something else. We had all that and a garden on little more than half an acre. It seems like things were bigger back then.

We would catch the rain water to wash our clothes and water the animals. One day when I was about twelve, I was playing with the washing machine, the old ringer type; well I got my hand caught in it. It did some damage but when I prayed over it, I soon got better.

We also had one old billy-goat who'd always chase me up the fence and then onto the shed. Then I would have to wait until William would come out to get the goat so I could get down. It was wild. I don't know why that goat didn't like me.

One day a distant cousin came to visit. He would do chores to have a place to stay, and do a little work with other people to get his wine.

Well, one day my cousins and I were jumping up and down on this old chair that my mom had thrown out and the bottle of wine came out. So we thought it must taste good because Lenny drinks it. So we all decided to taste it. It was nasty. We all started throwing up. My sister told on us and we got a whipping.

The same thing happened with smoking. My Aunt Lillian smoked all the time. She eventually died of cancer. But when she was at great-grandma's, and our grandpa was there, we saw them chewing tobacco and dipping snuff and smoking a cigarette. So we asked if we could try it and see how it tasted since they did it.

Well they let us. Never again. We all turned green and threw up. I tried to smoke years later but only got choked up.

I would watch my mom's younger brothers and sisters get on the bus in the mornings and get off in the evenings. I thought that must be fun. But when it came my turn to go to school, my mom must have discussed things with someone in the family and she decided to take me back to Harlan to live with my great-grandmother, Parlee, on the mountain where some of my cousins lived.

And I don't know if they were drinking or what but three of them came down the hill and one looked at me and said, "I'm going to get you little girl."

I was so scared I told my mom I was not going to stay. A short time after that my great-grandmother got ill and I guess the cousins and her daughter couldn't take care of her and so she came to live with us.

I didn't go to school until the truant officer came and told my mom she had to send me to school.

She told him since my birthday fell on a certain day and with my great-grandmother being sick she had forgotten.

When I was about eight years old, mom took me down to the beauty parlor and had this woman give me a permanent. I did not like it one bit. I remember it stunk and felt like it fried my hair.

She also took me to the discount store and bought me three dresses. One was blue and white striped, one red and white striped and one green and white striped. I wore them most of the year.

In the winter she let me wear pants under them, and she bought me a snow-suit. It was pink and squeaked when I walked. I was so embarrassed when I first got on the bus. But the first thing my mom said was for me to keep my mouth shut and not to say anything or they might harm you. I sure did not know what that meant. It was later that I learned in the old days if people thought you had Indian blood they would try and kill you, so we were told not to tell anyone about that either. At least that's what we were told. When the Trail of Tears began, some of our ancestors went in the mountains to hide and didn't say they were Indians. They cut their hair and learned how to speak English. So they were always told not to tell who or what they were.

So when I put my first foot on the bus this red headed boy said you look like a rooster. Every one was laughing. I thought that's what my mom meant so I just cried.

One of my uncles told me I had to learn to fight. I didn't know anything at that time.

I went to school and sat where the teacher said to. My first grade teacher was named Mrs. Allen. One day she went out of the room and the boy who sat in front of me turned around and started coloring on my desk. I told him to stop. He laughed and kept doing it and so I smacked him. I was in trouble then because the teacher came in just at that moment. And of course, since

I got in trouble, she called my mom. I told them what happened but no one wanted to listen. The teacher had me stand in the hallway all day and even eat out there. It was raining outside. And I told my mom she made me stand outside while it was raining and then I got in trouble for that. So all through school I got in a lot of trouble.

In a way I liked school. I made a couple of friends, one girl who was taller than anyone in class. Her name was Brenda. She had to have a taller desk than the rest of us. No one wanted to talk to her much, but I did. She wasn't in any of my classes after that, so I thought she had moved. I saw her at a bar after I got in my twenties. She looked almost the same. We talked for a while. I was going to go back and see her several months later but I heard she was murdered. They found her in the trunk of her car. I really was sad for her. I prayed justice would be done for her. She was a nice person.

There was another girl name Heather, and a friend of hers name Adrienne. Heather got mad at Adrienne. One day, we got our lunch because they brought it to the room. Heather told me to put my foot beside hers, so I did. When Adrienne walked by she tripped and her face went into Edwin's food.

Heather just sat there and laughed but I was the one got in trouble for that too, and a whipping when I got home. So the teacher moved me around and I didn't sit by Heather any more. She didn't talk to me much afterwards either. She said I had tripped her friend. I was so upset.

I don't remember too much after that only that it was the same old same old that year.

In the second grade I had Mrs. Willis; she was nice.

I don't remember getting into any major trouble but at recess one day I was playing jump rope and I looked at this one girl and said to her, "I will miss you when you leave."

She said, "What you are talking about?"

I said, "I see you moving. Your dad is going to get a job somewhere else and I see a big truck in front of your house."

They just looked at me funny. The next day the girls said you can't play with us anymore. I asked why and they said because I was a witch. I just started crying; I didn't know what a witch was. They said I was bad.

But within the month the girl moved. And the teacher said that Wendy moved because her father got a job somewhere else.

The whole class just looked at me. One girl said I made her move.

I told my mom, and again she told me not to tell people things. So I quit telling people about what I saw. I got blamed for almost everything if I did it or not.

Because I spoke with a really thick country accent the kids would pick on me. Most of the time I would ignore them and would not answer the teacher because they would laugh at me. I told them I talked this way because we were poor. I did not know what to say. The only thing my uncles would say was to punch them out, that's what they did. They stayed in trouble all the time too.

They would say because we came from the mountains no one liked us. I said let's go back to the mountains. My mom of course said no; she did not like the mountains anymore. She said it was too hard of a life to live there, and too many snakes.

One day I asked my great-grandma, "Can you see the shadows?"

She would say don't speak of them and they won't be able to hear you.

I thought what was the big deal? She said that they were warnings and omens.

She would sit and play some games with us from time to time and she would have us smack her hand and she would grab it and tickle us. She also saw a lizard on the house with a blue tail. She said they were poisonous and she took a butcher knife and stabbed at it, but only cut its tail off. She said it would grow its tail back. She said that if you cut your hair you would lose your glory, so she never cut her hair. She took herbs and spices and made medicine for herself. I tasted it one day, it was nasty. But I guess it worked on whatever it was for at the time.

One day my sister Sandra said she saw a man that looked like the television character Hoss Cartwright standing in the room, so she covered up her head and said to the spirit, "Don't take me; take my sister first."

She always slept in the same bed with me, close to the wall because she was so afraid of seeing things. She just figured if anything was going to get us they would always have to get me first and she would be saved. Crazy.

I told her I would just hand her over to them. I would tease her a lot.

I sat outside most of the time and wished one of the space ships would come and get me and take me out of there I was so depressed.

My grandpa bought great-grandma, which was his mother, a little trailer and set it up in his yard. She liked it better there. She didn't have to put up with anyone.

She had raised about ten kids but only three were hers, the others were from three other wives great-grandpa had. I don't know what happen to all of them. I know a couple of them (his wives) died.

I would ask my great-grandma Parlee if I could stay with her. She said she would let me. But my mom said no. I loved her so much, it seemed like she was the only one willing to talk to me or try to make sense out of what I was seeing or feeling.

I would sneak over to see her when I could; she would tell me some things that she used to see, like ghosts.

My great-grandma said one day there was a man that shot this other man. Well, when it got back to the family of the man who was shot, the man who was named as the shooter was the wrong man. But her husband, my great-grandpa (I never got to meet him, he passed away before I was born) and a few more went to shoot the wrong guy that someone had told on. Anyway, as they were all walking down the road, out from behind a bush stepped my great-grandpa's dead mother and everyone saw her. And she told them out loud to go back; they had the wrong man. It was really so-and-so. They all turned white and dropped their guns and ran home. And the next day they found out she had told the truth. My great-grandma said not everybody could see the ghosts. She would tell about others that different people saw in the mountains.

I remember when I was seven years old, all of my family heard a woman and baby screaming and we all ran out to see what was going on. One of my uncles said he heard a car crash. But there wasn't any. They decided it was an omen or warning that something was going to happen.

A week before that my mom and a couple of my aunts went to a woman they called a fortune teller. And she told them a dark haired brother or sister was going to get killed in a car wreck. The next day my grandmother, her sister, and one of my aunts and cousins were going to another great-grandmother's house because she was sick and they were going to sing for her. We called her 'Mam' and her husband 'Pap'.

Great Aunt Edna dropped everyone off except Aunt Anne and her baby Nick. Anne was about twenty-one and Nick a few months old. They were going to the other two sister's homes to pick them up so they could sing too. But on the way to pick them up the car skidded on the gravel road and turned over and Great Aunt Edna, Aunt Anne and the baby were trapped. Great Aunt Edna got out, but Aunt Anne had a broken neck. The baby was saved. So the pre-warning happened. Everyone was devastated. For a long time a lot of them were angry at Great Aunt Edna for asking Aunt Anne to ride with her to pick the others up. But I think God or Spirit knew what might happen because we all heard it the night before. My mom went into a great depression over that and was not 'with it' for a long while.

Third grade was kind of quiet. I would keep to myself and go sit in the trees and talk to the trees and sometimes fall asleep sitting in them.

One day at school I went to say something to my teacher, who was sitting on the hill with another teacher at recess and somehow she gave me a mean look and I fell backwards and tumbled all the way down to the creek. It was a long ways down. No one came to see about me, they just laughed. I wasn't treated very well by any means.

One time I had to go to the bathroom and the teacher said I couldn't go. I told my mom and my mom came and ask the teacher why she didn't let me go and she lied and said she told me that I could go if I wanted too. So I got a whipping because the teacher said I lied. But I hadn't.

When I turned eleven years old, I was in the fourth grade and Mrs. Rice was our teacher. In the fourth grade I got into some fights because these girls started calling us names. My cousin Dawn was in the same grade, so was Freda and my cousin Donnie, but we were in different rooms. At recess we all played on the swings and sliding boards. One day I got stuck on these bars. So the teacher had to get me down. I was used to turning summersaults on this little bar. And I forgot I had grown that year so I wound up with a big goose egg on my head.

That was the year I found out some people ate paste. This sneaky boy in the class would eat this white paste we had for art. I tasted it too to see why he did it all the time. I thought he was crazy or hungry, because it sure didn't taste good to me.

I told my mom about it and told her that they were more poor than we were, because all he had to eat was paste. I took my lunch to school and I asked my mom if she could make him a sandwich too. She did a few times; I would try to share with him. He didn't really want it.

I continued to see spirits out of the corner of my eyes at school and some-times head on. But I would just pray to God in my head and hope they would go away.

In the fifth grade, I found out my teacher, Mrs. Mullins, liked polk salad. It's a plant that grows almost anywhere. Well she knew we were from the country so she asked me if I knew what it was. I said yes. She said if I could bring some to her, she would give me something for it. So I got a big paper bag and filled it full. She said I will give you a quarter. I thought I was rich. So I asked her every week if she wanted some. Back then you could buy a soda for a nickel and a candy bar for a nickel or penny candy. So since my mom couldn't afford to buy us these things, I bought it with the money I made from the Polk.

Her husband was blown up at the Army ammunition plant that year. Some-one was smoking and dropped a cigarette around the gun powder. Mrs. Mullins had to take off from school for a few months. I really like her though. We had a substitute during that time. I don't even remember her name.

This was the year I won a black and white Polaroid camera. I was very excited. I had entered my name in the Key Market store contest and my name got picked. I took it on a school trip. We went to the zoo.

In Mrs. Mullins's class there was a boy named Harry. He decided he liked me. He was the cutest boy there. I guess the other girls got jealous and started calling me names so I told him I didn't like him and he never spoke to me again all the way through school. Then my uncle got in a fight with his uncle and I wasn't allowed to talk to Harry even though I wanted to so much. I wish I had talked to him but I was so bashful at that time in my life. Later, he told someone he wanted to get married and have ten or more kids. No way could I have done that. I talked to his sisters through the years. Most of them were nice. I told the oldest one I did like Harry but he had met someone else by then.

At different times in my life I felt so alone and I felt no one loved me. In fact, I was very convinced that no one did.

We were kind of forced to go to church and Sunday school. Sometimes I would hear the song 'Jesus Loves Me'. And I would think Jesus was singing it to me. I thought how could Jesus love me, no one else does. Everyone else I knew said I was ugly or they didn't like me for some stupid reason. But I always had a strange feeling maybe He did.

Mr. Godfrey was our sixth grade teacher. He was okay. Dawn and I collected bubblegum cards and records of a music group called "The Monkeys." You could buy a five-cent piece of bubble gum and some cards would be in it and when you got enough cards they would make a puzzle like a poster.

When it rained at recess we were allowed to play with them and make a puzzle from the cards. The other kids had games to play to but there was this one boy I kind of liked named Greg, and he came over where we were and picked up our cards and threw them in the floor. And then he said what were we going to do about it? I threw back my chair and grabbed him and threw him up against the register-heater and hit him and he hit me and I gave him a bloody nose. The teacher came in the room and at first I got in trouble and then he got in trouble and then we both got detention. Later I found out he was a distant cousin of ours. I felt like I was related to everyone. Weird.

During the sixth grade, the family heard a loud noise that sounded like the front awning fell in front of the house. We went outside and didn't see anything. About an hour later we got a call that one of our cousins had been killed in the coal mines. When he was coming out of the mines a boulder fell on top of him.

Each time something like this would happen, we would hear something similar or a rooster would come to the door and crow and we would hear of a death.

I would see or feel things that would happen before they would happen more often at this time of my life. I would tell my great-grandmother sometimes. I would go over when I was allowed to, or sneak over and talk to her and do some chores, like wash her windows or something. She had skin cancer and it went through her nose and then to her brain. My mom was afraid we could catch it. I didn't care at that time. I just wanted to be around her.

I saw different spirits, or ghosts, from time to time. I would even see strange things in the sky; I thought it was space ships, or some weird planes. I would be upset over something and look up and say please beam me up. I had some weird dreams and now I think I was beamed up but sent back.

I couldn't tell any one except my great-grandmother, Parlee. She would listen.

"If you ever see an angel at the foot of the bed, don't answer," she said, "They have come to get you."

So I never said anything to the ones I saw in the house. I would just cover my head and pretend they were not there. I asked Jesus to make them go away. We were made to go to a Baptist church. So I learned about Jesus. I would pray. And I did not do anything wrong that I knew of. I tried to do right by others.

But the kids at school did not like me. I stayed by myself, except for hanging out with my youngest aunt and cousins. I would go and sit in the trees and sleep or sing or just dream unless of course I had to do chores which were everyday things but when I was done I would head for the trees. I never thought a snake or something would attack me. And luckily none did; only a wasp or a hornet chased me a few times.

One of my cousins told me that she felt a hand come out from under her bed and grab hers. Of course they looked and couldn't see anything. And the grown ups told us we watched too much television. I told her I believed her. And sometimes even the grown ups who would tell stuff they saw in the mountains didn't want to believe us. I guess they thought that only stuff like that was in Kentucky and not Indiana. I think that's one reason they moved to Indiana, not just to get work at the Army ammunition plant.

People also said there was a ghost in there too. They found out different though. During the war they had some German soldiers held there and some of them died from something, and so some of their ghosts were there.

One of my uncles, Jesse, got married and moved in this big old house. They all saw ghosts there and it scared all of them. He shot at one; he said the bullet just went in the wall. They moved months afterward because they had to find another place. He said he would hear footsteps up and down the stairs and no one would be there.

Then different members of my family would see things at different places. Down the road about half mile there was an old house. We would see an old lady in the window all the time. People said no one lives there and we would say, "Oh yes they do; we saw an old woman."

One night my Uncle Jesse came running up the road yelling and busted the door down because he said a ghost was after him. He was scared. There were a lot of haunted places in the world.

In seventh grade I started going to high school; that's where things got really rough. I had a lot of different teachers. We had lockers that I could barely get open. I was really frustrated because it took me longer to change books. I walked fast anyway, but now I got into a routine to walk really fast, so I became the fastest walker in school. I passed everyone up going to the classroom. When the bell rang, out the door I went and I would be there for the next class.

I only got in a few fights that year, because they would call me names and tell me they wanted to try me. So they started it, and I finished it. I would try and keep by myself.

Eighth grade was about the same. That year of course I had different teachers and some were not so nice ones. There was one teacher, Miss Frye, who didn't like me from the get go. She would wait until I came to class and then have me clean the dirty dishes from the class before me. It was funny because one time she had us to make and cook biscuits from scratch. She said she was going out of the room for a while and we better have it done when she got back.

So we started and the girls asked me, "Did she say we use baking power or baking soda?"

Well, I forgot or something, and I said soda, and those biscuits were hard as rocks. Well, the teacher came back and was mad. She thought I told them that to be funny. So she made us eat them. I tried to sneak mine down the sink but she caught me and I still had to eat it. It was nasty and hard as a rock.

She failed me that time and I had her each year after that. I told her one day you must like me because I have to keep repeating your class, but she didn't really because everyone had to take it. I still can't cook very well. She sure would like to take all her frustrations out on me. I tried to skip class when I could because no matter how hard I tried she would still give me an F in her class.

During this year, a lot of country music singers came through town. I became really inspired and wrote two songs. They were called "The Country Life" and "Please! Please!"

In ninth grade, we had an additional class where we had to try and make clothes. Mrs. Townsend, Mr. Evans the math teacher, and others, they were even rougher.

Mr. Dixon, the history teacher, was always picking on me. My feelings were easily hurt back then and one day I told him off. Of course, I got in trouble and three days detention.

At that time my Aunt Susie decided to foster this girl name Beth. Well, she got in trouble a lot by smoking in the bathroom. So one day we just decided to leave school for the day and go to the root beer stand and hang out. She had saved up a little money and I borrowed a couple of dollars from great-grandma.

Well, we were going down the hill and she fell in the creek and came up muddy from head to toe. She started crying and the only thing I knew to do was call and get Susie or my mom to come and get us. I went to a lady's house and ask to use her phone, the lady looked at both of us and said I could come in but not her, so Beth started crying. I asked her if Beth could stand by the door. She finally said yes. I called my mom and both she and Susie came to get us. Boy, were they mad. We both got a whipping. We also got suspended from school for three days.

I would play like I missed the bus a lot so I could walk home, because every time I would ride the bus some of the kids would start to pick a fight. So to avoid it when the days were pretty and not so cold I would walk home. It was almost three miles to our house. Along the way I might stop at my cousin's house or if I sold some cinnamon candy at school I would stop at the little store on the way home and buy a candy bar and a Pepsi.

We learned how to make cinnamon candy and we would use muffin pans or the kind of pan that looked like corn for cornbread and put the mixture in it and let it harden and then we'd take it to school in Saran Wrap and sell it for a quarter or nickel or even dime sizes. We would break it up according to the money the kids wanted to spend. After a while the teachers made us quit though.

I remember times when I was making the candy I would hear a voice and they would tell me how to make it a certain way and what colors to blend. I thought it was my imagination at first, but I would see a spirit sometimes and thank them for the info and then they would disappear. I learned that if I told anyone about the spirits they would say I was crazy so I kept my mouth shut and didn't let it bother me.

I saved enough money one time to buy some new shoes and a few clothes for school. When we didn't have food, I would buy a loaf of bread and bologna and then my mom wouldn't be so mad.

About the age of fifteen or sixteen, I had save a little money and started going to wrestling matches. Freda and I were going to become wrestlers but some of the wrestlers discouraged us. When they said why, we were disappointed. They said half the wrestlers were fakes and if you got in with the wrong people they could get you into all kinds of trouble. I also thought one time I'd like to be on the roller derby. But anyway, at that time we were getting these wrestling books. And advertised in it were other kids and people that wanted to have pen pals. So we started writing to some of these people. We would write about the wrestlers and school, a little about our families. I ended up with over 300 pen pals. So most of my money I earned then was for paper, envelopes and stamps. Lucky things were cheaper back then. One boy from Louisville, Kentucky, wrote me a lot. His name was Dean. He was afraid to drive and I had just gotten my drivers license at sixteen and a half. Dean called me a lot during the next couple of years.

Another boy that I wrote to, George, came to see me. He was going to leave for the Army. And I think he was going to be stationed at Fort Knox . So he came and saw me, and while he was there he was going to help my mom give my poodle Elvis a bath and Elvis didn't like his feet touched so he almost ate George up.

(I named my poodle Elvis because in our family tree we found out we were related to Elvis Presley. I think he would have been a fourth or fifth cousin to me. Anyway, I thought he was cool and loved his music).

After George left for the Army he only wrote a few times. I think he was killed in Vietnam because he said he would come and see me when he got back from the war. We all felt something happened to him. I wrote to a lot of people at that time because I felt I needed friends.

About that time one of my aunts' friends killed her lover. Of course, the woman went to prison and her relatives sold her appliances and furniture.

Well, my Aunt Susie got the washer and dryer. Early one morning, Beth and Susie woke up and heard the washer, and since her friend Ivey was there they thought it was her washing clothes. Susie asked her what she was doing washing clothes at three in the morning.

She told Susie she hadn't; that she had been asleep.

Well the next night the same thing happened. So Susie got up cussing Ivey out; she thought Ivey was sleep walking or something. The same thing happened the night after. They finally sat up until three in the morning and it was then they saw a woman standing at the washing machine, starting the washer. It was the dead woman that had been murdered. So they freaked out. Susie wrote a letter to the woman in prison and told her about it. The woman wrote back and said that her partner always washed clothes at a certain time and she guessed she still was. Well they got rid of the washer and the woman left.

Susie had met all kinds of people in her life and she was very intuitive too. She would tell people stuff that would happen to them before it did, and it would happen. She and the others still didn't refer to it as being psychic or clairvoyant. She didn't use the cards until later.

She was soon to get married and move. At that time she married some guy name Hugh, it didn't last long. Then she married a guy name Conrad. That didn't last long either. Then she married Leno; he was from Texas. They lived downtown.

We had some neighbors across the street named the Watt's. They had five children. They stayed there until I was thirteen and then sold their house to an older couple named Coolidge. Before they moved, we would all play games and ball together.

But one day, I remember kicking the ball and it landed on their house, and the woman came out screaming. My mom said the woman called me a bad name, and threatened me for some reason. Well, she and my mom got in a fight and my mom broke Mrs. Watt's finger. It was a big mess because we all lived across the street and the Watts kids had to cross our yard to get on the bus with us and go to school.

One day the Watt's just up and moved. The Coolidge family was from out west, I think Oregon. I thought that was neat. But I did not like them too much because they would buy our rabbits and some goats and kill and eat them.

They sold a little part of their land to Susie and Leno, and they put a trailer on it. Leno would play the guitar and sing for us and taught us some dirty words in Spanish. We all liked him.

One day Mr. and Mrs. Coolidge had a party and invited us all to come over; Susie helped them out a lot. They had made some Applejack wine. We thought it was punch; so all of us kids drank a big cup full. We all started laughing and laughing; and then I saw a lady walk through the house that looked like Mrs. Coolidge. At least I thought it was her until Mrs. Coolidge came in from outside as the other lady walked into the next room. I told Mrs. Coolidge I thought she had just walked into the next room. She said you must have seen my dead mother.

"What?" I asked.

"That's what we are celebrating," she said. "We buried her ashes in the garden yesterday."

Well that scared me and I told my mom. She asked me what was in that cup. I told her it was punch; and then she asked where I got it. I showed her and she started yelling at me and made me go home.

"You're drunk," she said.

"No, I'm not," I said. "And this doesn't taste like Lenny's wine."

"Well, it is wine," she said.

So she thought I saw the spirit of the woman because I drank some of the wine. But after that; days and weeks and months and years, I would see that woman's spirit walk around over there even after they moved and my grandpa and grandma bought the place. Not only did I see her then, but some of the other family members saw her too. They said she really didn't bother them, only when they saw her they were a little scared.

Now my youngest uncle seemed like he was possessed at times. He would think that people were talking about him or something and wanted to shoot them. He shot Freda in the back with a B-B gun, and got in a major fight with his brother Billy Ray.

After that Billy Ray moved out. I didn't know how to pray the spirits over to the other side then. He picked a fight with me and wanted to shoot me but grandma grabbed the shotgun out of his hands.

I thought the old woman's spirit made Hubert act the way he did, wanting to fight with all of us, for no reason. I had seen a show on television where the dead person was there and the people ate food around the body and took on that person's sins so they could move on. When I went to church and found out what all the sins were, I thought we all took on that woman's sins to us and she had been haunting us ever since. So afterwards when someone dies, even to this day, I don't eat or drink anything after the funeral.

It was a rough life. As I got older I got picked on even more, and the kids would snicker when I would read out loud or the teacher would ask me a question and I would answer. After a while, when the teachers would laugh at me too, I would no longer answer or read. I would just bow my head and say nothing. Some of the teachers would get very angry.

When the kids would pick on me too much, I would tell them, look if you don't quit I will fight. Well I spent over half my time in the principle's office because I would end up in a fight. I told them. I warned them and they kept on. So this is what happened - year after year, month after month, and day after day. Every week I was in at least three or more fights. They would not leave me alone, calling me mean names and laughing at my accent.

Every year the carnival would come to town and the year I was sixteen, almost all of the family was there. Someone started a fight with one of my uncles because of his wife. We thought she had been flirting with a worker at the carnival. She was the type.

Anyway, everybody was fighting. A carnival man jumped in and grabbed a stake out of the ground which held down a tent and said, "I am going to kill those (so and so)!"

I grabbed him and said, "You're not going to kill anyone!"

Then he grabbed me and said, "You're coming with me!"

About that time Susie showed up. She was tough and carried a gun. Susie told the man to let me go or else.

He cut my arm and started running. One of my uncles got his guts cut out and they had to sew sheep guts in him. Another uncle was cut within a quarter of an inch of his jugular vein. We were all hurt, but the other guys were too.

The ambulance and police came and loaded them all up to take them to the hospital; and they fought in the ambulance too. Wild.

When we went back to school, all the kids were mad at us. Because of the fight they said there were not going to be any more carnivals to come to town. And there hasn't been since.

Of course they would still pick on us at school, trying us; now more than ever.

I wore a dress to school one day after many years of just wearing pants. But in grade school I wore pants underneath my dresses. I didn't want anyone to see my legs. My uncles used to call me spider legs and granddaddy long legs and say I was ugly. And since I was called a witch, I thought they meant I looked like that mean witch on the Wizard of Oz. Then everyone in the family told me to quit being a tomboy and wear a dress instead of pants all the time. So I did.

Well, that was a big mistake. I tried to be more like the rest of them; but no, a girl jumped on one of my cousins calling her names and making fun of how she walked and my cousin couldn't fight too well. So she came to me to get the girl to quit calling her names and of course the girl and I went to fighting. My dress went up over my head and all the kids were in the hallway started hollering and laughing at me for that. I was so embarrassed. I didn't wear a dress the rest of the year.

I had a few teachers that hated me for no reason, although they said it was because of the family getting in trouble a lot, but we just took up for ourselves. A lot of teachers just did not like my family.

One time one of my teachers made me a couple of dresses, and they were pretty. I found out later she felt sorry for me. But after that fight with the girl, she kind of made fun of me too, so I refused to wear them anymore.

Obviously I got into a lot of fights in school; one day twelve girls jumped on me and my Aunt Freda. The principal and vice-principal wanted to expel us instead of them. But I told them off.

A black girl called us white trash and a white girl came up and stuck a baby bottle in my face and squirted milk on me at lunch time while I was trying to eat. Well, Freda and I started to get back at them. The only thing was they both ran when the teacher came in. My mom and grandma had to come down there and talk to the principals.

A short time after that, near the end of the school year, Freda and I had a class on Friday that was dissolved. That meant we could go to the store or whatever. So we had a little money and decided to go to the laundry mat down the street from the school to get a soda pop.

Well some of the other kids went too, including one boy named Steve. He decided to call us sexy and we thought he was talking dirty to us and Freda pushed him into an on-coming car. He lived; the car barely hit him, but he never said anything to us after that.

We lived a sheltered life and were ignorant on a lot of levels. Of course when we were growing up, my grandma (Freda's mom), told us to never kiss a boy or we'd get pregnant. We believed her. I don't know why they told us dumb stuff. We didn't know any better; we figured, "Why would they lie to us?"

In eleventh grade it was more of the same old stuff. Freda, Dawn and I, along with some other kids, took Driver's Education. That was a strange class because I thought you practiced what you preached. We had this teacher; he would say don't drink and drive. I thought he meant anything. (He didn't say alcohol). He asked all four of us if we wanted something to eat or drink. I told him no because we weren't suppose to drink and drive. He gave me the funniest look.

Each morning he would have us stop at a donut place so he could get a cup of coffee. If you made him spill it while you drove he would take points off the grade. One day it was my turn to be first to drive which also meant I would be the first to see if my driving would make him spill his coffee. When we went down the road there was a turtle in the middle of the road and he said to just run over it. I told him no; I would straddle it, and I did. I told him if I can prevent hitting any animal I would. I asked him if I could pull off the road and take the turtle to the side and he told me no, so I thought he was mean.

One day my mom and William walked down to Mr. and Mrs. Fox's house. They would go to visit from time to time. It was getting a little late so I decided to drive and pick them up. I found mom's keys and rounded up my cousin and sister to ride with me; they decided to sit on the hood and trunk of the old white Chevy she had. I drove slowly and when I got there I told her I was saving them some walking because it looked like rain. Of course that was my excuse to drive the car by myself without her in it yelling at me. All the kids said I drove well but I got a whipping anyway. I think she just liked to whip me. I ask her if she would let me drive back, and she said no.

When I turned eighteen, Dean asked if he and a friend could come over to see us. So I asked my cousin Dawn if she would like to meet his friend and she said she would. Well, they came over with his friend named Phillip and we all went riding around. He had a convertible and Dawn liked to wear wigs for some reason. Well he started driving faster and her wig began to fly off so she had to hold on to it. It was funny. Dean tried to hold my hand and I smacked him; he asked me if he could kiss me and I told him no, that I didn't want to get pregnant. They thought we were crazy. I told him my grandma and aunt said if we kissed a boy we would get pregnant. (I was stupid back then on many things; I thought they had told the truth).

So they decided to stop at this little restaurant in town. Well as soon as we ordered our food, Dawn's dad shows up in his pajamas, cussing us out. Dawn started crying and got in her dad's car and left. So the boys took me home. When we got there Phillip said he like me and Dean liked my sister. They came only a few times to see us and just talk.

When I got to the twelfth grade in 1973, the girls made more fun of us because they dressed more feminine while Freda and I dressed more like tomboys. Like I said, mom started me in school late. Freda quit but my mom made me keep going. I didn't go to the prom; the other kids told me that I was not welcome and none of the boys would ask me to go.

One night before I graduated, our family went to this country music show in Otisco, Indiana. There I met Tom. He was with some other guys. Naomi, one of my cousins, told me to look over at those guys.

I said, "Yeah, one is cute."

She said she was going to go over there and tell him what I said.

I told her no. But she did anyway.

So he came over, and asked me if he could sit by me. I told him only if he wasn't shorter than me. So I stood up and saw we were about the same height. He was about one or two inches taller than me. I still tried to get out of letting him sit there because my mom was giving me a dirty look. He asked me if he could he call me to go on a date. I told him to ask my mom; I thought she would say no. But she said yes. So he started calling me. It was almost time for me to graduate.

In May 1973, my cousin Dawn and I, and of course, the rest of the class, graduated. Dawn took off with this guy Kirk and got married right away, and moved to Kentucky.

CHAPTER 3
∞
PROPOSALS

My mother's brother worked on cars and would go to the auction from time to time, so my mom gave him some money to get me a car.

My first car turned out to be a 1967 Pontiac. It was white and I put a sticker on it that said 'Giddy-Up-n-Go'. And I thought it was fast.

Right before Dawn moved she received a white Catalina for graduating.

I got a job at a drive-in restaurant as a car-hop. I didn't like it. The manager was not a likeable guy. I was cutting off the tops of strawberries and throwing away the rotten ones and he told me to mix them up with the good ones and put glaze on them. I told him that would make people sick. He said to put the glaze on anyway. It wasn't the best paying job; people would not give us any tips; they would rather throw the trays across the parking lot. I just figured I was jinxed in life. It seemed like nothing went well for me.

Then, to top it off, my mom told Phillip and Dean where I was working and they rode down on a chopper motorcycle and Phillip asked me to marry him and go live on this little island in the middle of the river. I told him he was crazy. After they talked for a while, I found out he belonged to some "Grim Reapers" motorcycle club. I told him "NO!"

It was a good thing I did because Dexter, Tom's little brother, told me a long time after that he and Tom had been sitting across the street watching me and if I had kissed the guy or got on that motorcycle he was going to shoot me. I quit the car-hop job soon after that. Freda and I then found jobs at a ceramic place trimming statues.

I worked there for a few weeks. Tom became jealous because Freda wanted me to sit with her while she talked to one of the guys; he said his name was Jesus but pronounced it differently. They were from Mexico. We were also waiting for the supervisor's husband to come pick her up as well.

Well, Tom was drinking and came down there. I told him what was going on and he got mad and ran his car into a semi-truck tire. It mashed up the front fender. He followed us home but I was so nervous I ran a red light and so did he and almost got hit again. I tried to break up with him. He begged me to keep seeing him. I did.

My mom had told me I probably needed to keep him because no one else would have me. She was always saying stupid stuff to me, lowering my self-esteem more and more. I prayed to get away from her at times. But she was good too. She had a hard life.

When Tom decided to take me over to his house to meet his parents, it was scary. I had a bad feeling; I should have listened to my gut instincts; I didn't know much about the world and was a little scared.

One reason was because when I was eleven years old, I decided to run away, and I felt I needed to tell my great-grandma. So I went to tell her about wanting to run away because mom was whipping me a lot - it seemed like mom went a little nutty when Aunt Anne got killed. But great-grandma told me not to go because it was dangerous out there. She and my grandpa both said there was no place like home.

Mom had me scared; none of the other girls would run away with me. Mom said if I ran away she would send me to a girl's camp where they were meaner than she was. I should have gone there first and then run away. But then I figured I would be on the most wanted list or something. I watched too much TV. I was afraid of what would happen to me on my own. But I should have chanced it even though I was very nervous and naive at that time.

I still wrote to a few of my pen pals and kept their letters in the trunk of my car. One day, while he was driving my car, Tom had a flat tire. And it was raining and all the letters I had saved ended up on the side of the freeway. He threw all of them on the side of the road and it was a wonder that the cops didn't find me and give me a ticket for littering. (I wanted to run away then too, but dumb me, I didn't). He said he couldn't get the tire out; he had to move the letters to get to it and once the wind blew them out of the trunk they were too wet to put back in the car.

I didn't like to meet too many people because I saw ghosts around them and I didn't know what to say to Tom's family. What if I saw a ghost; what would I say or do? Well, I decided to ignore all of them, and pretended to be like other normal people who didn't see things. Well, I met them and his mother did not like me at all. We ate dinner and she asked me all kinds of questions.

I hated to tell her we were poor; I know she knew by the way I acted.

On the way home Tom decided he had to go to the bathroom.

Well he pulls over to the side of the road and walked behind the car. Then I heard this knocking sound. I thought he was trying to scare me. He came running back to the car and jumped in.

"Did you hear that?" he asked.

I said, "Yeah, you're trying to scare me."

He said, "No, I'm not!"

Then it sounded like somebody was in the trunk. The horrible sound came from the back of the car. We looked at each other and he took off really fast.

The sound finally stopped by the time we almost got to my house. He and I were really scared.

We told my mom about it. Tom asked her if he could sleep on the couch; that he was too scared to go home. She thought we were making it up. He told her to go out there and see for herself. She didn't; and, she let him stay the night on the couch. But the next day, there were four women missing. The authorities later found them cut up in the field where we heard the noises. Of course, they all said what we heard was a warning. That road has always been scary. They found the man that killed them. He lived down the road from where we heard the sounds and he had some of their body parts in deep freezers. Then I really got scared, and didn't know what to do.

Later, whenever I had to drive that road, I would pray or go the long way around to get home. Sometimes I would see people walking and they would disappear in a few seconds.

Well Tom and I married April 29, 1974, and soon afterwards we were having arguments over stupid things. I was going to leave but he wouldn't let me. One day I was watching some soap opera and when the woman had a baby their marriage was better. So I was outside that night and I prayed to have a baby. Soon after that I was sick. I thought I had the flu, but my mother-in-law said I was pregnant. I told her it couldn't be, that I must have the flu. She told me to go see the doctor. I hated to go to the doctor because they never believed me when I told them I didn't feel good. They would say I was imagining this. So I hated doctors. Anyway, I finally went and of course he said I was pregnant. I was doing pretty well except for morning sickness, and then that became all-day sickness. Every day, when I went to cosmetology school, I would throw up because the permanent solution was so strong. Back then I could not handle it so I quit.

I worked various jobs, like the tennis shoe factory. We drove fifty miles one way. There and back was two hundred miles a day because Tom worked there too but we had different shifts. I also worked at an ice cream store, but the man kept making passes at me so I quit. I did not know back then that you could sue people for sexual harassment. No one told me anything.

Tom finally got a job as a mechanic and I got a job at the fuel desk at a Mobil truck stop. All our jobs paid anywhere from one dollar to three dollars an hour, poor times for sure. We were both working and struggling. I worked only a few weeks or months at each job for a while.

There were some places where I worked overtime, and I was tired all the time. That's when I chose to ignore the noises and filmy gauze stuff that I saw floating in the air.

I went to the doctor and he gave me some tranquilizers to sleep and diet pills, or pep pills, to stay awake when I worked. I just quit the different times when it would happen.

When I went to work at the fuel desk of a truck stop, the guys that worked there were my age or a little younger. I was nineteen; they knew I didn't know much about life and the world, so they would play stupid tricks on me and tease me.

One day two truck drivers came in and the boys were blowing up condoms and flying them around the room. I though they were balloons; they were laughing so hard. I thought they were just messing around. The drivers told me to come over there; they needed to educate me about life. Well they told me that they were Amish and had run away, and then told me why.

And then they asked, "Do you know what those boys are doing?"

And I said, "Goofing around, flying balloons around, I guess."

When they told me what they were really doing, I got so mad I chased one of the boys around the truck stop; I was going to whip him good.

After I told my boss about it, different people told me things about life and the people in it. I was shocked.

My great-grandma became more ill and I went to see her.

"I saw you at the end of my bed last night," she told me, "but you would not speak to me.

"What was going on?" she asked.

I told her I hadn't been there. But she insisted she saw me standing there, that a light had been around me. Then it hit me she saw an angel and thought it was me. I knew then she was almost ready to die. I was so upset I started to cry. I told her I would be back, that I had to go outside and cry. After a while I went back in and talked with her for a little while and told her I would come back to see her and that I loved her. I hugged her and left.

A day or so went by and our clock went crazy like it was falling apart. I asked Tom what was going on. Then it hit me, grandma was dying. I went up there and the ambulance was already there. They were putting her in it.

She was screaming, "Don't let them take me!"

I was in shock and trying to get them to let her out of the ambulance. Tom and my mom pulled me away, I was crying so hard. I prayed she would live to see Jason born, but she didn't. She died in November, 1974. I had just turned twenty-two months before.

On December 15, I gave birth to a boy, Jason Lee. We had a hard time. He weighed ten pounds and four ounces; and I was really sick. We were in the hospital for almost three weeks. He was a "blue baby" and almost died. He was also two weeks late and couldn't breathe well and had colic and jaundice. They had to keep him in an incubator. My bladder had fallen and they had to dilate my bladder every day and use a catheter.

There was one nurse who would take Jason out of the incubator every day for a little while and rock him every day. When they asked me what his name was going to be, I told them Jason Lee. All the other women having babies there at that time named their babies the same thing – Jason. They would have different middle and last names, but the first name was the same, it felt weird. I asked the nurse why all of these people wanted to name their babies after mine. She said they just liked the name.

When we got home we put Jason's bed next to ours. The back bedroom was always cold; at the time I didn't know why. I guess it was better that I didn't know back then. Tom just said something was wrong with the furnace.

After Jason was born I went to visit my mom; after talking with her for awhile, I walked over to my great-grandma's house and started up the steps. My mom started yelling at me.

I turned around and asked, "Why are yelling at me?"

She said, "What are you doing?"

I told her I was going to show Jason to Grandma.

Mom came toward me. At the same time, she told Tom to go after me, because he was in the house talking to my brother. He didn't know what I was doing either. So they both came over.

I just stood there and looked at them and she said softly, "Grandma died; you know that."

Inside, I felt like, "No, I did not know that."

I was in so much shock or denial I just sat on the steps and cried and cried.

Tom finally led me to the car and we went home. After that, every time the clock would act up, we knew someone was going to die. And within a few minutes to an hour we would get a phone call and find out that someone had died.

One night something woke me up. I saw a weird white cloud thing hovering over my baby. I tried waking Tom up, but he wouldn't budge.

So I prayed and told it, "You're not taking him."

It finally went away. I had to rock Jason to sleep every day and night. He and I were sick for months. I finally got a new doctor and he got us straightened out.

Then one other night I woke up to see this ghost lying on top of me. It looked like a man dressed from medieval times or like some Musketeer-type person. I started screaming and screaming. Tom was lying beside me but didn't hear me. I started praying and praying. And I guess GOD or Jesus took it away. I sat up the rest of the night and when Tom finally woke up, I asked him why he didn't wake up earlier.

He said he didn't hear me. I thought he was lying. I was getting afraid of the trailer. I told him this place was haunted. He said I was just dreaming.

One day, while I was still sick from giving birth, Tom said he was going somewhere with a friend of his. So he kissed me and went out the door. I looked out the window and saw his friend and two women in the pick-up truck. He said there was no one in the truck but him and Jimmy. I don't know if they were ghost women or what. It was awful. I told myself at that time I would never have another child. I loved my son, but I was not well enough to have another, not physically or emotionally, or mentally anyway.

I went back to work and Tom's mother and my mother took turns watching Jason while we worked. At first I went back to the truck stop. They had an assistant manager by then but he couldn't stand me and I didn't like him very much either. So Bruce, the boss, put us on different shifts.

The assistant manager had a daughter who wanted to work there so he told Bruce to hire her. So one shift later there she was and it wasn't long before my hours were dropped back while hers were increased. Then some paperwork was altered and she accused me of having taken twenty dollars from the drawer. (Although I believed she might have actually taken the money). I told the boss about my suspicions but he said he didn't know what to do.

"Well, since you are letting them take over," I told him, "I will just quit before I whip her and get in trouble anyway."

He said he hated that this was happening but he would write me a letter saying I was a good worker so I could get a job.

I went to the other truck stop and the lady manager there knew Bruce and she called him and he said I was a good worker and she hired me.

I worked there for a few months and found out that the corporate office was going to go bankrupt and close. Before I left there, I noticed several ghosts that walked around that place. Sometimes I would see something and it would disappear; some of the other people there confirmed what I saw because they saw them too.

Times were hard and Tom and I argued about really stupid things and the lies his mother told. We both worked different shifts and were always tired. We had arguments off and on, usually over petty things, but for young people it was major in ways and we did not have any one to counsel with us. We did go to a counselor one time and they just didn't do any good. The person would just sit there and then kind of fall asleep. If Tom became too angry he would tear up things.

One day I was giving Jason a bath; I had him on the counter top and I reached over to get the soap and something jerked him out from under my arm and he dropped to the floor. I panicked. Tom came running to the bathroom. I had already picked Jason up and his breath was knocked out of him. I was screaming; Tom thought I did it on purpose. I told him what had happened. He grabbed Jason and ran to his mother's and told me not to touch him. Of course I was a nervous wreck.

We took him to the doctor and he said Jason was all right. But I think one of the ghosts grabbed him away from me. It was strange. I had seen a strange image in the mirror but dismissed it. I thought it was my imagination.

Weird things happened over the next three years. I told Tom I was going to join this health spa. I thought maybe he would stop ignoring me if I got my figure back. He told me to go ahead, so I did.

At the health spa I met this woman name Lucy. She had three children and would talk to me and invited us over to their house to socialize. Since I didn't really have any friends, I guess I adopted Lucy to be one.

My cousin and I grew up together and she had married and moved away and so had my youngest aunt. It seem like all of us had gone our separate ways. Sometimes Tom and I would go and visit my family that was in Indiana, and we would visit some of his. We even visited my dad in Tennessee and some of his brothers and one of his sisters.

Then I got a part time job at a school in the filing department and met a woman name Millie and she was like a friend too. So Lucy and Millie were the only two that would talk to me about life and things.

It was during this time that Tom and I separated for the first time. I told him I was not living with a bunch of ghosts.

One day, with Jason standing beside me, I began packing to go see my dad in Tennessee. We looked around and we saw a man standing by the coffee table. He looked like a Colonel or General in the Confederate Army. Jason said that was the same man he saw on a horse the other day. He was halfway in the hallway and halfway in the bathroom. After he said that, the man disappeared. That's when I realized why Jason didn't want to sleep back there. I was shocked. Jason was only three or four at the time. So I thought, oh no, he's like me and sees stuff too. I didn't know what to say, or how to explain it to him.

I told Tom and he said he thought something like that was going on. I told him we needed to move but he wouldn't at the time. So I stayed for a little while longer.

I began baby-sitting for this woman's twelve year old daughter. Her name was Nina. She would watch Jason for me while I hung some clothes out on the clothesline.

One day, while I was hanging up the clothes outside, she and Jason came running out hollering at me, saying there was an old witch sitting on the couch. Jason sounded like he was in a panic. I thought one of the older women had come in to see us from the neighborhood. Sometimes one would just come over to visit in the small town we lived in. But they both said no; it was an ugly old woman. Jason called her a witch. He was about four at the time.

I told Tom we need to go to a church to find someone that could help us. We went to several different denominations looking for answers but no one seemed to have any. One preacher said I guess you have a gift. I told him I did not worship devils; that I was afraid of them, and that I only prayed to God.

I was going to different churches to find THE ONE, but I never found it. I was very discouraged. I even felt like life was a big lie. There was nothing else. I told Tom we needed to move but he wouldn't.

My intuition or gift or whatever you want to call it kept coming. I would see more and have more visions. A lot of them I did not like. So I moved out to an apartment. Later Tom moved in with me. He said the ghost was out to get him. I told him we couldn't go back. (I felt like I was in a twilight zone or a nightmare all the time. While we lived in the apartment I saw images walking through the wall at times. I grew so tired of seeing these things all the time).

Tom and I still had problems. We had our arguments and I would tell some people I had met and they talked me in to thinking all kinds of stuff and that I should get a divorce.

One day Tom was working on his motorcycle. He asked his little brother to hold a part that was to be put into the machine but he dropped it on the ground. I figured he would pick it up, dust it off and put it in. But Tom got so mad he picked up a sledge hammer and beat the motorcycle all to pieces.

Tom's sister Claire was getting a divorce and she moved in with us. Big mistake. She ran our phone bill up several hundred dollars talking to some guy in

Kentucky. So he and I also had arguments over that. I think if we could have just talked to a professional counselor (one that didn't fall asleep) we might have worked things out.

One day I took one of my cousins to Kentucky and a rain storm came up. It rained so hard I couldn't see the road, so we were late getting home. When we finally arrived, Tom chased me around the cars with a gun. I had him locked up at the time. I called and told his mom and she got him out of jail the next day. People around me said he would come after me first and then probably kill himself. I was so tired of the emotional rollercoaster ride I told him to go ahead.

It seemed like my life was a vicious circle of lies, fears and chaos. His mother was always saying negative things about me and then other people would tell lies about me. Being very naive and gullible in those days, I didn't know which end was up half the time. And seeing the ghosts just added to it.

One day, after some people kept saying I was crazy, I just packed up my son's stuff and took him to my mom's and left. I was going to drive my car off the bridge and drown myself because I couldn't swim. I figured I would just do that and end the chaos in my life.

CHAPTER 4
∞
I MEET JESUS

So as I was driving to the bridge, I had to cross a creek before I got to the town where the river was. As I crossed the bridge over the creek, I heard a loud voice say, "Turn around; I love you."

I jumped. I looked behind the seat and saw no one there. I heard it again, so I pulled over. And then I saw a golden image.

I asked, "Who are you, speaking to me like this?"

The voice said, "Jesus".

I said, "Are you *the* Jesus in the Bible and is there *really* a Jesus?"

He said, "Yes."

And then I asked, "What church *am* I suppose to go to? Which one is THE ONE?"

He said, "None of them."

I asked, "Am I crazy?"

"No," He said, "Turn around and I will lead you, and show you many things."

I said, "I want to know it all, all the truth. I see things and no one can help me; and grandma died."

And I went on and on. And finally I said, "I want to know everything."

My head was filled with so many questions. Back then I never heard the words psychic, clairvoyant or any term except fortune teller. But He said for me to go see a fortune teller.

I said, "In the Bible it says not to see them."

"There is one you must see," He said. "She will help you understand some things."

I asked him where this person was and He said I would find her.

Well, I remembered my mom and her sisters went to that old woman when I was seven, so I went to my mom's and I asked her where the woman was.

"You stay away from her," she said. "She warned about Anne and you don't need to go there."

Well I was upset. I didn't keep up with a lot of my family, but I did know my Aunt Susie. I wanted to see her but thought she was away. She had been out of state for a while then traveling with her new husband. She didn't keep them long. She had told me one day that she would marry seven times in her life. I thought that was bizarre. Maybe she just wasn't satisfied or just wanted more husbands than anyone else. I didn't know. I also didn't know she was back in town and remarried.

Well, I was backing out of my mom's drive way with Jason when my cousin Tonya pulled in behind me.

She said, "Hey, guess who's back in town!"

I asked her who and she said Susie. When we were kids, Susie would have us make phone calls to her boyfriends and give us a quarter. She was kind of a wild child. But everyone liked and loved her.

I told Tonya to take me to her. So I followed Tonya to Susie's house. She and Leno had moved away and eventually divorced; then she had married a man name Larry. Later, she thought Larry was cheating on her, so she divorced him too.

I found her, a friend of hers and two guys remodeling this duplex. She told me she and her husband had divorced, and that she now had another one who was Mexican. His name was Julio. I introduced myself and Susie started telling us a little about her adventures. After a while, I got around to asking her what happened to the fortune teller that she used to see. She asked why. I told her I would like to see what she could tell me. I was afraid to tell Susie what had happened to me and Tom for fear that she would think I was crazy or something.

She said, "Well, she died and left me her powers."

I said, "She what?"

Susie said, "I went to see her before I left to travel and she told me that when I came back she would have left me something and she would have moved down the road. Well, I was playing cards with a group of women. And Larry was with the men in a business meeting. I started seeing things about the women and their families and telling them what I saw and felt. And they said I was right.

"So when I came back here, I went to see the fortune teller and she had moved to the grave yard down the street. The neighbors had burned her house down with her in it. The neighbors said she was a witch because she read the cards."

I wondered how come Jesus had not told me this. Then I thought, well maybe He meant for me to come and see Aunt Susie.

So I asked her, "Well, will you read for me?"

She said, "Why?"

"I just want to know what you can tell me," I said.

She said, "Bring me two dollars on the weekend and I will read for you. But there is another woman that reads named Myrtle, and I will give you her number so you can go see her."

Well, I was so dumb I didn't know that there were other people that could do this. So I prayed about it and felt a strong urge to call Myrtle. So I went and paid her twenty dollars and she took several hours with me and told me what had happened in my life and that Jesus sent me, and told me about things that only I knew, things I never told others. At first I thought Susie called and told her what to say, but Susie did not know a lot of what was happening in my life at that time, so she couldn't have. She told me the future to a degree, some things I could not fathom. She told me about Smokey. That he was an Indian guide for me and I was to talk to him and that he would help me. She also told me that one day I could do healings and would become a minister.

This was in 1978 and I was ordained by her in 1990. It took that long but it did happen. She became a mentor. I called her my second mom. When I felt I needed to go to her, she told me about my gifts and how to use some of them. I felt like someone in the world finally knew me and knew how to help me. Jesus would appear to me and I would hear his voice when I chose to listen. I went in a lot of depression because Tom and his family would put me through stuff. They would put doubts in my head and we argued.

Of course, there were people who would say, "You are not dealing with God. You are dealing with the devil."

And I would say no, and then I would get confused again, even though I found out that Tom's mother was supposedly wishing us bad luck and sending us negativity a lot because she didn't like me and saying she wished I hadn't married Tom. With her attitude I sometimes wish that I hadn't either. But I have my beautiful son; that's what matters to me.

I would go to the spa to meet Lucy. We would be there about the same time and talked a lot. She would invite me over to her house. Tom told me that maybe I needed a friend. So he let me go over there and spend a little time with her. We drank coffee and the kids would play and just talk about our families.

She and her husband started having trouble. She felt he was cheating on her and she asked me to help her move. Eventually she moved to Frankfort, Kentucky.

Finally, I got so tired of things with my life and marriage, I asked Tom for a divorce. He only wanted to believe his negative mother.

First, I went to Lucy's apartment in Kentucky. But Tom found us. I don't know how, but he did. I guess he just asked for her name. He threatened us. He said if I didn't come back he would hurt Lucy.

So I went back; I went back to the trailer with him. I couldn't handle it, so I went and borrowed money and got an apartment. There was a lot going on with people around us, family, work and we were stressed out to the max. I decided to leave again. This time we decided to get a divorce.

Later I met a guy named Arthur. This was a huge mistake but I was still naive and gullible for some stupid reason. He ended up being a major jerk. We moved to Lawrenceburg, Kentucky. Lucy lived about ten miles from there. I worked three jobs, two during the week and one on the weekend. There were no days off. I found out later that Arthur hurt himself on purpose to get out of working and so he could party with the neighbors.

I went to work at a pizza place in Frankfort. In the back they had a bar and I was a waitress. The bartenders taught me how to make drinks and then I would experiment on my own and create different drinks. I should have patented them, but again I didn't know how. So I did bartending too, kind of a self-taught one.

One night I was driving home and it smelled like my car was on fire. Well, it was all the smoke in my hair. It was awful.

While I was in Kentucky, I saw strange images on and off. I worked three different jobs so I thought I was hallucinating sometimes. I would just pray and hope for the best. I didn't know who to talk to since my grandmother passed away. And it seemed that I could not reach Myrtle.

CHAPTER 5
DARKNESS APPROACHES

When I let Arthur talk me into going to Florida with him, I thought maybe a new start would change things. I hadn't been there yet and it sounded exciting, but a part of me said no while the other part said yes. I went.

We moved into this little white two-bedroom house. Arthur's sister lived about twelve miles away but that was close enough for us to visit. He was supposed to work in construction with his brother-in-law. Well, all of that turned out to be a lie.

While we were in Florida, I got a job at a local food mart. At first, the people were friendly and helpful. Then after about a month everyone started acting weird. Once when I went toward the kitchen, I saw a woman hanging in there. So I did a lot of praying. I told Arthur we needed to move.

I found out he was again playing like he was hurt and going to the neighbors in that town like he had in the others, smoking dope and doing who knows what all.

He took Jason with him over to the neighbors and Jason told on him. But before Jason told on him, Arthur tried to bribe Jason by taking him to his sisters and telling him we would give him a pony of his own.

Jason would tell me that he had a pony and the people wanted to keep him. Tom came and visited but on the way he got a speeding ticket in Georgia and they threatened to put him on a chain-gang. That whole episode was weird.

He also said he saw ghosts walking on the side of the road with chains on them. He had driven down for Jason's sixth birthday and gave him a Christmas present since it was only ten days away from his birthday.

Arthur and I got in a big argument and he started the augment so he could leave. He left us stranded. I worked two shifts for the same company, but different stores at different hours. I did not quite understand what was happening because I was so tired. I had some girl watching Jason for me for a little while then I had to take him to the second job with me and he would sleep in the office on a blanket while I worked. I couldn't seem to get enough money to leave the place. No one we knew back home answered my letters or phone calls.

One day my cousin Tonya came down on a bus with her son Joel; he was only three. Jason was going to start kindergarten. I told her she could watch Jason while I worked and then maybe we could go somewhere else. The house was starting to literally fall down and I told my boss and she told us where I could rent a trailer. So we moved in to the trailer. It was on a sandy dirt road. I put Jason into kindergarten. It got to where Tonya would oversleep and Jason would miss the bus. So I had a lot of trouble with the school.

We had a sliding glass door on the tub and every time Tonya would get in the tub to shower the door would fall in on her. Several times I had to go in and pick it up off of her. We just thought it was loose or something.

Then she said she saw a man standing there watching her one day. When she screamed, he disappeared.

She, Joel, Jason, her poodle Clyde, and I all slept in my king-size bed that night.

I remembered Susie told me to put a cross in the Bible and say the Lord's Prayer when weird things happened. So I open the Bible and prayed. I laid the cross in it open and lit a candle – a seven-day candle.

We were all in bed when we heard footsteps walking up the hall. We saw an image of a man and it went in the living room and blew out the candle. It threw the cross in the floor and slammed the Bible shut.

We did a lot of praying that night. I don't think we got any sleep. We tried to call Susie and my mom and then her mom the next day. But we couldn't get through. So when I had to work two shifts, I took Tonya and the boys to work with me at night. I would make the kids a pallet on the floor in the office and they would go to sleep. I guess we had this weird thought that ghosts only came out at night.

Good thing I didn't know too much back then. I don't know what I'd have done. We met some guys that were interested in us as girlfriends, or so I thought, but it turned out they were out to kill us.

The first person I made friends with was a local cop; Jake, he was nice and would come into the store and just talk to me. He told me to watch some of the people that came in, that they would buy a bottle of cheap wine and a can of dog or cat food to eat themselves.

"You're kidding me," I said.

"Ask them."

So about 6:30 that morning after I had opened, and Jake had dropped by, this person came in the store still dressed in their pajamas and house shoes. They went and picked out the wine and the can of dog food. So when they came to the counter to check out I asked them what kind of dog they had.

They said, "I don't have a dog; this is for me."

"Why?"

"It's got a lot of vitamins," they said, "and it's better for you than regular food."

I was shocked. Finally, I just said, "Oh well."

I mean, what could you really say? I finally decided these people were crazy or just alcoholics that didn't know better.

Jake looked at me and said, "See, I told you."

"You probably put them up to say that."

But every morning after that, several people started coming in and buying wine and dog food.

Working two jobs, I didn't have any time to date. I was trying to get enough money to get out of that town. But every time I tried to save money I would have to spend it on something.

Different people would talk to us. I tried to get a telephone but they said they couldn't put one in because we hadn't live there long enough.

I asked the guy we rented from about the trailer. He said someone had hung themselves in the bathroom. He couldn't keep people there. I was so angry, if I had known that before we moved in I would not have rented it.

One day at the store, Tonya met Sam. He was a nice person. He said he was going to loan us his shotgun. He also said that since the phone company would not let us have a phone he would find us a citizen's band radio.

In the mean time, we had written several letters to Tonya's mom and mine. I had even written to Tom. But still there was no answer from anyone. I put the phone number to the store in the letters but no one called or wrote. Everyday and night we would call Indiana to talk to someone. But we couldn't get through. I figured something was wrong or they just didn't care.

The kids got sick and couldn't go to the bathroom, so we made a doctor's appointment. We went and were the last ones there. We overheard the doctor and the nurse talking about how to give all of us a shot and kill us. They said after the shot took its toll on us they would bury us in the woods where no one could find us.

Obviously we left without going into the next room.

I told Jake the next day at the store; he came over that evening and said he would fix them. He put his hand over the stomachs of both children, balancing out the energy around third chakra of the solar plexus. Then they went to the bathroom. He thought we might have mistaken what the doctor had said. I was sure we hadn't. That place was getting weirder by the day.

Arthur's sister gave Arthur an Ouija board, and he had left it in some stuff. When we moved it was in one of my boxes. I don't know how it had gotten there. Well, when Tonya saw it she wanted to play with it. I told her I didn't know how; I had never seen or played with one before. She said she had seen somebody work with it one time.

Well, Jake and some other guy came over and they all wanted to play with it. When we started, Jake and his friend thought the whole thing was a joke and they started laughing at us. Well, the thing practically moved by itself. It started telling us stuff; then it said on a certain day at a certain time that I was going to be sacrificed. Then we asked it what their name was and it said witch, and we asked if it was a good witch or bad witch. And it said 'bad'.

When it said that, Tonya threw the board up in the air and it landed on me. Well, I started feeling kind of strange, and the one guy still laughing at me said you look like a witch and I pulled a knife out and told him to quit laughing and leave. He just kept on and Jason started screaming so I dropped the knife.

Jason said, "Mom there is something over you."

I was praying and fighting the thing away from me and then I heard Jason say, "There is an angel that is taking it away."

Well, I tried to throw the board away and it was back the next day on the door step, so we wrapped it in some white towels and put it in a closet that we didn't use. Then a different weird thing happened that week; loud noises would come from the closet at times.

I did meet a guy named Craig; he worked at the dog track. Earlier in his life he had been pushed out of a pick-up truck and hurt badly on the head, but he was still coherent.

It wasn't long after we met that he told me, "I tried to leave this town but they won't let me. That's why things are happening to you, you are in a place of devils."

With all the strange things that were going on I believed him. I told him I would help him get away. So I took him home with me and told him to stay with Tonya and the kids until I went to work and got my check and we all would leave. Well, while I was at work, someone sabotaged my car. And it was sounding strange.

Tonya went to the neighbors and called me at work and said Craig is acting strange. He was running around the yard naked and howling and saying strange things. She didn't know what to do. So I told her they must be controlling his mind. Go and take a sheet and put around him and talk nice to him and try and get him back in the house. So she did, and I prayed to get home okay.

When I got there, he was just sitting there and staring out into space and said, "They won't let you take me, I am their's. You try to go. Take me to the track."

He wanted to go to the dog track because he had a room to stay there.

"Let me look under the hood of the car first because it's acting strange," I said.

About that time some guy pulled up in the drive and asked if we needed help. I told him we did.

He said, "Here's your problem; someone has pulled these wires loose. I'll tighten them.

"My wife and I and some other folks just moved here and we know it is evil. You need to try and get away from here as fast as you can and don't look back. They will not let you leave if you stay too much longer.

"It looks like they sabotaged your car."

Well, I just stood there and listened and he had no more turned around to get a screw driver than he was suddenly praising the place and saying how good it was there.

I knew then we were in trouble. I offered him some money but he refused it.

He said, "Take your friend home while you still can."

By then I was a nervous wreck. I didn't know what to do. But I took Craig home and helped him feed the dogs.

He told me if I couldn't take all my stuff to leave it with him and I could come back later and get it.

Well, I went to get a U-Haul but no one would rent one to me. When we learned this, Tonya and the kids just started crying.

So I went back to work. Tonya continued to stay with the kids. When she cooked, she would put a large amount of grease in the food; I mean everything she cooked and we could not eat it. So she wasted the money and the food. I think she was under some kind of spell.

We lived twenty miles from town, and I would have to go back and buy more food and it would take up more of our traveling money and then we still had to pay rent, electricity, a water bill and insurance - it was a never ending cycle.

After a few weeks went by I was feeling stranger. We had been in this town for five months and had had no contact with anyone we knew from Indiana or anywhere else. I even tried calling my dad in Tennessee and Lucy in Kentucky. Still, no phone operator would put us through.

The day came that the witch who spoke through the Ouija board said that I was to die. Tonya begged me not to go to work. I told her I had to make money. If anything did happen to me, she was to somehow get Jason and Joel home even if they only took their clothes and got on a bus. I should have done that anyway, but somehow in my head I thought I couldn't leave without my stuff. I had sold a big wardrobe, sewing machine, and some other things to get money for food.

Well, I went to work and the day went kind of okay. The boss said she would give me a raise and I could become a manager myself. I guess she was bribing me but I was only twenty-five years old. When she said that I thought maybe all the stuff that happened up until then had gone away and everybody was okay. Boy was I wrong. All I remember after that was I started to turn out of the parking lot after work to go home and the next thing I knew I was sitting in this long drive way. I could see a big three-story house at the end of it.

I wondered how I got there. Did I take the wrong turn? Because I didn't see anything that looked familiar, and I didn't remember turning or anything. It was like I came out of a weird sleep. I thought I would just drive down to the house and ask these people where I was and how to get back to town.

All of a sudden I heard a loud voice say "NO."

I shook my head and then I heard the voice say, "Back up and turn around".

So I did. I thought maybe I was talking to myself and I didn't want to feel dumb by asking these people where I was. Then I wondered which way do I go, left or right?

"Left," I heard.

Well I drove and drove. I thought I would stop at a gas station and I heard "Keep driving. Soon you will be back in town."

I drove a little over fifty miles. The courthouse was in the middle of the road and there were streets that went each direction from it. As I approached the town, everybody stopped and looked at me, cars pulled over and stared and people walking just stopped and stared. I thought that was strange; and wondered what they were looking at. Did they know I went the wrong way?

I kept driving around until I saw the store where I worked and then drove home. I was lucky I didn't have to work that night. I was so tired.

Tonya said she was afraid that I had been killed. I asked her why. She reminded me of what the board had indicated.

I told her about all of the weird stuff that had happened and she said, "They were going to get you in that house and kill you."

"Well God, or something, told me to turn around and I did," I said.

A day or two later when I was at work, a truck driver came in wanting to use the telephone to call the police. I asked him what had happened.

He said someone walked in front of him and that he had hit a curb and lost the load. The whole truck had turned over along with the trailer that was carrying brand new cars to a car lot. The man was shaking so hard I told him sit down; that I would call the police for him. And I did. They took the man away and I never heard or saw him again.

Finally a so-called friend of the guy named Sam came in. I ask him where Sam was. He was supposed to get us a CB radio but we hadn't heard from him.

He said he was in jail and he needed me to give him the gun Sam had loaned me. He needed to pawn it for his bail.

Well the so-called friend lied and we never saw Sam anymore.

I told Sam's "friend" he could follow me home after work and I would give it to him then.

He said, "I know where you live; we all do."

I though that was strange, and I told him I didn't want him there unless I was there because my cousin was scared of strangers.

Well, he didn't listen because when I got home he was already inside, sitting in a chair and laughing. Tonya was screaming and Joel had a red mark on his forehead that looked like an upside down star and his eyes were rolling around. Jason was crying and saying this bad man hurt Joel.

"What the hell did you do to him?" I yelled.

"You all think you're going somewhere, but you're not," he said, "You escaped us the other day but there will be another one."

I didn't know at that time what he was talking about. I forced him to leave and told him he'd better not come back.

I got a soapy wash cloth and went to wash Joel's face but it wouldn't come off.

Jason said, "Mom, that man was a devil."

At that time, I remembered (or my guides told me) "you have some holy water in your jewelry box", which I did.

A lady that I had worked with in Louisville at the pickle factory came up to me and told me I would need it one day, that it was water from Lourdes, a holy place overseas. I took it from her with no questions asked. She must have been psychic.

So I went and got it and started praying over Joel and rubbing the red stuff off, it look like smoke coming off his head and he screamed like it was killing him. But it was taking whatever it was off of him. After a while, when the red stuff was gone, I helped Tonya give him a bath. I told Jason to get a bath too.

He said, "Mom, I knew he was a bad man and I wouldn't let him touch me."

"The man said for me to take your son back home," Tonya said, "and leave my son with my cousin. They were the ones they needed."

I couldn't figure it out. One day I thought because I dyed my hair blonde and Joel's hair was already blonde, maybe they didn't like blondes. I still don't know. I knew when I was little my hair was naturally blonde and that's when that other bad person tried to kidnap me. And ever since I dyed my hair blonde I had the worst luck.

There was also a fat guy that drove a station wagon that came in the store one day. He just looked at me and asked if I would be his girlfriend if he bought me a new mobile home.

"Yeah right, are you nuts?" I said.

"No, I mean it."

"No, I'm not interested," I said.

The next thing I knew he had followed me home. I looked around and there he was. I told him to leave.

"Who's the girl behind you?" he asked.

"I'm her cousin," Tonya replied, "What's it to you?"

"I would love to buy your cousin a mobile home if she would be my girlfriend," he countered.

We just started laughing.

"If you give us a new mobile home and a deed to it with our names on it we will consider it," Tonya said, "And I want a purple car."

I just looked at her, stunned.

"No way," I told Tonya, "I'm not *that* desperate."

He said in a few days he would have it.

"Don't come back unless you prove it," I said. I felt he was lying.

Then this other guy came into the store and offered me a bracelet and said he would lavish me with jewels if I would marry him. I wondered who was putting these nuts up to this. One lady standing there said I should take him up on it, that he was rich.

Again I felt they were lying and trying to trick us in to something to harm us. Later, the fat guy brought some phony papers in that look like a deed and said he was going to put it in my name. I just told him to stay away.

I talked with Jake the cop about these guys and he said that the law was looking for the fat guy. I told him I just wanted to move somewhere else.

Another week or so went by and suddenly Tonya's mom, brother, grandma and grandpa showed up.

"How did you find us?" I asked.

The first thing they said was, "Why haven't you all contacted us?"

Well, we told them what went on, even about the Ouija board. So the first thing her grandma did was go get it and break it up and throw it into the garbage. Then we went with Tonya's grandpa to get a U-Haul to tie to the back of my car. I couldn't fit everything in it, so I left some stuff with Craig.

I stopped by the store and the boss suddenly told me she had decided to promote me to manager. Then this weird feeling came over me to send Jason home with Tonya and for me to just stay there.

Shirley, Tonya's mom, said, "No, you're going with us."

So when she said that I kind of snapped out of it a little and told the manager I had to go home. We went back to the trailer to load up. There was a dog that had been given to us but it acted crazy too. I tried to get it in the car and it ran away.

We started down the road. Shirley rode with me and Jason and Tonya. Joel and Todd rode with Tonya's grandma and grandpa. At the end of the road a pick-up truck full of men stopped us and asked where we thought we were going. I told them I was leaving and they couldn't stop me. We turned around. The group leader said we'd be back, that we were part of the "family" now.

I was mad and scared. We drove down the road briefly when the U-Haul suddenly started whipsawing back and forth. I started praying and it straightened out. Then it felt like something was choking me and I said I had to go back, but Shirley said to keep driving, that someone was working a spell on me.

Jason said, "You have to go back with me mom."

If it wasn't for that I don't know what I would have done.

When we got back, I went to my mom's first. Tom came over to see Jason and asked me to come back to him. He wanted us to try again and Jason said he wanted to be around Tom. So we got back together, back to the haunted trailer.

Since Tom was working as an auto mechanic he drove my car in to the shop to see what all the weird noise was.

Later in the day, he called me and told me to get in his car and get over there now. Well I did and he was white as a sheet and shaking. I asked him what was wrong.

He said, "You!"

"What did I do?" I asked.

"Look at that car; it shouldn't be running, let alone start," he said. "Look at all that sand."

I reminded him that I had lived in Florida on a sandy dirt road.

He said several things were missing and the motor was full of sand. The car should have never started; God or someone must have been watching over us.

He decided to quit for the day and we went home. I told him all the weird stuff that had happened. It was still hard to believe.

After everything that had happened, Tom thought we needed to do something to get away. He thought maybe I should take up truck driving; that I should go to school for it. That way he and I could drive a truck together and take Jason with us in the summer and on holidays. He said he always wanted to travel; that we might as well get paid for it. So I agreed and found a truck driving school in Memphis and signed up for it.

Before I left for Memphis, I kept seeing strange things and people that looked like some of the people that had been in Florida. My cousin also saw them. It was strange, we thought, that we were being followed. But my guide, Smokey, said that the people down there were projecting images to us and trying to draw us back down there. Well, whatever they were doing, it was strong. I had started to meditate a little and I would hear the voices in my head. And one day shortly after that, I felt a strong feeling to go back to Florida to get the rest of my things that I had left with the guy named Craig.

I went to see Myrtle and before I could get the first word out of my mouth, she told me everything that had happened there and I asked her how she knew all of that. Actually I had forgotten some things to tell my family about from that journey.

"I can see it like a movie," she said.

I told her I thought I should I go and get the rest of my stuff, but she said not to, that they would try and kill me.

Well, then I went to see my Aunt Susie and she said she didn't believe that we went through all of that and lived.

I told her I would borrow some money and go down and get my stuff and take her with me.

She said she would drive and so she, her friend Ivey, and I went. Tom tried to talk me out of it but it was like I just had to go, the pull was so strong. I told him that maybe I was supposed to rescue Craig or something.

Before we went, Myrtle made me wear a wooden cross, and she told me to never take it off. So I wore it in the shower and slept with it on. And I kept it on even years after.

Anyway, I managed to gather six hundred dollars together and we set out, just the three of us on the journey. We even towed a small trailer.

When we got to Georgia, I started feeling kind of strange and when we got to Craig's I had a dreadful feeling.

He lived at the track and next to it was a hotel with a restaurant. We went to get him and then walked over to the restaurant to get some coffee and to eat.

We talked a little while and this man came over and asked how we were doing.

"Great," I replied.

"I know you all have to be tired so here's a key to one of the rooms," he said. "Go and get some rest and spend the night. Since you're a friend of Craig's, you don't have to pay."

Well I thought that was very nice; but that's when Susie got suspicious. But since we had driven all day and part of the night she agreed to the offer.

She and Ivey went to the room, and all of a sudden this feeling came over me to get Craig to take me to the store where I once worked. I felt I had to say hello or something. Bad mistake.

"Be here at eight tonight or I will leave you," Susie said.

I asked her why; the man said we could stay all night.

But Susie said no; she was starting to feel strange things. Craig had told her what had happened to us and him. She told us to hurry up and do what we needed to do; that we needed to leave. She was starting to believe what we said was true.

So we left and went to one store. The lady manager was there, and so was Jake. He looked very surprised that I was there. I told them I just came by to say hello.

Jake was also working there now.

She said I could have my old job back and she would train me to be a man-ager if I'd like. When she said that, this overwhelming feeling came over me to say yes; it was like I was in a daze. I told her a part of me wanted to but I had no place to stay. She said I could stay with them. I almost said yes and then it was like something jerked me back.

I told her, "No, I have to go. My aunt will be waiting for me."

It was already five o'clock in the evening.

"She's not leaving until eight," Craig whispered.

"No," I told him. "If I'm not back there by six, I heard she will leave me. Something is wrong."

And then the woman's face kind of changed to look very old, like something wicked.

Craig wanted to hesitate but I said, "Let's go."

So we got in his truck; I told him they were trying to trick us – or worse.

He started to daze out and then said, "I am their's and if I go with you then you will be in danger; they told me already they will not let me leave."

I began to get very nervous. When we got to the hotel, Susie and Ivey were in the car and the motor was already running.

"Get what you want," Susie said. "We're leaving."

I told her what had happened.

"Just do as I say and get in the car," Susie said, "If you hadn't come here by six I was leaving."

We had a small trailer on the back of the car but even though I only had a few things, nothing would fit. So again I had to leave some things. I only brought back two things, a cedar chest and a small end table.

She told me to drive, so I got behind the wheel. My cross was choking me. I told her I needed to take this cross off because it was choking.

"Don't you dare take that off!" she yelled.

So I tried to bear with it and as I drove away all the street signs said the same thing.

Suddenly, we came upon what I thought was an accident. It looked like a truck had dumped a load of chickens with their heads cut off all over the road.

I told Susie those were the biggest chickens I had ever seen. She just said to keep driving.

"But all the street signs look the same," I told her. "And we need to turn around to get directions."

Again, she just said to keep driving.

Well, we finally got to the Georgia line and I pulled into a gas station and filled up. I was still feeling the choking around my neck.

Susie asked for directions and we got back on the main road. After we had driven on into Georgia, the choking eased up some. I asked Susie what that was all about.

"When you went with that guy Craig to the store, I saw a man pull up and take a box into the room next door," she said. "All of a sudden, strange noises started coming through the wall. I told Ivey to get up; something was going on. It was then I saw faces coming through the wall and I saw devils dancing, so I knew then it was voodoo.

"God told me if we didn't get out of there before seven we would never get out; that we would be killed."

"Didn't I tell you these people were evil?" I said.

"And your crazy self wanted to go running around," she snapped back.

"They must have put it in my head," I said.

"They must have," Susie said. "I have seen some evil in my day but this was going to be the worst ever. You still have to be careful; they will try and use others against you."

After we got home safe, I told Tom what happened and I apologized to him for being ignorant, but maybe it was to make sure I didn't make this up and for my aunt to finally believe me. I had told her I didn't lie about things.

When I went to my cousin's house, I told her what had happened and all of a sudden a huge black hand like a claw came up on the wall and went across the ceiling back and forth several times. I got up and closed all the curtains but it was still there.

She said they were coming after us and became hysterical. I told her to calm down; that we would pray. She looked out the window and saw our brothers coming up the street. I called them in and ask them if they saw anything, just in case we had been hallucinating.

They became wide-eyed and said they had seen a devil. Both of them then ran out the door. So we prayed and prayed and finally it went away.

I went back home and told Tom; he said we needed that break we had talked about earlier. I agreed.

CHAPTER 6
∞
JERKS BEHIND THE WHEEL

I finally heard back from the driving school in Memphis and received a student loan. I started in the middle of January so Jason stayed with Tom; it was a six week course. The school told us of a place that would rent to us. There were six women and lots of guys, so the women and I were placed in a trailer that had bunk beds in three bedrooms.

A lady named Kelli shared the same room with me. She was shorter than me but she took the top bunk anyway.

I told the women that I was going to go and do some trading, and asked if any of them wanted anything, or wanted to go with me. They all looked at each other and me as if I had five heads or something. They asked what I was talking about.

"I forgot," I said. "You're not from the country are you? When we go to buy groceries we call it going to trade."

And one gal asked, "What do you call it if you buy clothes?"

I said, "Shop."

They all started laughing.

"And we call a paper bag a poke," I said.

They thought I was nutty.

One girl went with me. She asked me what it was that I traded. I said money for food. I asked her why she asked. She said she was just curious.

All and all they were okay. There were a few people in class that had attitudes but the classes were kind of easy. It was like a light bulb lit up in my head and things would come to me out of the blue and it would happen.

I remember it snowed and the city was almost shut down and no one drove even though it was only like an inch or two deep. I thought that was strange because I was used to driving in several inches or even feet of snow at times. I figured the big trucks could move through the little stuff.

My back would start to itch when a police man was within a mile. It was weird, I would tell the instructor there was a cop down the road; that they better slow down a little and then, sure enough, there they would be.

Three students would be in a truck with an instructor at a time. Some of the guys would laugh at me.

I thought, "Oh heck, just like in regular school, being made fun of."

I was shy. One guy, Bobby, liked me and he had me over to his mother's for dinner one night.

After the fourth week the women found out for sure that Kelli was gay. She had quit because the other women felt uncomfortable around her. But something happened at her home too. I thought they were just prejudiced. But she said some things were going on at home that she needed to attend to anyway. I felt bad that she didn't get to finish.

One of the instructors told me that she thought I was a good person and she hoped I didn't hold anything against Kelli. I told her no because that was her life. I thought she was a nice person and never said anything out of the way. They made me feel uneasy too, so I rented a room from Bobby's mom. The people there were nicer to me.

It came time to finish school and we had tests. It was so funny, when we practiced, we all performed the turns and everything perfectly, but when they used the word "test" we all flubbed up. One woman backed the fake dock all the way into the road. My straight was a jackknife and my jackknife was a straight. I told the instructors that the word test must scare a lot of people and they needed to grade us on the practice parts instead of the test so they talked it over and agreed. If they hadn't we all would have failed.

Then there were some people that came over the next day from different companies to hire us. NLR near Little Rock talked to me and hired me. They said I needed to work with them first because I was a rookie and I needed some more training.

So I called Tom and told him what they said. And he said to go ahead; he would see what he could do on his end to get this other job so we could drive together. So I went to Little Rock.

As soon as I got there they introduced me to this guy named Marvin that I was scheduled to ride with. We were going to New York first and the route we were driving would take us through Louisville.

I told him I lived close by and about how my aunt read cards. He said he would like for her to read for him, so we went there and Tom and Jason came up to see me. My mom lived next door and we went there and waited until his reading was over. This gave me time to spend with the family and get something to eat. Tom brought me some more clothes. He also gave me a .38 caliber pistol in case I ran into any trouble.

Before we left, Marvin told me to come over and ask my aunt to tell me what she saw on the road. She told me she knew if we didn't stop thirty minutes before three o'clock that morning, and wait for thirty minutes after, we would experience a bad wreck and probably be killed.

I told Marvin we'd better listen because I had a weird feeling too.

Well, as the time came closer, we looked at each other as if to ask each other if we were stopping. But before I could say anything, he said, "Yes we are. I am not taking any chances. One time this other woman told me things and I didn't listen and wished I had."

So we stopped at this truck stop. It was foggy out and there was only one parking place left beside a truck that had just hit a skunk. It was awful.

We went in the truck stop for a while and waited. Then when it came time we left.

As we went down the road about twenty miles, there were trucks slung all over the road on their side and some cars piled up on each other. We were lined-up for a long while.

Marvin said he was going to ask someone what time this happened, so he got on the CB and asked about what time this accident happened and a man came over the radio and said it was around three o'clock.

Well, I thought Marvin was going to have a heart attack. He was sweating and praying. He said since this part came true, he would believe the rest she told him.

I told him she was pretty accurate.

As we continued on, we had to go through Pennsylvania. The roads were very bumpy with lots of holes. We had to go through a lot of tolls and I began to get angry. I thought those people they needed to take all that money and fix those darn roads. Well about that time I hit a hole in the road as big as the tire but I managed to hold it on the road and finally came out of it.

When I got down the road a little further, a lot of people came over the CB and said, "Great job; great job."

When Marvin told them I was a rookie, they were shocked; they said most rookies would have jackknifed and wrecked. I just told them I was a good driver. Someone said good driver or not, God was with me.

Then right before we got to New York, I was going up a hill and snow was on the ground and it just kept coming down. Marvin looked at me and asked if I was all right and I told him yes. I asked him why he asked. He told me to just pull over at the top of the hill and park.

Again I asked him why.

"Please, just do as I ask," he said.

So I did.

He turned the inside light on because it was dark out. He was sweating to beat the band.

"Oh my God, are you having a heart attack?" I asked.

"I don't know; all I know is that it's you."

I asked him what made him say that.

"You're weird," Marvin replied. "Don't you know we don't have any brakes?"

"No, I hadn't noticed."

"I felt them go out back there and you got us here," he said. "I can't believe it. God or someone is watching out for you."

"Yes, He gets me out of some awful situations," I assured him.

I told him a little about my experience in Florida. That scared him. When we finally got back to the terminal, he went in and then came out later and told me that they wanted to see me and for me to get my stuff. So I got what I could before that turkey left me there. As I went gathered my clothes, I noticed my fringe jacket and a watch were missing. The company wouldn't reimburse me or talk to him about where they might be. And because I was new they only paid me seven cents a mile. I sure didn't make much.

Then they put me with some other nut named Marvin. In my mind, I referred to him as Marvin Two. This method actually turned out to be a good thing. By the time my truck driving adventures were over, I began to think there was a curse on that name for me.

I had to go to California with him. It was my first time out west. Well, it was not fun. My nose would itch all the time when I tried to sleep, so I didn't sleep much.

I saw deserts and mountains. Wyoming was kind of neat. I would have liked living there at that time. We were on top of a mountain and when you looked down it looked like the ground was a patchwork quilt.

Marvin Two told me we were going down there so I needed to hold on. It was scary. I noticed there were runoff sidings as we headed down so that if the truck was a "runaway" for any reason we'd have to try and pull on to the side of the runoff ramp, which wasn't much at all. I just prayed we got down without having to do that. And we did. It was beautiful in the valley; it had a big lake and beautiful landscape.

I would have dreaded the trip back if we had to go back up that mountain, but we were headed on to Oxnard to get celery.

When we first got to the California line, it was day break. I was in the passenger seat and I looked down and saw a convertible next to us with its top down and a stark naked man driving. I thought I was seeing things, so I shook my head and looked again and there he was beside us at the stop light.

I looked over at Marvin Two and told him to look over in the next lane; there was a naked man driving a convertible. He said that was nothing; they did that all the time out there. I was shocked. Then I was glad the light changed.

I wondered if all I was going to see was a bunch of naked people. I did not like California. Well, as we got closer to our destination, I did see people with clothes on.

I said, "Thank God!"

Marvin Two said, "What's the matter with you?"

I said, "There *are* people with clothes on."

He just laughed.

We had to wait in line to get a load of the celery because there were other truckers there for the same thing going different places with it. I looked over and a man with a silver food wagon drove up, raised the side cover and started cooking hamburgers.

Marvin Two said that's where we would get something to eat. So I went over there and again my backwoods country accent got me in trouble.

Where I grew up, when you wanted a hamburger with everything on it like lettuce, tomato, onion and mayonnaise, you called it a "dressed" hamburger. So I went over and asked for a dressed hamburger.

The man ignored me and said, "Next!"

I thought he got my order and was gathering more so he could cook them all and then dish them out.

Everyone got something but me, so I said. "Did you not hear me? I ask you for a dressed hamburger."

He said, "What the heck are you talking about? Are you nuts?"

Well, I got confused and went to the truck mad with tears in my eyes. I was already upset from his angry voice, and I was really hungry too.

Marvin Two asked me what was wrong. So I told him, and I had to explain to him what a dressed hamburger was.

"Give me your money and I'll go get it," he said.

So he brought me one back.

"These people out here don't talk like you," he said. "They call everything something different out here."

Well I didn't know what to do then. Were these people never going to understand anything I said?

I told Marvin Two to do all the talking before I got in trouble.

We headed back east to Delaware to deliver the celery. Then we had to go to Canada and take some glue. We barely got over the border when we had to wait for one of their drivers to take our trailer, deliver it and then bring it back to us.

Back then a lot of men were really prejudiced against women driving. Those men up there did not like me. They said women needed to stay home, barefoot and pregnant.

I was really angry at that time. I told them I had as much right as they did. Marvin Two told me to go get something to eat at a restaurant down the street and keep out of trouble. So I went there and I had to explain what I wanted in detail. I didn't like the way they cooked, but I was hungry so I ate it. I would eat some meat back then but I wish I hadn't.

They asked me what I was doing there and I told them. But they criticized me too. One lady said I just rode with my husband – probably to get them to shut up. I was glad to get out of there. At the loading station they didn't even have a bathroom for women.

Then we got another load of something and headed to Portland, Oregon. On the way we had to get another permit to pass through a couple of states. Well, he was getting aggravated with me because he had to explain to several guys why he had a woman riding with him instead of a man.

It started getting dark when it became my turn to drive while he slept. Marvin Two told me to stop when we got to the truck scales so we could get the permits. I told him I would.

Well, I drove and drove and drove. Finally he woke up and asked me if I stopped at the scales. I told him I hadn't seen the truck scales yet. He asked where we were. I told him all I know is that we are in so and so and we were already a hundred miles into the state. He was furious. He said those guys were right; women needed to stay home, and he said some other nasty stuff. I just ignored him. He said I should have stopped at the Port of Entry. I told him he didn't say those words and I didn't see that sign either.

Well, the next truck scales stop was around this other mountain. Marvin Two said we needed to stop at the other end and tell them what I did; they would probably give me a five hundred dollar fine.

Well, I got there and went in and explained to the man and woman what had happened and they said, "Well, it's another world out here but we'll let you go. Just be sure to stop on the way back through."

"No problem since I know what to do now," I said.

They wished us a safe trip. I went to the truck and Marvin Two was laughing and asked me how much they fined me. I told him they didn't fine me at all. I proceeded to tell him what else they said. He was so mad.

We drove on and Marvin Two went to sleep. We had to come off an exit ramp and a car stopped in front of me. I had to slam on the brakes and Marvin Two came rolling out of the "doghouse". He was so mad, he grabbed the steering wheel and told me to run over her. I pushed him back and told him no, there were children in there. And I wouldn't have run over her anyway.

Well, Marvin Two had a lot of choice words to say. All along the way, as we would go through each state, I would buy a bell with the name of the state on it and put it into a bag. Well, he grabbed my whole bag and threw it out the window. We cussed each other out. We got to our destination barely talking.

On the way back, we went through Reno. It was the first time I played the slot machine. I won fifty dollars. It was lucky I kept it. I played one machine and the bells were going off and it said I had won the big truck. It was beautiful. But the man who ran the place told me that it was a mistake and that I couldn't do anything about it. I was so mad; no one would help me.

When I finally caught up with Marvin Two he had lost three hundred dollars. I let him borrow thirty dollars from me just so he'd shut up.

We were headed back to Arkansas when we came upon these guys who wanted to race us but I told Marvin Two no. So he made me let him drive and I told him he was going to get in trouble with the police. He told me that I was crazy because the road we were going to travel on hardly had any cops on that road.

Well, here we go. I told him my back was itching and that he would get a ticket.

He said, "Well, where are they? I don't see them!"

I told him they were about a mile down the road. Well he wouldn't listen and here they came. After they pulled us over, he even tried to tell them I was driving. He hardly spoke to me after that.

We got to Flagstaff and the snow and ice came. I dreaded that. We put chains on the tires and started out. I was driving when we went up this hill and the brakes went out. Again, I got to the other side of the hill. On the other side of this town was a strip mall. I pulled into it and Marvin Two asked me who was watching over me; he said anyone else probably would have wrecked.

I told him that's what the other Marvin had said, and like I told him, God and my guide Smokey ride with me. I then told him a little bit about some things. He couldn't handle it, I don't know if he snapped or what.

But whatever happened, his following actions were those of a desperate person and caused me to fear for my life. I knew that no matter what happened, I had to find a way to get away from him. I just prayed and asked God to get me out of this situation.

Then I heard a voice say, "Tell him some things and he will let you go."

So I just opened my mouth and God spoke through me. I didn't know anything about these people and their past, but God did and when God, my guides, and the angels finished, these people let me go and had me promise not to tell anyone at that time what had happened. (I am telling this now because it is part of my life's past).

I guess when we are in trouble just pray and have faith that God will get you through it somehow. (God, the angels, and my guides have saved my life many times as you have read and will read in the next few chapters).

Of course, when we got back to the terminal he requested to change riders. But he also requested a vacation.

The boss asked me, "What are you doing to these guys?"

"It's not me," I said, "they're just crazy."

When I found out the next one they partnered me with was also named Marvin (the third one), I told them they must be kidding.

The boss said he was the only one available at the time. So I asked him where we were going. He said California; had I been there yet?

I laughed and said, "Oh yes."

I told him what had happened and he just laughed.

So off we went. Well, we get down the road and he pulls out this cigar box that was full of marijuana. He said he had a really good batch. I freaked out. I told him I didn't smoke and that what he was carrying was illegal.

Well I just made enemy number three. He said I better not tell anyone. I begged him not to smoke while we were driving. But I had no luck with that. I coughed and coughed. At the truck stop I called dispatch and told them what had happened.

But all they said was, "We don't have another driver right now to trade you with. So I guess you just grin and bear it and try not to get caught."

I was furious. We were headed to California. We had to go through Flagstaff. It was snowing to beat the band.

When we got to the top to get fuel we all got a call on the CB from dispatch instructing all drivers in the Flagstaff area to meet up with Caroline.

Marvin Three knew her and called her on the CB. We went to meet her.

I wondered what had happened. Did she have her own truck and they put a rookie guy with her?

Apparently what had happened was after she and her driver had slept together, they got to a truck stop and she went in to take a shower. While she was doing that he had called another woman and she came and got him and they stole all of Caroline's stuff out of the truck, even her CB, all her clothes, her coat, money and gun and whatever else she had, even her blankets.

When we got there she only had a short sleeve shirt on and a pair of pants and flip-flop shoes.

I asked her where her regular shoes were. She said she left them in the truck and he had stolen them too. She just wore the flip-flops to get into the shower.

So I gave her my velour blanket to put around her.

"I know those that I rode with took stuff from me too," I said. "Now this jerk wants me to smoke dope and have sex and I don't want to do either one."

I suggested to her that we make them let us drive together and we wouldn't have to deal with the nutty men. So we went in and called, but they said the company rules were driving teams had to be a man and a woman.

"That's baloney," I said.

"I tell you what," Caroline said, "we're all headed for the same town and we have to lay over there for three days. I'll ride with Marvin and you drive my Peterbuilt."

I was happy then. She let me drive by myself. It was the best time I had on the road, being a truck driver. We got to our destination and Marvin Three got soused and she spent time with him and let me sleep in her truck. I dreaded going back on the road with him.

Somehow she kept my blanket, but for what she did for me, keeping that nut away for a few days was worth it.

Later, it was back on the road with Marvin Three as we headed to Oxnard to pick up a load of produce and take it back east. The whole time I could hardly sleep. Each time I laid my head down, he would reach back there and pull on my clothes telling me to "give it up". I began to hate him, so I would get mad and stay awake. I never gave it up. Well when it came time for me to drive I was extremely tired, and frustrated. Without anything to take to keep me awake, I would go to the restroom when we stopped for fuel and close my eyes for a few minutes trying to rest them so I could see to drive. He told me since I wasn't "putting out" he was not going to let me sleep.

So I prayed a lot to God to keep me awake. I called home and finally got in touch with Tom. He had also been trying to reach me.

I told him a little bit about the guy. I knew if I told him everything he would kill him. He told me that they didn't pass him on his physical and if I wanted to get my tubes tied I better come home. So I told him I would be there soon. I knew we had to go through Indianapolis and I could meet him there.

I told Marvin Three I had to go home and he got furious. He was very obnoxious and told me I couldn't leave.

I told God I had to lie my way out of this one.

And a voice said, "No you won't; we will give you the words to say. It is called using strategy to get out of harms way."

So I agreed; I needed a way out of this quick. So I open my mouth and the words flowed. I still wasn't allowed any sleep. I was so tired I stopped at a rest area to go to the bathroom and I closed my eyes for a while, maybe five minutes, to get my second wind.

But when I got in the truck I must have forgotten to push the button down to start the truck going again. The truck started bucking like a horse. Then I did it to reverse and it bucked again.

Well that woke him up. He cussed me for all it was worth. He climbed up in the passenger side and I just stared ahead and he said, "Push the button down stupid!"

Well I did and then started to back out. I didn't know he had the door open and was peeing out the door onto the ground.

I backed up and he had to grab the door and it slung him out in the air. Of course he cussed and cussed.

"Well, you said let's go," I said.

I wanted to laugh so badly but was afraid to. I was awake though, all that cussing woke me up good. That lasted for another day.

So for four days and four nights I did not get any real sleep. On the fourth day the road looked like a monster trying to gobble me up. I was hallucinating badly. We were almost to Indiana and I called Tom and told him we were almost there. He drove over a hundred miles to come to the destination to pick me up. I thought we were almost there.

I got back on the road and realized we were in Springfield, Missouri, not Springfield, Indiana. Well, Tom was so mad when I told him that he went back home. Of course, Marvin Three just laughed about it and made bad remarks like "if you're willing to put out I will let you sleep."

I just told him no. So I drove on again. I told him that driving without sleep and breathing that dope he was smoking could cause us to wreck. He said it would be on my head, not his.

When we finally got to the destination, Marvin Three said I could not have any of my stuff; he would keep it until I came back and rode with him. I told him that if he kept my stuff, my husband would hunt him down. He said I had to promise him that when I came back I would ride with him. So I used strategy and said okay.

I finally got out of the truck and had to wait for hours for Tom to get there. He finally got there; this was in March.

I called the trucking company and told them what had happened and that I quit.

CHAPTER 7
∞
MY HUSBAND PASSES

Our trailer had caught on fire while I was truck driving and Tom had put it out but it still smelled strongly of fuel oil. And since it made me very sick, I went to my mom's with Jason.

While I was gone, Tom's mother had Jason convinced that if I had another child I would love it more than him. She spent a great part of her time speaking against me and causing trouble between Tom and me.

So about a week after I quit driving a big rig, I went in the hospital and had my tubes tied. The operation made me so sick that I had to stay a couple of more days in the hospital.

While I was in there an older woman was brought in and they put her bed in the same room that I was in. I was by the window. That night I saw a huge tree hitting the window, like the wind was going to blow it down or blow it into the window and break the window. I got up to close the curtains, thinking that if I didn't the glass from the window would go all over me and the woman. When I got up to close them, I looked out the window to see how bad the storm was but there wasn't any storm and there was no tree. I closed the curtains anyway and jumped in bed and covered my head, very scared and prayed.

I heard a voice say "death is coming for the woman tonight."

I was so scared. I stayed awake all night with my head covered up. I heard noises all night.

About six that morning, a nurse's aid came in and tried to wake her but, of course, she would not wake up. After a while a lot of people ran in the room and took me to another room, I was afraid to say what I saw and heard. So I kept my mouth shut.

Tom came in to see me and I told him about it. Then he helped me get ready and took me to my mother's. I told Tom that we needed to go to other doctors and see what they said about his health. (It turned out that Tom had a dark spot on his lungs. The doctors said it might be cancer. But Tom told me he was not going to go through the chemo like his dad did).

He said the spirits in the trailer were out to get him and he had no choice. He had me all confused. I was so sick, I begged him to stay with me at my mother's but he said no. He said he would probably have another fight with that boyfriend of his sister's. (He had gotten in a bad argument with one of his sisters and her boyfriend because he kept climbing in and out of her windows at night). He also said I might as well kill myself.

I cried and told him not to do foolish things. We all begged him to stay with us. I didn't know later on that he told our seven year old son that he was going to kill himself. I was furious. I had all kinds of emotions!

The next day, my friend name Bobby came up from Memphis to see how I was doing. Because he found out how bad a time I had driving the trucks, they sent him to another company and they didn't treat him right either. I had told him a while back about Tom's plan to get a job with this company with flatbeds and he came up to talk to us about it; he thought he might get a job there too.

When he got there, I told him what had happened while I was in the hospital and about the woman, and what Tom had said before he left. Bobby wanted to take me over to our trailer to talk some sense into Tom.

I tried to call Tom's mom but she didn't answer the phone. So I got in the car and we drove to the trailer. I knocked and opened the door and yelled for Tom. The lamp was on and I stepped up inside and there he was lying there dead, all purple looking. I was shocked and started screaming.

Bobby had just gotten out of the car when I opened the door and stepped up inside the trailer. He ran to me and I yelled for him to call the police. He asked me where there was a phone, but I ran out the door and over to Tom's mother's across the yard, opening the door and said Tom was dead, and that I had to call the police.

His mother and three sisters just stood there and looked at me. She said she hadn't heard anything when they came home last night. She said the lights were off in the trailer.

I called the police and my mom, and went back and sat on the steps to wait for them. Bobby just stood in the yard and paced. I cried and cried. Bobby didn't know what to do.

None of Tom's family came over until the ambulance came and finally his sister Glenda walked over and just kept walking around in the yard.

I said, "Your brother is dead, don't you have anything to say?"

"No."

Finally his mother came over there after the ambulance loaded Tom up and said to the police that she didn't see the lights on.

"The lamp was on when I got here," I said, "and I did not touch anything."

She told the police she wanted her son's tools. Tom had a bunch of Snap-On brand tools. They were expensive. I told her to just take all of it and sell it to pay for the funeral since I didn't have any money or insurance. Tom had some but when it would be ruled suicide they wouldn't pay.

I told her I just wanted mine and Jason's stuff out of there. She told me I had better get it soon or it wouldn't be there much longer.

After the police questioned Bobby and me, my mom and Aunt Susie came over.

The police let us go. At that point we left. Later I went to the funeral home to make arrangements. It was awful. Jason could hardly keep from crying.

"Daddy told me not to cry at his death," he said. "He doesn't love me."

I was so upset with the whole situation that I had a mild heart attack. I was only twenty-seven at the time; Tom had been twenty-nine.

The day after the funeral, Tom's mother sent word for me to get my things out of the trailer. My sister-in-law, Paula, and I went over there and I prayed for Tom's spirit to go to heaven to be with God and for God to forgive him if he did commit suicide. As I was praying and crying a huge white dove swooped down over my car and up in the air and disappeared. Paula and I just looked at each other and I said he must have gone.

Later on, Bobby called me and wanted me to come to Memphis. I told him I wanted to go back on the road for a little while to clear my head and Jason was going to stay with my mom. That was another bad mistake. She never sent him to school, so he failed that year.

CHAPTER 8
ON THE ROAD AGAIN

Back on the truck driving scene, my former boss called me to see if I wanted my old job back. I told him I would consider it but I didn't want any more crazy people to ride with. Well, that was all they had. Another guy named Marvin (the fourth one), he was an older guy, at first he acted like he had some common sense. (Marvin Three had heard that I wasn't coming back and took a baseball bat and beat up his truck). Well, Marvin Four was talking about how he would like to start his own business some day.

All I could say was, "That's nice."

Then all of a sudden a voice said to me, "He is saying in a round-about way he wants you to be a part of it. And he will tell you that he use to be a sheriff in a certain town and went to bring in a criminal. The guy shot him when he walked up on the porch with a double barrel shotgun and he fell backwards but he lived through it and still brought the guy in."

I thought that I'd just gone off the deep-end when I heard that. I thought I was under so much grief and turmoil that I was hallucinating. Well about two minutes after I heard the voice say that, he said it word for word. I almost fell over. Then I heard the voice say other things. I can't remember all of them but after I heard the voice say something, then he would turn around within two minutes and repeat it.

Well we went to New England first and picked up a load. Then we dropped off that load and went somewhere else and picked up some baby milk formula. We took turns driving and when it was his turn, I fell in to a deep sleep while he drove west.

We were not supposed to go there; in fact, we were over a hundred miles off course.

When I woke up and I found we were parked but he wasn't in the truck. I looked around and I saw Phoenix this and Phoenix that.

"Well, it's just a name," I thought to myself.

He finally came back and I asked him where we were.

"Welcome to your new home," he said. "We're going to get a plumbing and drain business going and you're going to be my secretary."

I thought, "Oh my God, the craziest one in the bunch and I'm riding with him."

I thought what the heck will I do now? If I say no, will he try and kill me like the other ones or what?

"You are going to use strategy and get out of here," I heard a voice say. "Listen very carefully."

So I did. I had to convince him that a lot of babies might starve to death if we didn't get this supply to them. So I told him that I would work for him after we delivered the milk. He finally agreed. We got back on the road after several hours. We had to get going because we were late.

After we delivered the formula he said I needed to give him my money. I told him I didn't have anything except for a few dollars; and, that we needed to drive for a while longer and make some more money so we could get the business started. This he agreed to.

Well, we got a call to go to Los Angeles and pick up a load of produce and deliver it elsewhere, and while we were in the area we went to see the Queen Mary ship, and of course, he said at one time he was the captain of it.

With all the stress I was under, it was a wonder I didn't just keel over. After that we headed to the heart of southern California to pick up another load. On the way there, he said he was going to show me how to shift the "fifth wheel" while driving. And before I got the word "no" out of my mouth, he did it, throwing me up against the windshield. It felt like a boulder hit us.

When I came to, I asked him what happened; I was still dazed.

"I am going to tell them you did it," he said.

When we stopped I opened the truck door and said the heck with this, I was out of there. Another truck stopped behind us and the driver got out and asked me if I was okay. By that time I was in tears and I told him what had happened.

And then Marvin Four got out of the truck and tried to convince the guy that I had been driving at the time.

But the other driver said, "Buddy, it looks like the pin is sheered. Get back in the truck and I will follow you to the garage."

So when Marvin Four got back in the truck the guy told me he would keep him busy talking when we got there and for me to go call my company and tell them what happened and that he would back my story up.

I told him I didn't want to get back in the truck with Marvin Four; but he said it would be okay. So I barely got back in the truck when that nut drove away as I climbed in, barely shutting the door. I thought if I get out of this I will never drive a semi again. There are too many crazy people out there.

Well, we got to the garage and I told Marvin Four that I was going to the bathroom; but I went straight to the phones instead. I called the company and told them what had happened. And I told them I wanted to go home.

The dispatcher said they didn't have any other drivers out there to bring me back. Then he wanted to know what I was doing to these guys. I told him I wasn't doing anything to them; they were all crazy.

All of a sudden a man on the phone next to me became all upset and started crying. Another person asked him what was wrong. And he said his son had an accident and he was going to undergo surgery in two days in Pennsylvania; that he needed to get there right away.

I asked him if he had another driver and he said no.

"You do now," I said.

I told him I could drive a few days without sleep, because I had done it before; he would just have to drop me off in Memphis; that's all I wanted. I told him of the other nut I was with and he said okay, but he had to drop me off in Texas and then pick me back up because he wasn't allowed to have anyone in his truck and if they saw me at the terminal he would get in trouble.

I agreed. I told him my name and he said his name was Marvin so-and-so. I almost passed out; another Marvin! I grew more scared and nervous; I wondered what kind of nut he would turn out to be. I was now convinced that all men named Marvin were crazy.

I told him I would go and get my stuff from Marvin Four and tell him that I was leaving. He said okay and told me where to meet him. I went and told Marvin Four I was called home for an emergency and had to go.

He was furious; you could see the devil in him come out. The other driver that was keeping him occupied got between us and told him not to lay a hand on me and to calm down. I had to promise him I would call him before he would calm down. I hurried and got my things and left.

The other Marvin (the fifth one) was polite to me and treated me with some respect. He told me that there were a lot of negative ones out there. So I felt a little safer driving with him. He was mainly concerned about his son so we talked mostly about him. When it came time for me to drive it was getting dark and we stopped to switch over and he fell right to sleep, so I just turned the radio on and relaxed for the first time and drove.

I heard some people coming over the CB and saying that they were seeing a UFO.

Suddenly the radio and the CB went off. I turned the knobs off and on but nothing worked. I yelled at Marvin Five but he wouldn't wake up.

Then there was a banging on the door and it look like some little kid was jumping up and down in the seat beside me. I started screaming: "Wake up Marvin!" over and over. I tried to pull over and couldn't. It felt like they were trying to take the steering wheel away from me. So all I knew then was to pray.

It looked like a big ball of light in the sky was following beside me. Since Marvin Five would not wake up, I just prayed that it would go away. And I prayed that God would help us and God would help Marvin Five's son come through surgery.

The ball of light followed me all the way to New Mexico for almost seven or eight hours. It was about six that morning before it disappeared in a snap.

I pulled onto the scales and the guy at the window told me I looked like I had seen something.

Then Marvin Five woke up and I told them both what I experienced. He asked why I didn't wake him up; he had always wanted to see "them". I told him that I had screamed at him off and on but he just snored away. The guy at the window just laughed and told Marvin Five he'd better drive, now that I was out of it. He said that there had been all kinds of sightings out west that night.

After we went through New Mexico, we wound up in Abilene. And when we got there he dropped me off at a restaurant. It took a long time for him to come back, but he finally did. I was relieved; it was getting dark and was my turn to drive. I was almost afraid that the UFO would come back so I prayed that they would stay away, and as far as I know they did. My nerves were not ready to handle any of that just yet. I guess they decided to give me a break until later. We finally got to the truck stop on the other side of Memphis where Bobby picked me up.

CHAPTER 9
MAJOR ADJUSTMENTS

Memphis

Bobby and I rented an apartment in Memphis together. It was okay for a little while, about four months or so. We lived three doors down from this couple and two children that wanted to be friends with us. I thought it would be all right.

Bobby went to work as a mechanic where Don worked. Don's wife, Dawn, and I talked casually; they had two sons.

I awoke one morning to find Bobby cowering in the corner scared out of his wits.

"What's the matter with you?" I asked.

"You!"

"What'd I do; kick you?"

"Your body - it was hovering above the bed!" he said, holding his hands about two feet apart.

"You must have been dreaming," I said.

"No! I woke up when I felt you moving...*up*!"

I just looked at him.

"So I just got up and stayed up all night," he said, "to see what else you'd do."

"Well, was I hovering all night?"

"Most of it," he said, "then you dropped back down just a little while ago."

I thought about what he'd said. I wondered if spirits had been working on me, maybe they had lifted me up.

Finally, I just told him, "Well I wish I could do this when I'm awake."

Later, I heard Spirit say, "Your body was acting spontaneously while you were asleep."

My body did this the following two nights and Bobby was so afraid he moved to his mother's.

Returning to Indiana

A woman named Amy, who I knew from Kentucky, called me one day and wanted to come for a visit. I told her that would be fine. Well, soon after Amy came to visit, I decided to move back to Indiana. I really didn't want to but

Jason kept on saying he wanted us to go back and be around family. So we began to pack up.

I carried everything down the steps by myself because Amy said she had a bad back, which wasn't quite true. But she was willing to drive my car while I drove the moving truck.

We lived on the third floor and I had a portable bar. That thing was very heavy. As I took something down to the truck, two guys walked by. I told them I had a portable bar up there and if they would help me get it in the truck I would give them twenty dollars.

They burst out laughing at me and walked on. I got so mad I picked up a second wind and all this adrenalin started rushing through me. So I went up the stairs and picked the thing up by myself and carried it down and put it in the truck.

Amy's eyes grew as big as silver dollars. She asked what happened. I told her but she couldn't believe it.

"I know you can carry some little stuff," I said, "so get off your rump and let's get going."

"You aren't waiting until morning?" she asked.

"No, we're leaving tonight," I said.

She, Jason and our little Cock-a-Poo puppy, Peaches, rode in the car with some small items while I drove the moving van. I only had a pair of jeans on and a blue-jean shirt. It was February and cold and raining. I had become so worked up during the packing that I had gotten hot and had packed my jackets and coats away, not realizing I would need them later. Well, we got about an hour down the road and Amy pulled over to the side. In my rush to jump out to see what was going on I didn't realize the truck door had shut and locked behind me. Of course, I had left the truck running too.

It turned out that Peaches had gotten sick and thrown up. So we found some napkins and cleaned up the mess. I told her to wait until I got in the truck before she took off. Well, when I got back to the truck, I couldn't get in. I tried to pry the wing window open but it wouldn't budge. And it was like forty or fifty miles to the next exit.

So I told Amy to go and call these moving van people or see if someone at a gas station would come and help get this thing open. So they took off.

It started pouring down rain. I guess I needed to get soaked for some odd reason. It just made me more angry. I tried flagging down cars and trucks but nobody would stop. I broke off small tree limbs trying to pry the wing window open. Nothing would work.

So I sat and prayed and the lock on the back door of the truck unlocked; even though I knew I had locked it. And I had tried it before but I had found it firmly in place. Then I heard in my head "turn around and lift the door up."

Well, I turned around and grabbed the latch handle. It opened and I lifted the door up and out fell the dog's toenail clippers. I heard "use these to get the wing open" so I tried and the wing window just popped open. I stretched my arm through the window and was able to reach the door lock, pull it up and open the driver's door.

I had to sit there because I didn't know if Amy was on her way back or not. It took almost an hour before she got back. Some man was following her and I told him what happened and I offered to give him money for coming out but he said not to worry about it.

So we went on to Indiana. I was drenched. Luckily, I had a heater in the truck.

We got to my mother's the next morning; it had been about an eight hour trip. We only stopped to get gas and I was very careful not to shut the door unless I had the keys in my hand.

After we had some sleep and had rested, I unloaded my stuff in her house and took the truck back.

A Year of Mind Control

After about a month I found an apartment. But my mom introduced me to a guy who I wish I hadn't allowed into my life at all. She kind of forced him on me and I was stupid and gave in.

His name was J.R. and he was good looking but he was mean in a way that he would cheat on me and tells lies. He almost broke my back a couple of times. I would tell him what I felt was going on and he said I was hallucinating all the time.

Finally I went to a doctor and I asked him if he thought I was crazy. I told him what was happening and he told me I wasn't; but he thought I should go see the city prosecutor and get J.R. out of my apartment before he destroyed me. So I did.

He didn't want to leave; he even tried to come back several times. And I let him come back but I could not understand why.

Well, I found out later why after I had hidden some money in a photo album. It was about the third one from the bottom of my stack. I had about forty albums full of pictures at that time and I had put eighty dollars in one so I could have some money toward the end of the month.

Well, when I went to get it only twenty dollars were in there. I became very angry. When I confronted him about the money, he told me that I could not hide anything from him because he could read my mind, and could even put things in my mind.

So I went to Myrtle, the psychic lady, and asked her what I should do, she told me to make my mind go blank. Well, with a little practice I did and after a short while I finally got him out of there. But before he left, he had taken my broken down car to some guy he knew so it could be fixed. He would go up there everyday and told me that he and the guy were working on it a little at a time (it took almost a year).

It was then that I told him the vision I had seen; I told him I knew about him sleeping with another man's wife. He told me that I was hallucinating. I told him to just bring my car back and get out.

Later he did and told me I was right about all the women that Spirit showed me.

He said he was a spirit that had been sent to get rid of me in anyway it could. And he thought he could torment me to death; or drive me crazy to where I would commit suicide. That was the devil's plan. I told him to hell with the devil's plan, and his. I told him he needed to just get out of my life.

He brought my car back and had a bucket of bolts that he said was left over. He and the guy put it together just enough to get it to my apartment and leave it.

But I drove it. The spirits said it was being held together with spirit "safety-pins and band-aids". I could not afford to take it to a mechanic so I just prayed it would take me wherever I needed to go until I could get it fixed, or get another car.

Myrtle said my Indian guide Smokey was working to get me to a new place.

My First Move to Lexington

Later, Jason and I moved to Lexington. Lucy had moved there and I went to see her and she helped me find an apartment. I hadn't seen her in about five years so we decided that I should move there.

In Lexington, I got a job at the Funland Bowl-a-rama as a bartender. It was an interesting job but one of the bosses did not like me. His name was Dick, the owners' son-in-law. He would always find fault over something even though I would do my best to keep everything the way they wanted. I even worked overtime when I didn't have to in order to help out. I lived down the street from the bowling alley so most of the time I would walk to work.

I hated working the weird hours because Jason became what they called a "latch- key kid." But I made him call me when he got home. A lot of times he would come and play the video games and wait on me to get off work. I just felt he would be okay. I prayed for him every night and still do. (There is never a night that goes by that I don't pray for him).

I worked there until one night the register came up all sixes. That scared Dick. He turned white as a sheet and asked me if I did that on purpose.

"How would I know how to do that?" I asked him.

"I have been feeling weird all day, like something is going to happen," he said.

I thought that was strange, that he would say that to me, because I had told him a little about the ghosts in the building and some other things.

He asked me what kind of feeling I had.

Well, I had an eerie feeling and decided to go home to see about Jason.

He wasn't there when I arrived. I panicked and called the police; I thought someone had kidnapped him. Well, the boys finally came home and I yelled at both of them. He and another little boy had decided to go out on the town. They said they just wanted to go out and talk to people; they were only 10 years old.

But a tragedy did happen to a man that lived in an apartment three doors down from Lucy. Some people he knew robbed him. They drugged him and took him out and tied him up to the back of the car and drug him around and set him on fire. It was all over the news.

My friend was working late and came home and the police were swarming all over the place. So there was evil working that night for sure. I heard the next day that something had happened to Dick, or one of his family members, that night also. So I guess the sixes on the register were indeed a warning. I began to pay more attention to more things like that.

Major Adjustments

When I turned thirty, it seemed like everything amplified. More things started coming to me and Smokey started talking more to me. Or I just started hearing better. I got my first grey hair. It felt like my whole body went in to some kind of metamorphosis or something. It was weird; I didn't know what to do so I went to see Myrtle. She said more of my physic powers were kicking in. She said I should come back to Indiana and attend some of her classes and help her with opening her own church. And that her father's spirit told her to do this.

I told her I needed time away from Indiana but that I would come to her classes each week.

About that time, I decided to move to the other side of town and get a different job. So I found a factory to work in for Christmas and then went to work for a temporary service. I liked that because it seemed like I was not satisfied for very long at any one place; so this way, I had a variety of places to go and not become too bored.

When I didn't make much money, I donated blood plasma for gas money and had enough to go to Indiana and back for the classes.

I also met a guy Lucy knew named Howard. We were all talking and he said he knew a medium that channeled spirits.

I said I wanted to meet her. At first he said no; he didn't want anyone making fun of her. We begged him to take us to her and he said if he did and we made fun of her he would not speak to either one of us again. We promised, and he said to meet him at a certain time. We did and went to the channeling session.

Her chair sat on a platform and had a rope across it so no one would touch her. She went in to a trance. The first spirits talked to a man on the end. And then each spirit went to each one that was in the row. When it came my turn Smokey came through her.

I was amazed. She did not know me. Smokey told me I would be doing many things. One would be to help heal others. I could not grasp a lot of it. I was still digesting the things that Myrtle had told me I would be doing.

Then another spirit came through and said he was Dr. Rogers. He said I had a lot of grey areas that suggested I couldn't grasp or comprehend if this was real or not.

I told him that was true.

He said, "I am a philosopher for you and I will teach you what is and what isn't."

So he was with me for a long while. He would phrase things so beautifully that if it wasn't true, the way he spoke it made you think it was. But I have since found out all that he told me was true.

He said he was there to get me through the doubting phase of my life. He said Guides came into a person's life to teach and show the way. Once the person understands and trusts what they must, the person doesn't need the Guide any more and they move on, or sometimes they go to teach others.

One day Dr. Rogers "graduated." I guess his job was done, so he moved on. I miss him from time to time.

Some guides stay with a person all their lives, and some don't. I have had so many to come and go, and to be a guide in any form one must earn the right. The other reason guides come into our lives is that some come to work off some karma with the person or others so they can move on in peace. There are many reasons why we receive a guardian angel or Guide to help us in life. Babies and children can see spirits. It's only when we are conditioned in the belief systems and fears of others that we lose that connection. Parents and others tell the child that the person they are talking with is just an imaginary friend. And then one day the child is convinced that their friend does not exist; that the person was just their imagination and that now it is time to grow up and not believe. How sad.

Meeting Sitting Bull

One day I made an appointment with Viola and she did a chakra balancing on me and told me that Myrtle's classes were going to be good for me. She also knew Myrtle.

I had worked a few more places and one day Spirit said, "Go to the mall, Viola will be there. You are to work for her."

So I went and lo-and-behold, there she was. She had a wagon-type kiosk set-up and a stool. She read cards and sold books and crystals and little things.

I hadn't heard from her in quite a while and she hadn't returned my phone calls. So I went over to her and told her I had been calling to get a reading but had never heard back from her.

She said she had been so busy and had started this little job; and now she needed someone to work for her for a week. A family member was ill and no one she knew could substitute for her. She asked if I had a job.

I smiled and said, "No, but the spirits said to come here today, that you needed help."

She said okay; she could pay me five dollars an hour. So I agreed. She said for me to do some readings for people too. I was shocked.

"I can sell your books and stones but I don't know anything about the cards, and I don't think I can remember that book," I said.

She laughed and said, "You *are* clairvoyant; and you don't need the book. The cards are only a tool and you let the person pick one for a dollar and see what you feel from the person. Your Guides will help you."

I said that maybe I would try.

She had a tall stool to sit on and I went the next day, opened the little wagon up and I heard a voice say, "I am Sitting Bull."

"How did you get here?" I asked.

He said, "I have come to help you."

"How can you help if you were in a body and died and are now coming to me?"

So he explained that once you are in the spirit world and cross over in the light, things change and with the karma he had, he needed to help someone in an unusual way. So he was going to teach me the proper way to read the cards and tell me what to say.

I thought to myself, "Okay, this should be interesting."

First he said, "You must sit up straight. Put your hand on this big crystal and the energies from it will help you to amplify and see visions."

I thought that was cool, but scary too. But I did what he said.

That week seventy people came and received a reading. What Viola or Sitting Bull did not tell me at the time was the need to keep people to a time limit. So when Viola came back she said she was disappointed in me.

"What do you mean?"

"I had these people over here at the next booth watching you and they said you did full readings and cheated me," she said.

I was furious.

"If you are psychic you can ask your Guides," I said. "I don't know how to put those cards together. All I did was what Sitting Bull told me and seventy people came and all of them said that I read very well for them. I did not cheat you. You said charge a dollar a card and that's what I did. Ask your guides."

So she did. She looked at me and said, "I didn't tell you to say a few things and stop."

I said, "I didn't know there was a time limit."

She apologized and said, "I didn't know you were so sensitive. You were only supposed to tell them a little bit then charge more when there was more time involved."

Well, she hadn't told me that part, and she apologized again. She proceeded to tell me how to only talk about their life or what they wanted to know for a short time. But I never did get the hang of it. Even today, I go in to the space of spirit and time changes around me.

"Myrtle wants to teach me some meanings of the cards," I said. "Do you recommend it?"

"Yes," Viola replied.

I thought at that time it was all so cool. I would go to the bar where Lucy worked and tell people what I could see for them. I did it for fun.

One day Spirit said, "You are going to go to the bar but not dance tonight, I want you to observe others."

At first I thought they meant to watch others dance, maybe they didn't like the way I danced. So when guys asked me to dance that night I said no, I am resting. But what happened was I felt energy and spirits in the bar; one even played with my hair. Then other spirits started talking to me.

I asked what this was all about. My guide Smokey said he was there to protect me but for me to be aware that there were more spirits around. Some were not so good and many were earthbound.

So then I started learning about different spirits.

Ghost Whispering

There was a woman named Kim that would hang out with us from time to time.

Actually, there was Lucy, Gwen, me and Kim. But one day Kim called me crying. She had been dating a truck driver from Pikeville. She got the news that he had passed away drinking moonshine and she couldn't find anyone to go with her to the funeral.

I told her since Jason was in Indiana with my mother for spring break I would go with her. So she rented a car and paid our way there and back. We got into this little town outside of where her deceased friend was from and arrived at the funeral home early. The people let us in and we saw him in the casket. Kim went up to put a teddy bear in it with him. I sat down and looked at the flowers. They all looked dead. I made a comment about it and all of a sudden they all came to life. And above the casket was this man's spirit. He looked as real as we did. I looked at the casket and the body just laying there.

Kim turned around and asked me what I was looking at.

I said, "Him."

She came over and sat down beside me.

"He is talking to me and telling me to tell you some things," I said.

Right now I don't remember all that he said but he told me things about their relationship that I didn't know. She asked me how I knew them.

"He just told me and he says he loves you and for you to move on with your life," I said.

Then all of a sudden he disappeared.

I had to get some air. When I went through the door there was a man standing there that looked like him. At first I freaked out before he said he was the deceased man's brother. I almost fainted.

When the service started I almost didn't go back in but Kim kept asking me to, so I did.

I heard a voice say "Pay attention to the preacher and what he says because you will be doing this one day."

"Oh no, I won't," I said.

Well, I couldn't wait to get out of there. I told Kim we were not staying for anything else; everything was too weird.

We headed up the mountain on the way back home. We stopped for gas at a station and I told her if she would go pay and get me a candy bar, that I would pump the gas.

She looked at me and said she never knew her friend's middle name and hadn't picked up a card at the funeral home. Out of my mouth came the name Francis.

I told her I didn't know where that came from. She got out of the car, went in to the store and came out with a newspaper shaking it. I asked her what the matter was now.

She pointed to the newspaper and said, "Look."

There in the obituary was his picture and his name, Walter Francis Jenkins. I almost passed out.

"Let's get out of here," I said. "This might be one of those witch towns."

But something would not let us go. I was directed to go into the store. I only had seven dollars on me and when I went in I saw the headpiece of an Indian woman.

I heard, "You must buy this."

I couldn't put it down. It didn't have the price on it and when I asked the lady how much and she said, "With tax, I will let you have it for seven dollars."

Well, I came home with it. It was to represent one of my new Indian guides, named Rain Tree.

When we got home, of course, I told Lucy and Gwen but I also felt I had to go tell Viola.

"It doesn't surprise me," she said.

"Well, it does me."

She said, "You'll be seeing and doing a lot more than you realize."

I was flabbergasted. And then more things came to me.

Past Lives and Dramas

On one of the occasions when I worked for Viola, she started having me work once or twice a week. I started to meet more people that could do different things. I was amazed. Some of them talked about being hypnotized, and about past lives.

A man named Ken came for a reading. He said he was a hypnotist and I noticed he wore this big blue ring. I told him I had always wanted to be hypnotized to see who I was in a past life. Ken started turning his ring on his finger and said my energy was strong but that I needed to tone it down. I didn't understand what he meant. He told me but I still didn't comprehend. Then he offered to come to my house and hypnotize me.

So I had Gwen come over to be with me during the session. Ken started out by telling me a word to remember and that this would be my word to go under. I was so naive and gullible at that time. It's a miracle I am still here.

So I went first to an Indian lifetime and I saw myself pulling a travois, and I saw a large number of Indian people all walking in one direction. We set up for camp and I was going to have the children come and go to sleep when all of these horses started running. The dust was everywhere. I grabbed the children. And then out of the blue a white man with curly blonde hair came up to me and stuck a sword in me. It was Custer.

I felt the pain and I was dying, at twenty-three years old. I must have been dying in real life because Gwen screamed and cried that I was dying. I saw my spirit rising out of my body and into the spirit world. And I heard Ken say you are twenty-one...twenty-two...twenty-three...twenty-four and then something else until finally I came back.

Ken said this had been the most authentic hypnosis session he had ever encountered. I told them what I saw and felt. It was wild.

Gwen said she saw my face and that it appeared I was dying in the here and now. I told her it felt like it.

We all talked for a while and then Ken asked if I wanted to see another one. Dummy me, I said yes.

So then I went to a lifetime where I was a boy. That confused me until it was explained that your spirit is androgynous and you can go into a male or female body at birth and then experience that gender in that lifetime.

So I thought, oh well. In that life my name was Andropolis. I heard this woman calling to me. I was about nine or so. I had a tunic on and these other children came and wanted to go into this cave like place. So I went inside and in this place was a Minotaur, a half-person half-bull being with horns. It came charging after us and it killed me.

Ken had to talk me up out of that one too.

Gwen called a halt to the past-life regressions; it was too much and she was concerned that I wouldn't come back from the next one. She was actually scared. I agreed; no more regressions.

Ken's ride had gone home and I had to take him back to his apartment. But before he got out of the car, he said the word he had asked me to remember again and this time it was weird. Suddenly my guide Smokey came in to me and said, "You be still; let me speak."

I thought, "Okay."

Ken said, "You were my slave and every time I say this word you will do as I say and you owe me karma from a long time ago."

Smokey said, "You are not controlling my instrument and you will never come around her anymore in this manner. The word you use will be revealed to her and you will be exposed to many of your evil ways."

Well, I did not know what Smokey was saying, but Ken did and he got out of my car and ran.

Smokey stepped out of me and told me where to find out what this foreign word meant.

The next day I went to Viola's and before I said any thing, she said, "I just got some new cards in. One is in French. See what you feel with them."

I looked through them and saw the one that meant devil. It was the word this guy was saying to me and I told her about it. She asked me who he was and I told her how he came and received a reading and what happened as a result.

She was very angry. She said he had been conning women for a long time. And a friend of hers got involved with him and had experienced all kinds of bad luck.

So Viola called her friend and had me to tell her the story. And she put a stop to being around him and exposed him to many people; he wanted to prey on woman.

He showed up in our lives about a year after and apologized to me and said it was wrong of him to do that.

"Yes, it was," I said.

Kim was with me at the time and she said she would like for him to hypnotize her. I told her I didn't recommend it; but she kind of put the move on him, so he said he wouldn't use any negative words. He said after that Indian came in to me he was afraid of me and him. He agreed to be on his best behavior.

So he came over to Kim's house and I met them there. He was outside waiting on me and I asked him what the matter was. He said there was something going on in Kim's house that was strange. I told him I knew what it was. The previous night a man came in my dreams as if he was being seen through a television set and said his name. He was in Kim's house but he didn't mean to hurt anyone and to please help him. I told Ken I felt him in a nearby room and that he needed to leave, but I didn't know how to help him.

Ken said he did.

About that time Kim had seen us outside talking so she came out and we asked her if anything strange had happened in the house.

She said as a matter of fact something had. She had bought this wardrobe a few months before and some ghosts were in it. She said every time her daughter Wendy got a boyfriend their pictures would be thrown on the floor and the whole room would be rearranged.

I told Kim the ghost came in my dream and said he wasn't there to harm, but I thought we had better go see.

We went in and I was guided to just sit in a big chair. Ken walked back to the rooms to sense him.

"Come here and feel this energy!" he said.

"I can already feel it," I told him. "And he is walking into this room right now."

The man's spirit said his name was Harvey and that he was in love with Wendy, that she was his.

"No, she isn't," I said. "She is flesh and you're not."

Harvey said he wanted to talk to this man I was with, he couldn't hear me.

So I asked Ken if he could hear Harvey. Ken said no, which I thought was strange.

Ken suggested I let Harvey speak through me so he could talk to him.

After a moment, I agreed and asked Smokey to protect me.

Harvey sat in my lap with my spirit and then his spirit was inside me. He spoke to Ken and said he was killed by a man at a bar and his body had been placed in this wardrobe and even though his body had been found, his spirit had been there ever since. Now he wanted to be with Wendy.

Ken told Harvey he didn't have a body.

Harvey said he did now.

"No you don't," I said.

And Ken said, "You are talking through a woman and Wendy doesn't want a woman."

That was when Harvey said he would take Ken's body.

And Ken countered by telling Harvey he was sending him into the Light.

At that point my conscious mind and my spirit called Smokey in to help push Harvey out. And they took him out and sent him to the Light.

Back then I didn't know how to send a spirit over. It was scary. I learned the hard way about things and trusted Smokey to be my protector more than anyone on the planet.

I started dating a guy named Daniel and fell in love with him. Every time I looked into his eyes I melted. Viola said we were supposed to get married. So I had moved to a different part of town and he came to see me from over sixty miles away where he lived. It was like we were soul mates. I could tell most of what there was to know about him but he was good at hiding secrets too. I could sense him before he came to see me.

The other girls where I worked were jealous of us and I found out later through another person that one of them kept telling lies about me and wanted to cause trouble. I don't really talk to any of them anymore because Lucy is dead now. And I don't know where the other two are.

One day he had a wreck and blamed it on me because he was going to break up with me. I told him I had done no such thing; I loved him too much.

But, we didn't see each other anymore and I felt devastated. I worked a little at Keeneland, the thoroughbred race course near Lexington. I later moved back to Indiana and regretted it but I had to leave, there was no work available. I guess things changed for a lot of reasons. Even though I did not like the changes, they happened anyway. I think Spirit wanted me to move but Jason was doing well in the school there.

CHAPTER 10
SCHOOL DAZE

The Sweat Lodge

One day later on, I went to Lexington and saw Viola for a reading. She said that the Harmonic Conversion was going to be happening soon and that I needed to attend this ceremony that would only happen every one hundred or so years. Spirit told me not to attend, but she kept saying yes. I doubted what I was hearing and went with this girl named Lisa to the gathering. Well, Viola didn't tell me she and her husband were having trouble and the real reason she wanted me to go to this ceremony was so that I could spy on him. She just strongly urged me to go to this gathering. So Lisa and I went.

First we went to my mom's and Aunt Susie's. I left Jason with them so we could go. Aunt Susie said she didn't feel I should go; but because I knew some of my family had gotten a little jealous of me, I thought she just wanted me to miss out on something great. I invited them to go also, but neither of them wanted too. I was so naive and gullible back then, maybe I still am a little but I really try to listen to the spirits now.

Well, Lisa and I had traveled down the road about seventeen miles when her car quit. We asked some guys if they would look at it for us and when they did, they discovered we needed a starter. At the time, I just thought the dark side was trying to keep us from going. So I called my sister's husband and he came and put a starter on it.

I said, "Well, come hell or high water we're going."

What a wrong and foolish thing to say.

Anyway, when we finally found the place, we had to drive across a creek. Fortunately the water level was low at the time, and we crossed it without any trouble and arrived just before they began the ceremony. I told them Viola had urged us to come. They invited us to come in; they were getting ready to hold a sweat lodge and prayers for good things to happen in the future. So we went into the sweat lodge. Everyone sat in a circle where there was a hole in the middle of the ground. They put a large hot rock in the hole and poured water on it. The hot steam rolled throughout the interior.

A red-headed man started saying prayers and told everyone his wife was part Indian. I wondered where the real full-blooded Indians were that Viola told me about.

I saw her husband sitting there with a few women. At first, I didn't think anything of it and then when they started getting cozier, I finally figured it out. I still didn't know whether to tell Viola or not. After the first set of prayers I felt a little dizzy but okay. Then they passed a pipe around; it was long stemmed and had a bowl shaped somewhat like the Indians used in the old days. They opened the flap to the doorway and let a little air in and told everyone that this was the first door. They said there would be four "doors" and if anyone needed to go outside we could do so at that time.

I thought, "I'm okay; I'll just sit and see what happens during the next door."

Then they poured more hot water on the second rock that was in the hole. And more steam came up. I felt like I was in a sauna. I thought maybe it was like when you sweat out the bad stuff so good can come in. So I sat through the "third door" and Lisa said she couldn't take it any longer. So she and a couple of others left. I thought if I am here to be purified I might as well sit through the fourth one and not leave. So I did.

They put in the fourth rock and poured more water on it and more steam came up. I just sat there and prayed to be purified and for good things to come into my life. After the fourth door, they ended the prayers and I felt weak. I crawled out of the lodge and went and sat by Lisa on the ground. The others went to the other side, kind of like they were talking about us. I couldn't figure out what the deal was. I looked over to the lodge and saw this huge Indian man come out of the sweat lodge and he looked at Lisa and me.

I looked at Lisa and said, "Where did he come from? I didn't see him in there."

She didn't know. He was dressed in full regalia and looked like a Native American chief from the 1880s, just in new native clothes. He waved at us and I told her I was going over to talk to him. He looked as solid as we did; he walked down over the hill and disappeared. (Later I learned he was the spirit of Apache Chief Cochise).

I went over to the group that was there and asked them where he went. One guy suggested I sit down and drink some water. They thought I was hallucinating. I told them what I saw and another man said after a person sits for all four doors they should stay there all night and rest. I told him I couldn't; I had to go to work the next morning.

So Lisa and I just gathered our things and got in the car. We had just started across the creek when what looked like a large deer, or maybe an elk, came walking down the hill. It stopped right in front of her car and stared at us. Then instead of walking across the road it turned around and went back up the hill with its head held down. I thought that was strange and so we went back to my mom's. Susie was over there and she said the spirits were angry that we went. I said that was hog wash.

Well, we went back to Lexington. I got Jason ready for bed and I went to sleep on the couch. The next morning I woke up and could not move. I called in sick to work but they fired me for not coming in. I sent Jason on to school and just laid there and cried and prayed.

The next day this lady I knew, Gwen, a Hidatsa Indian, called me and said she had just returned from South Dakota where she had been visiting her family. She asked what I had been doing. As soon as I told her the story, she said she was on her way over. When she finally got there she said I looked awful. She asked me if I had smoked the pipe. I told her only one time. She said I should never smoke a pipe, especially with a mix of people, men and women together. At that point she said in her tribe, they perform separate ceremonies for men and women. And the woman does not smoke the pipe.

I told her my family had stopped practicing native ceremonies a long time ago and also stopped teaching the old ways. She said for me to let her call her mother to see what they could do for me. She started speaking in their native tongue. I said okay.

While she was on the phone, my guide Smokey came in and said he had been to a spirit council meeting to plead my case. He told me to let Gwen's people help me and to do exactly what they said. I told him I would. (No more disobeying spirit world). He said the wrath had come upon me for going. I asked him if he told them I hadn't understood at the time and he said they did.

When Gwen got off the phone with her mother, she said I had to make a personal sacrifice and that meant cutting off some of my hair, taking it outside and burning it. Then I had to promise never to go into a sweat lodge again. I said I would. And then she said I would have to cut meat up in little squares every night and beg for forgiveness. I said no problem. So she helped me get up and get the scissors and cut my hair and take it to the balcony and burn it and say prayers. I felt a little lift after that. Then I went and took some lunch meat and cut it up in little squares every day.

I told Viola about it and said I was very disappointed in what had happened. She said her husband had confessed; they were going to get a divorce and she would move away.

I thought, "Well, so much for that."

But the experience at the sweat lodge had taken my powers. I couldn't get a job anywhere. And that's when I moved back to Indiana and took the bus job.

I figured I couldn't trust anyone. And I got talked into going back to Myrtle's church.

The School Bus

So I went to live in Jeffersonville, Indiana, and found a job driving a school bus in Louisville. It was one of the hardest jobs I ever had. I got up early and had three loads of children to get to schools by eight o'clock.

First, I had the high school kids, they were the worst. They like to throw things and cut the seats up. I had to turn them in everyday. I was so mad; the job only paid six dollars an hour but for those days it was good. For all the stuff I had to put up with it, it should have paid six hundred dollars an hour.

Well, the first day I was downtown and on my way to pick up the second load of children when the bus quit on me. It just simply broke down. So I radioed it in. The school sent another bus to collect the children and I had to wait. The other bus finally arrived where we were and I took it and picked up the rest of them.

Every time it rained the kids would get riled up; some of the other school bus drivers said it was the negative ions in the air. So every day I prayed for sunshine and if it was to rain I asked for it to wait until night time. It was crazy.

One day this boy cut the seats up and threw a potato at me while I was driving and I almost wrecked. I stopped the bus I was so mad. I drove him back to the school and made the principal take him to the office. I was wearing an amber whale necklace and when I went into the rest room it just broke all to pieces. And I heard Spirit say the boy's anger did that. So the stone had taken on his anger instead of me at that point.

The grade school children weren't too bad, although they had their moments. And the kindergartners liked to jump all over the seats while I was driving. There were no seat belts in busses back then. I was so frustrated.

This went on day-after-day. Four months had gone by when I got a letter from Jason's school. They wanted to know what was wrong with him because he had missed so many days. I had always set the clock for him to get up and go to school after I left for work. Well he wasn't getting up when the alarm would ring. It was another set back; I was so mad.

One day soon after that, I was driving to work and stopped at an intersection. When I looked to one side to check for traffic, I saw what looked like a man in a robe sweeping the sidewalk at five in the morning. I thought he was crazy. He wore what appeared to be a monk's robe. But what I found strange was that when I passed by I couldn't see his face.

When I got to work I always had to climb on top of the front bumper of the bus to check the oil and water and such. Well, this particular morning I fell off; I slipped and down I went. I wrenched my arm hard and couldn't drive so I had to stay home for a while.

My Aunt Susie came by and said she saw me being killed on the bus; that I better quit while I could. I reminded her that I still had to work.

The arm sprain had laid me off from work for about three weeks, but then the contractor for the county school bus system wanted me to drive with a hurt wrist. I had a supervisor who had a crappy attitude and he didn't care about anything but himself and money. He put me back to work and gave me another route; it was on the west end.

For the most part the West End kids were okay. Only a couple of them gave me a little trouble, but I wore my crystals. There was one child, a fifth grader, who asked me about the crystal. I told him a little about it. I asked him if he liked crystals. He said he did, and then he asked me if I told fortunes. I ask him why he wanted know. He said he had always heard if a person wore crystals they could tell the future.

"Well, maybe," I said.

Then all the kids started saying "tell my future" and stuck their hands out. I got tickled.

"So all of you know about this?" I asked.

And they all shook their heads yes. They ranged from the first grade to the sixth. And all of them wanted to know what they were going to become and how many children they were going to have.

One little boy said something smart to me and kicked the seat. I told him that if he kept doing that and having attitudes, he wouldn't have much of a future. He said he was going tell his brother and his brother would bring his gun and shoot me. Then an older boy said that's what had happened to the other bus driver. She had taken him off the bus and his brother bought a gun and was going to shoot her. And she quit, and that was how I got the job.

I said, "Oh really, well I am not afraid of your brother or anyone else for that matter. You're going to do as I say or I will just sit here and you all will be late for supper."

So he apologized and didn't give me much trouble the rest of the year. His brother didn't come either. The other kids were amazed, although I still had trouble out of the high school kids. The kindergartners were good some days and on rainy days they just jumped from seat to seat.

The one little boy who had kept asking me about my crystal told me one day that he would like to have this old flannel shirt I wore on the bus. It had a red and black check pattern. I felt the day before I quit that I should go ahead and give it to him. The day I quit there must have been something in me that knew something was going to happen because he said he wanted my shirt when school was out. I asked him why. He said he didn't know; he just wanted it, maybe to remember me later. So I said okay. He must have known I would not work there anymore.

The Wreck

I had a wreck one day while carrying the kids. I had just pulled up to an intersection, and like I did every morning, I made sure to look around the bus to confirm that nothing was coming from any direction. Well, I went to pull out to the left and out of the blue, a van hit the bus and bent the heavy bumper in front backwards and the van went spinning out of control across four lanes of traffic. It then slid up into a yard and stopped right before it would have plowed into a house.

The woman in the van was thrown to the floor. She had had to pull on her handbrake to stop the van. But the woman in the van managed to jump out, run over to the bus and ask if we were okay.

She said, "I thought I could beat you."

The lady in the house that was almost hit called the police and brought us a soda because she saw me shaking. I was so confused but another bus came and took the kids. Then they made me drive another group home that evening.

I was so weak and shaky by the time I finally got home I literally crawled out of the car onto the sidewalk and then up the steps to get into the house. At the time, I didn't know I had hypoglycemia, low blood sugar. I just went to sleep.

I went in the next day and the mechanic kept telling me that accidents come in three's. I told him to quit saying that; he was cursing me. That was the most stressful job.

The second incident had occurred when I was going around the curve on this one street and a boy plowed into the side of the bus. He got out and said I had run into him. I was so mad that he lied. He knew he ran into me.

That was when the mechanic had said, "See, that's number two."

Well, the month of May finally came and I thought, "Great, only two more weeks and its over."

Then came that Friday that I was headed back into the station where we parked the buses and as I went upon the ramp a car hit me in the backside. Inside was a group of east Europeans. I flipped out; I couldn't believe it. Some guy stopped behind us who saw what had happened. I was so shook up I couldn't move the bus. Then the police came and bitched me out for just sitting there. I told them I wasn't moving it because it was not my fault and I wanted them to see that. It turned out that the people in the car could not read yield signs; it wasn't my fault. I finally got the bus pulled over to the side and finished with the paper work and called dispatch. I quit that day. I said no more. I couldn't take it. So much negativity was thrown at me from so many different people.

Back to Church

During the three weeks I was laid off from work for my sprained arm, I started going to the metaphysical church, the Fellowship of Truth. My sister Sandra went to a channeling session at the church to see two ladies channel spirit guides. They called the spirits their "joy guides." They said their joy guides came to them as children to help bring joy into a person's life. I thought that was cool. I told Sandra I wished I had a joy guide because I needed joy in my life at that time. She said she did too.

When they started, one woman asked all of us to speak our name. There were thirty of us. Then they said in order to raise the vibration, we all needed to repeat the sound of "Ohm" several times. As the people would say the Ohms I would feel strange. The more they said the Ohms the more I felt my Guide Smokey with me. It was like I had two heart beats and two breaths. I heard Smokey say the energies were drawing him in and that he was not there to hurt me.

"I am to protect you from other spirits in the room," he said.

Well, I didn't know what that meant at the time but I felt afraid.

When Myrtle and Joan finished and came back to themselves, my sister kept kicking me and saying, "Wake up!"

I could hear her but I could not respond.

Then one of the other ministers came running over to me and said Spirit told one of the people in the group someone would go into a trance but did not say who it would be.

I was thinking, "What do I do now?"

Somehow Jill took me in to the next room and she worked the energies to separate Smoky and me. I don't remember what he told her through me, but he told them of "earthbounds" in the room. And when they got the tape rewound and played it, you could hear someone growling and asking for help. So they went to the church and said prayers for the spirits. Myrtle said I needed to come to her classes and train with her and the others.

I felt inclined to agree. I told her about meeting Viola and she knew her.

I got to meet others that played a role in my life. Good and bad. I went to the church every week and on Sundays to understand this more.

Myrtle's Church

Back then, before I was ordained, Myrtle started her church by renting out a little building that used to be a small airport guiding tower. It had two stories to it. The church part was in the top and other areas were in bottom. We stayed there for two years during which I learned more about meditation and channeling.

I used to be what some would call a "dead trance medium"; that's where I would only move my mouth and nothing else would move. The energy from the spirits of the light would be so strong that it would pull my neck back. I must have looked weird. I did my first service there. We had to practice since we were going through the program. All the students took turns at the podium. When it came my turn I was very nervous standing and talking in front of a crowd; and we had a red carpet, that didn't help matters much. The energy of red made me shake for some reason. I was used to the color blue and it was calming to me. I just had to adjust.

But Smokey pulled me through. He said to just let him speak some through me and tell a story of love and friendship; so he spoke and I spoke and I was okay. Afterwards, everyone said it was such a good service; some had a few tears in their eyes.

The church then moved into an old school in New Albany, Indiana. At least it was bigger and handicapped people could get into this building.

I did what I and some others called "faith healing". I would do a prayer and touch the pain in a person and it would go away. At church one day, this older lady, about seventy-five, came up to me and said she had visited the doctor the other day because she smoked and he told her she had emphysema.

"I prayed about it," she said, "and God said I was to come to you because you were going to heal me today. He said in a past life you were my daughter and a healer."

(I thought the doctor also forgot to tell her that she had Alzheimer's).

Finally Myrtle came over and asked what was going on. The elderly woman told her. At the time we were outside planting a tree for Joanne because she had died of cancer. So I just looked up at the sky and started praying and said, "God, if you told this woman these things you better get in here and help because I don't know what to do."

I heard this voice say, "Put one hand in front of her and the other behind her and pray."

My hands were shaking really fast and became extremely hot. In a little while, they stopped shaking and she started breathing easier; then she said she was cured. She went to the doctor the next day and told him.

Visions and images started coming to me after that and I would relay these things to the people who came to me for help or insight.

During the time I was a school bus driver, I met Ernie and we stayed together about six months, he couldn't understand why I had to go to work and come home and go to the church for classes. Well it was mandatory to get the classes in so I could become ordained. I started to quit a lot of times. I would get frustrated. Jason didn't really want another person in my life either, or for me to go to the church, but I would ask Jesus and he said I must go. Ernie finally said it was either him or the church and I chose the church.

As I looked back on it, I still felt, "What was the use?"

But Smokey pointed out I would learn the do's and the don'ts with all I came in contact with and that would include meeting a lot of my enemies.

I was really confused then. I thought what did I do to these people; and if it was a past life, what about forgiveness? Because I surely didn't understand. It seemed like time dragged on longer back then for some reason. It seemed like I had already lived a 100 years or so. But during that time at the church I was developing different skills, I guess you could say. I had to do a lot of meditation; and pray more than once a day and hope that Jesus and Smokey would not abandon me.

God had appointed Smokey as my protector. I once asked Smokey if he could do all kinds of things then why did I need the others. He said watching over me was like an assembly line. If he did it all, he couldn't focus on the protection part. Smokey said I had Alicia as my "joy guide". She was to help me lighten up and another guide, Penelope, was to address certain other things. And Sitting Bull, he helped me with the card readings, which was actually a clairvoyant reading because the cards would allow the person's energy on something so I could pick up on the person and tune-in to their guides and angels. I had Doctor Rogers as my philosopher guide.

Then I was introduced to THOR. He is one of the Olden Gods and he was there to help Smokey protect me and to shift earth energies. So he had to teach me how to do that by splitting the energies into a double-helix shape and then shift the energies and vibrations of the vortices and ley lines by turning them clockwise and clearing them out. Then Thor would seal them with a symbol from God.

Then came Geronimo. I was confused at first, because he was an Apache warrior. He told me, like Sitting Bull, he wanted to help people to understand him and wanted to help in a way of healing. So I asked Smokey about this and he confirmed that Sitting Bull was to come and introduce a healing head dress through me and when people would touch it the energies would allow the vibration to activate certain natural healing qualities in them.

So when I did any trance channeling sometimes he would come in and bring the head dress with him. That made a lot of people in the church jealous. One person asked why he picked me. And Geronimo said he picked me to do this because I was an Innocent and I had the power and that I would learn more when I got to know who I am incarnated.

A couple of years later I walked into a shop in Jeffersonville, Indiana, and I saw Viola, but she had changed her name and married another man, who did not have good energies either. We talked for a while and she said she was doing new and full moon ceremonies and would like for me to come. I told her as long as it did not involve going into any sweat lodges. I was forbidden to enter them and I told her what I had to do to even function again. She said this would just be a circle outside and prayers in the light of the moon. I asked my guides about it and they said it would be okay for the experience but not to do anything they told me not to. So I learned from the other one.

When I went there I really didn't like how they performed the ceremony. Viola's husband kept demeaning her in front of people and that did not sit well with me. But I kept my mouth shut even though I felt she had made another mistake. And I wondered why her guides didn't tell her about him before she married him. I guess they had some sort of Karma or sacred contract to work out between themselves. Like my guides said – a learning experience.

There were a few younger people there and a boy about eighteen named Blake. When I looked at him I kept seeing all these things about him and what he was to do when he got older. I didn't know this was his first experience; and, I didn't know he was scared of what I had said.

Well, I didn't go back to any of their gatherings but I went to their store to purchase incense and candles and crystals. It was the only store that had such things back then. Viola did a reading on me and said that she saw me doing different types of healings. People would think they were strange but they would be effective. I continued to go and visit her every once in a while and talk about spiritual things and I forgave her for sending me to that sweat lodge deal.

The Mantis Beings

One day, about a year later, I was in Viola's store and the young man named Blake came in. He said he wanted to tell me something; I told him to go ahead. He said I had scared the crap out of him at that meeting last year. He didn't know what to make of it but all that I had said would happen had happened. He wanted me to be his teacher. I told him that Viola was the teacher. But Viola said she had taught him all that she could, now it was my turn. She said she was going to divorce her husband here and move again. She didn't know where she would go. I asked her to keep in touch with me. I told her that all I could do was share with him what I have learned from her and Myrtle and my guides.

Blake called me a few days later and asked if he could come over. I told him he could. When he arrived, he showed me some large crystals he had brought over; he said they were called Celestial Crystals.

I took them in my hand and suddenly, out of the blue, I was lying on the floor channeling an alien. I saw myself on a ship of some kind and the beings looked like blue preying mantis. And I was freaking out. One of them told me to not be afraid; they were good beings. I told them I didn't care; I wanted to go home.

They said I would but one of their kind was speaking through me to the person in the room from which I came.

I thought, "Oh no, is Blake okay? Is my body okay?"

One of the beings said they were only sharing information about them to him. They were called the Mantis people. They were there to help humans to survive on the planet in the end days. I asked if the end days were happening right then. He replied no, but they had other skills. He explained they helped hold energies for the earth's atmosphere. I said I understood. He said they would contact me later and work with me.

The next thing I knew I was back in my body and barely moving. It took me a while to get back to myself.

Blake asked, "Wow! Do you know what happened?"

I told him what I heard and seen. I told him to get those rocks away from me. They scared me. Then I saw Jesus. I started asking Him all kinds of questions. And he told me not all beings that are not human are evil; that some beings do help out with what we need done in the universe. I told Him I didn't really feel comfortable channeling beings from another place, especially looking like that. He said I still had a lot to learn.

I told Him I didn't know there was so much.

Later Blake brought over some different gem stones and said I was supposed to work with these. I asked him how he knew that. He said he didn't know but he just knew I was. I told him it looked like he was the teacher. He said we were supposed to learn some things together. He had read that gem stones would open a person up more so they could talk to their guides and angels and he wanted to do that. Spirit had told me that someone would bring these stones for me to learn to work with.

He said, "Let's meditate with them."

I told him I didn't want aliens coming through that might be bad. Then I heard Smokey say there was a being that was a stone master that wanted to work with me. Smokey said his name was Moon Hawk and that he knew all about stones.

"Well, if you say so," I said.

So Moon Hawk started telling me about the different properties in stones and how our body had different frequencies and vibrations and that we had to match them up with the people. He went on to explain how I was supposed to put stones on the bodies' chakras and pull energies; and then after that, I was to place other stones on them to balance them.

Blake became the guinea pig. Moon Hawk told me to tell him in three days he would feel the effects. Blake became impatient because the vibrational change did not happen at the moment that he wanted it. But on the third day he called me and apologized and asked me to forgive him for acting like he did. I told him it was no problem but he had to learn like I did. This was new for me also and when they said it would take three days it would take that long. He continued coming for a while and we would practice readings and stone work and meditate and channel. He would bring some of his friends over and we practiced on them. Finally, one day Smokey told me I needed to advertise the type of healing I offered. So I did and gradually, more people began asking for them.

CHAPTER 11
∞
MAFU, UNIVERSAL MASTER BEING

Lucy's mom passed away that summer and she wanted me to go to the funeral with her. So I did. That's when I met one of her nephews. I told one of the little girls there that he was cute; so of course she just had to go and tell him. He was about four years younger than I was, named Luke. He asked me for my phone number.

When I went back home I started going to Myrtle's church and a guy name Jack was doing readings. He told me I would have a relationship with a guy name Russell, the relationship would be long-term and both of us would grow spiritually.

I thought, "Well, I don't know where he got that name; the guy I met, and liked, was named Luke."

Later, I received a letter from Luke stating his adoptive parents had named him Luke; even though his original name was Russell. I flipped out. I thought it was meant for us to be together. And for a while, we were. That was around the late eighties and we stayed together off and on until the early nineties. He was very attentive and loveable, at first. Then as we met more people he became just awful. I would teach him some healing work, reflexology and how to read the cards; and, he went to some classes and to church with me too.

After I was ordained, Myrtle held a channeling class and said it was to be a "cabinet trance" class. That's where the medium sits behind a curtain and the spirit uses the medium's ectoplasm, and sometimes the audience's ectoplasm, to manifest. Now, before the class started, two voices came to me. One said his name was Mafu and the other said he was Ramtha. Mafu said I had to choose between them. They were here to mobilize me.

"What does *that* mean?" I asked.

Alice, one of the ministers, asked me what I was hearing.

I told her and she told me who they were. She said there were other mediums that channeled these beings and wrote books about them.

I said, "Well, they can go back to them because I don't want to be mobilized."

She said I should feel honored.

I told her I didn't know what they meant to do.

Alice said, "All they will do is move your body around."

I said, "No way, I am afraid I will fall."

"Just relax," she said, "and let it happen."

Then Myrtle came over and Alice told her what the spirits had said to me. I told her to let them use Alice or someone else.

She said, "Just get in the cabinet and don't worry about it."

Then Dan, a young twenty-year old man from England, volunteered to get in the cabinet.

"Yeah, let the new people have a chance", I said.

So Myrtle offered, "If he gets in, then you sit beside the cabinet."

"Okay."

I thought I would be safe from those two voices that I had heard. Myrtle had wanted me to be close by because I carried a lot of ectoplasm.

Well, we said our prayer; the only light that was on was a night light in front of the cabinet. I think I counted maybe ten people in the room as we all started repeating our Ohms.

The next thing I knew I blacked out and the voice of Mafu began speaking through me. My spirit energy was beside my body and I heard Myrtle and Jane say that was the strongest spirit they had ever felt.

Mafu told them he was there to work with me and to mobilize me. He had another spirit to help Alice named Makia and that Makia would mobilize her; and, he said for Myrtle and Jane to sit and work with us. So they agreed.

Mafu then asked Alice to step up to my body to receive the spirit of Makia. When she did, she almost fell back because the energy was so strong. The spirits had to bring us up to their vibration. When Mafu was finished speaking, I almost fell out of my chair.

They told me what had happened, but I was still afraid. I kept wondering why all of this was happening.

Then I heard a voice say, "You are a chosen one."

I still couldn't quite comprehend. But it took off and on for four months to get mobilized and stabilized with Mafu. Until I my voice box adjusted, I sounded somewhat like him.

And my family was *not* pleased. They were afraid for me.

Smokey told me to relax, that Mafu was not there to harm me, but to balance the church and help me with a lot of things that were yet to come.

I didn't know there was going to be so much to understand, to learn and to do. During those four months, I looked like a robot walking around. Sometimes we practiced twice a week. That was around July of 1990. That was when Mafu decided he would be the one to come through me instead of Ramtha. Ramtha is a very strong spirit and felt too overpowering, where Mafu was more gentle.

One time, these people wanted two mediums to come to their business and do readings. I rode with Myrtle and Alice to the place and Mafu wanted to talk. Before Mafu said anything, Alice gave me a look that said "don't you dare channel Mafu."

Of course, Mafu said he would if he wanted to. I got in trouble a lot because Spirit wanted to speak through me. (Mafu is an Ascended Master; he is with the Hierarchy in the Spirit Realm).

Jesus approved those who came through me and those who came to teach me about the universe and the spirit world.

In June of 1990, I was ordained, and we did well together and then some of the people at church started getting jealous of what we had together, energy wise. I didn't understand at the time.

Then a spell was put on me in 1991. It was probably put on me before then but it took hold of me in January of that year. I had been warned about it; but since I could not understand why someone would do that to me, I guess it was a learning experience.

It came from this one couple that we thought were friends who started taking me to dinner and other places while Luke went to visit his family. They put in my head he was cheating on me, and he probably was; but they made it worse.

Luke came home one night when I had an ear infection. And this woman – we'll call her Lill and her boyfriend Gill – knew this old-fashioned way of clearing the ears with ear candles. This is where you stick one end of the candle in your ear and light the other end up and the heat helps the ear wax attach to the candle wax.

So I let her do this to my ears. Well, she looked down in one and said I had a lot of ear wax but she would take a bobby pin and remove what she could. Well she stuck it in and it punctured my ear drum. I came off that table screaming it hurt so much. I also had a low tolerance for pain.

I went to the doctor and he gave me some medicine but I just kept getting sicker and sicker. By the end of two weeks I had placed all the wax build-up and excess in a freezer bag and taken it to the doctor. He couldn't believe what had come from my ears. I pointed out that the ear waste even included a batch of parasites. They looked like little black bugs coming out of my ears. He referred to is as "voodoo." I was shocked. He left the room and I looked at Luke and asked him what we were supposed to do now. Then the nurse came in and said for me to take these antibiotics; and go see a priest or do a lot of praying, they couldn't help me anymore.

So we went home and I called Myrtle and my Aunt Susie since they knew about these things. I was so confused and hurt that this so-called friend would do this to me. I would see black figures in the night with their faces on them and we would wake up with little bite marks on us.

They had me not just praying but going to the cross roads and bathing in milk and doing all kinds of different things to get rid of it. We even performed a ritual using a lemon and the black things would come out of my ear into the lemon.

I called Myrtle when we got home because the black things were coming out of this rock that Lill and Gill had given me. And then they were coming out of the telephone; even Luke saw it. We threw the phone away. So I guess whatever was put on me was really bad. (I later asked Lill about this spell and she claimed other people's spirits were posing as her and her husband; I guess you could call them "spiritual imposters." Finally, I just told her until I could find out for myself I just didn't want to have anything to do with her).

Nothing worked. I grew more and more sick. It got to where I couldn't eat or swallow. Then my kidneys shut down and all of my body just collapsed. In those five weeks, I lost over fifty pounds. I felt depressed and betrayed.

The only thing I knew to do was pray. So I did what I could. I became very slim for my build, around one hundred and eighteen pounds. That was too skinny, especially for me.

Finally, Luke had to prop me up in bed like a rag doll. I could not lift my arms or move my legs.

Then one day I died. I thought I was having this cool dream; it was so peaceful. I was walking on top of this water and in the middle of this water was a man. He looked like a wise man or a wizard.

He said, "You are to come with me. I am Timothy, Timothy from the Bible."

"Okay."

So he placed his arm around me and we went straight up into this mist. We came to a place where I saw people in white robes and beautiful flowers. And I just stood there looking around. The next thing I knew I was looking at Luke. He was standing there screaming with sweat dripping down his face with tears looking at me and saying not to leave him. I told him I was only asleep.

"No, you were dead," he said.

The paramedic looked at me as if he had seen a ghost and said, "We'll take you to the hospital."

I said, "No, they can't fix me; and I don't have insurance."

Luke said he did not know how long I was gone before he got upstairs but the paramedics were there almost forty-five minutes trying to get me back. They said my heart had stopped and I was not breathing. Luke put a mirror in front of my face and I looked as white as chalk. I looked awful. I was so frustrated and angry that they called me back.

The paramedics left; Luke sat with me all through the night. The next day, Luke said he had to have a cigarette. I told him to go ahead and get a pack.

He said he had called my mom but no one answered the phone and the lady next door was out. I told him I would stay awake until he went to the store. So I laid there. There was nothing else to do.

When he left, I saw a big wolf come into the room. At first I thought I was going to be attacked. But then I saw the spirit of Grey Wolf with the wolf, and I knew him from meditations and journeying before. So I asked if he came to take me with him. He said no. I felt no one wanted me; so what was I supposed to do now? I couldn't move.

Then a big golden light appeared behind him and a really loud voice said, "I have sent you to do my work and you must do it."

"No disrespect," I said, "but I cannot move and I don't know what to do."

The Voice of God said, "You will take your spirit power name back and live."

Again I said, "I do not know what that is. If I did I have forgotten."

"Your name is Sha `La and mankind will call you Sha `La."

He pronounced the – a – in the first syllable with an "ah" sound and the – a – on the end as a long vowel, as in "day", so that it sounded like "Shah-lay".

"Uh, okay - how do you spell that?"

And he told me and said Grey Wolf would speak it every day and for me to tell others and have them call me this.

In a little while Luke came running upstairs and asked what happened. There was a strange energy in the air and he had felt something.

So I told him what had happened and about reclaiming my spirit name. He wrote it down. And as Luke wrote my name I felt a little energy.

"You were gone over forty-five minutes yesterday; are you sure you want to be doing this?" he asked.

"Well, they don't want me over there yet; and to break the spell I have to take my power name back from heaven," I said, "It's the only way."

He agreed.

In a few days I started getting phone calls from different people from the Enlightened Path Church. I told them what had happened and one girl said she was hearing for me to put the name on business cards.

"You know your family won't call you that," Luke said.

"I know."

But I told them anyway. My son, Jason, said he would come back home since I was feeling better. He had been staying with my mother.

I started getting my appetite back and started drinking tomato soup and water; then I gradually began to eat more solid food and getting my strength back. Grey Wolf stayed with me, speaking my spirit name over and over. I finally felt my kidneys working. Luke would carry me back and forth to the bathroom. Then by the end of the third week I felt better but not completely well yet.

The year before, I went with Blake to a psychic fair put on by a man name Max Loren. It was the first one I worked other than the events Enlightened Path Church put on. And I had read for some people that Blake had also read for in a different fair. He had told them about me and wanted me to come and do readings there. So I went. Many of the people who came said I told them a lot of accurate information. Sometimes my readings covered events that would occur during the coming year.

So anyway, the phone rang and a lady named Dotty from Birmingham called me and said she hoped I would remember her from last year; that I had read for her at the psychic fair in Huntsville. And all that I told her had happened. She wanted to sponsor me to come to Birmingham. She had eighteen people that wanted a reading. I asked her how that would work because I had never done that before and I had only read mainly at physic fairs. She told me I could come to her house and stay; that she had a room that I could work in. I heard God's voice come in and tell me to tell her I could only come if she introduced me as Sha `La.

So I told her I needed to tell her what God said. I told her the story and she agreed to introduce me as Sha `La. She told me to come in two weeks. So we borrowed sixty dollars and Luke took me there. I had the old Chevy and he had a yellow Ford. The Ford was in better shape so we took it. It was in my name but he claimed it because he worked on it a lot and helped pay for it.

I introduced Luke to her and she showed us a room. The next morning we got up, dressed and people started showing up. On the third day this woman, Sandy, came and said she had spoken with God. Her father had placed her in a hospital for treatment because of her claims; and now she had come to me seeking help.

I applied a stone layout over her and she began to feel better. After the treatment, and while she was in the bathroom, God told me to have her to sit directly in front of me and that he would send energy between us. While I was sitting there in the living room, two other women came in to receive readings; I asked the two women to sit patiently for a few more minutes so that Sandy could return and sit in front of me again. When Sandy returned to the room, I told her what God had said, so she sat down in front of me again.

Suddenly a huge white light came in through the window, drenching everyone. Then all I could see was a feathered cape draped around me. It felt very peaceful and I heard a Voice ask, "Do you accept?"

After all I had gone through, I was afraid to say no.

So I said, "Yes, I do."

At that moment, I didn't feel any pain or energetic residue from the ear parasites and resulting illness I had experienced earlier; I even began to feel strong again.

After the light lifted, everyone in the room commented about the experience. I told them what I had seen and they confirmed seeing the Light as well.

"What *was* that?" one lady asked.

I told her I wasn't sure but God had given me a special gift and then I described the feathered cape to her. Sandy said that not only had she felt the light, she had also received an extremely peaceful feeling. And, she added, the Voice of God had told her to be afraid no longer.

I saw thirty-two people that week and more wanted me to come back in the near future. We left for home at the end of the week; after we had been home for a few days, we attended a service at Myrtle's church. At that time, she told everyone she had a friend that owned a large farm where U.F.O. sightings often occurred and that we were all welcome to visit to see if any would materialize. She said we could all go there and meditate and send love to the beings above.

But I was still kind of scared because of what had happened with the Celestial Crystals. I told her about it, and about the encounter when I drove a semi-truck. But she said everything would be fine.

So Luke and I went to the farm. We all took blankets and sat in this field. I visualized pink light coming from my heart charka because Myrtle said to and I saw it go into the heavens.

Well, there I was again on a space ship. I couldn't figure out how that happened. It felt like my whole body was in the ship. I thought they had beamed me up. I didn't know if they had physically abducted me like before or actually taken my spirit. Again I was scared. They told me that they were the Ashtar Command group. I didn't know any of these beings.

And I thought to myself, "Just how many aliens were out there in the universe?"

They told me everything would be okay; my body was being used so Ashtar could talk to my commander.

And I thought, "Is the President down there or what?"

But they meant Myrtle, because she was the leader of the church.

When he got through talking through me, I was beamed back in my body and my body collapsed. I found myself lying in Myrtle's lap.

She said she knew I was going to fall backwards and she got behind me to catch me. I was so out of it four guys had to carry me to the car.

One jealous person, I forget which one, said I was just trying to show off. How ignorant. Besides, I didn't know anything about these beings. I knew it wasn't by my choice.

When Luke and I got home he told me that they told the group who and what they were about and they were protecting us from being invaded by some other negative beings at that time. (The way it seems now, I think some made it through).

CHAPTER 12
∞
A BOWL OF MIXED NUTS

Luke's brother wanted him to come back home for a while but he had left me for six weeks without any phone calls so I was very upset with him. And it seemed like he knew when I was to go to Alabama. He would always pop-up and take me. I was dumb and took him back. I would go to Birmingham and provide readings and apply stone layouts and channel every six months or so.

I connected with some of the ministers at The Fellowship of Truth. One older man was named Donny. He performed a lot of ministry work in Terre Haute. One day he called me and asked me to come and hold a workshop on color therapy one Saturday and to perform the following morning's Sunday service.

There was one man who attended the class on Saturday who had Aids. He asked for a stone layout after class so we worked on him. He was taking a strong dosage of a diuretic pill twice a day. After the healing work he got off the pills for a few weeks; later we heard some of his so-called friends stole his meds and he went off the deep-end and died.

Donny, who was more aware of the political situation at the church than I was, suggested that I go ahead and visit different churches and share my gifts. He was a genuinely nice man and helpful.

It was the time of the 'Awakening of the Planet'. Several groups gathered different places and created circles within circles and did prayers for people on the planet to expand their awareness and wake up to the truths.

Since I was to hold a workshop on Saturday and perform the service on Sunday I couldn't go to any of these places. Two days before I was scheduled to travel I was asleep in my bed when I felt it shaking. I woke up and thought it was an earthquake.

I called my mom and she said she didn't feel anything. Everyone I called said I must have been dreaming. Luke was at Aunt Susie's working on her car.

I thought, "Okay I'll just go back to sleep."

I was so tired. Then my bed shook again and I sat up and asked who was there.

All of a sudden I heard what sounded like a dog panting. I closed my eyes to tune into my third eye and I saw a big red Irish Setter.

Then I heard a voice say, "My name is Gladys and I am here to tell you about the Dog Star constellation, Sirius."

"Why me?"

"You are to know of us," she said.

"Okay, I know of you; now what?"

"I am here to let you know you will be encountering us in different forms soon and I am only one form," Gladys said. "We are to help protect you."

I thought if I tell a psychiatrist about all this I will be put away.

"You will learn more about the constellations and the heavens soon," she continued. "These are the golden years and you must stay alert and pay attention to your surroundings."

Two days later, Luke, Gayle and one other girl, I think named Peggy, and I went to Terre Haute.

At the Sunday service I saw all kinds of spirits and things in that place. There was even something strange about a woman that came in late. She was dressed in all white with a blue blouse and blonde-white hair.

After the service, the ministers of the church, myself, Luke and the other two that came with us, stood in the back and shook hands as they went out and said they liked the service.

Then the woman who had been late came in behind the others and told me she would like to touch my hands. I thought she might want me to pray with her. She put her hands about two inches above mine and told me this was the Golden Age and that she had gone to Tennessee yesterday for me. And she told me she stood in the middle circle for me and in the middle of the circle were dogs and they were there for me.

I couldn't speak; her eyes changed and I asked, "Are you an E.T.?"

And she said, "Sshhh! Don't tell anyone."

But of course I couldn't keep my mouth shut. The energies were pouring out of her hands and you could see it swirling between us.

Then she said, "Sign your name with this golden ink pen on this paper."

I did.

Then she said, "We will be in contact with you."

And then she left.

"What was that all about?" Luke asked.

He said he could not see her face at all. It was all light. I told him and Donny what had just happened.

Donny said there were lots of strange things out there. He had seen her there before but didn't know much about her. We left church flabbergasted.

When we got home, we discovered Jason had gotten mixed up with some kids and had been drinking; it almost killed him. We had to take him to the emergency room; it was awful.

His great-grandmother on Tom's side came and told me he was in danger. And that the death spirit was coming after him. I sat up all night in Jason's room and sure enough the death spirit came and I fought with it and made it leave and told God that if he wanted me to do the work for Him He had to keep Jason out of Hell and prison and safe from the dark side. Well, He has so far.

Jason has had a few close calls but has always pulled through. We even moved back to Lexington, where Jason started doing well in school.

Then my friend Lucy, Luke's aunt, was having pain and went to the hospital and they gave her a shot of pain killer. She went into a comma and died within three days. I was in the chapel and had been praying for her and her spirit came to me and said it was her time. I kept telling her no. She told me to call Gwen and tell her. It was three in the morning; she said to wake Gwen up and tell her to come and tell her goodbye; she would take her last breath in a few hours.

I was so devastated; and in shock. But somehow I went to the phone booth and called her and told her what Lucy had said.

Lucy's family took her to Hazard to bury her but they didn't really want me there.

I had told them about her coming to me in the chapel at the church. It was weird too; I had read cards for her daughter about a month before that and seen a death. I did see her but I told myself it couldn't be Lucy, maybe it was her grandmother. And even Lucy said I had been reading about her. I told her it couldn't be. And I left it at that.

I guess I blocked it out because I didn't want her to die. I was in so much grief I forgot how to get back to the apartment. Nothing looked familiar to me. It took a while to get back and I was only two blocks away.

At that time, I was also working at a department store in the mall. One day, I went to lunch in a little restaurant in the mall and saw an old boyfriend there. He asked me to sit down and talk with him for a few minutes, so I did. During the course of the conversation, he confessed that he had wanted to marry me at one time but Gwen had told him some stuff that wasn't true. I was so mad. But that was all water under the bridge. I knew he was telling the truth because spirit had told me that before and he confirmed it.

I went back to work and discovered a short little lady standing there. There were some clothes on the counter and I asked her if she was ready to check out and she said she was. I asked her if all of these things were hers and she nodded her head yes. So I started ringing them up and putting them in a bag.

My boss came over and, in a hateful voice, asked me what I was doing. I told him I was ringing up this lady's clothes for her.

My boss said, "Are you taking something!? There's no lady there! These are clothes I picked up off the floor and was going to have you put them back on the racks when you came back from lunch."

Well, I saw the lady kind of grin and then she looked a little angry.

I said, "Well, which ones are hers?"

And the boss said, "Who are you saying those clothes belong to?"

"That lady right there," I said pointing at the woman.

Then she called for a security guard and asked him if he saw anyone standing there. He said he didn't.

I said, "I know she's short but I can see her."

And then I described her.

And to the little lady I said, "I apologize to you ma'am; she doesn't like me and is trying to make me look bad."

By that time, the boss lady said I needed to go home and not come back, that I was "losing it."

The woman walked behind some clothes and disappeared. I was so mad I went home. I could not believe what happened. I tried getting another job and no one would hire me. A few months after that we moved back to Indiana. Again.

Back to Indiana

When we moved back to Indiana we got an apartment in Charlestown where I went to school and finished growing up. This time Luke left me again.

I went back to the church and found that several people had left for different reasons. I received a reading to get a better understanding of the bigger picture at work in my life. I didn't tell the person who gave me the reading about any of the recent events but they related back to me almost everything that had happened. And they explained that Spirit had sent the little lady shopper so I would need to move back to Indiana for a while, that something bad was going to happen if I didn't.

At the church, Alice said she prayed that Luke would leave me because she and the others didn't think he was any good for me. At the time I didn't think of all the reasons why but I found out much later that with him around he might save me from dying and staying dead. But like I said, I was lost and naive back then.

When I moved back, things turned bad with Jason getting in with the wrong crowd again. He was rebelling against me. And the biggest reason was because of my relationship problems with Luke.

There was a woman at the church who wanted me to go with her to Virginia Beach to the Edgar Cayce foundation to learn basic massage. Jason stayed at my mom's so I could travel for a few days.

It was awful. The lady kept doing things to embarrass and upset me. And the only thing I learned from Spirit was to ask for spirit gloves and gowns and spirit shoes to be placed on me before I worked on anyone. Because when I went to touch anyone it felt like I had stuck my hands in mud. And I really felt their pain. So I had to ask Mother Earth to pull it all out of me, and she did.

I went to meditate in this one area before class the next day because I was so mad at my traveling companion for embarrassing me in class. While I was meditating, I saw myself before God. I walked up some white steps and half-way there He said, "Look behind you."

And I saw the footsteps where I had walked were black and then the one I was standing on fell open and I went down this chute. Round and round and down I went landing on the step before him. And He kept changing from one form into another. He said, "I Am In Everything and Everyone. Now go and be angry no more."

I felt very peaceful and was able to finish the class that day. I saw a school of dolphins and wanted so bad to just get in the water and let them take me away – and then the woman I went there with started screaming.

I looked over and saw two giant orbs. They were beside her and we just looked at each other.

I thought, "What now?"

But they were there for a while and drifted back into the ocean. When we left there, we got turned around and were under those darn tunnels for a long time. It was getting dark and she finally found her jewelry she had misplaced.

We were a ways down the road when she said, "I see Mother Mary in the trees."

I said, "Good, she is to there to watch over us."

I was so tired. I told her we were stopping for a little while at the rest stop. We were in her little sports car and I had been driving. We rolled down the windows a little and went to sleep.

The next thing I knew this car was blowing its horn. At first I was agitated, but as I looked around, I saw this really big guy coming toward us with his hands up in the air like he was going to grab us.

Well, she started screaming and I tried to start the car. Finally it started as the man grabbed the hood of the car and tried to hang on. He was showing his teeth like he was possessed or something. I backed out hard then spun the wheels forward leaving the man standing and shaking his fist at us.

I finally got the woman calmed down a little. She said she had been raped before and just knew he would rape and kill us. I told her only if he killed me first; that I would have gone down fighting.

We returned home and most everyone at the church was unhappy because we went to the Cayce foundation instead of attending the monthly board meeting. The members didn't want to promote the lady who went there with me to the position of minister. The lady became upset towards me and I think blames me for it even to this day. We still don't speak.

Jason and my mom were fussing at me. Jason wouldn't go to school and I had to go to the office. They kicked him out of school a lot.

Back then I was dumb and let Luke come back. We went back and forth for three years. Crazy.

We went up to my mom's. Our cars weren't in the best of condition at the time and my mom said she had just received this budget paper in the mail. She said they might let me trade my car in on another one. I told her I didn't know, but she said we should try anyway. I told her before we go I felt the need to go to the funeral home and say goodbye to Adele.

She had gotten in a car wreck on the way to the house of one of my Aunts. Adele had known our family for a long time and I liked her. She was one of my aunt's friends.

So we went to the funeral home. Adele's body had a bright pink sweater on and it was winter time. I heard noises in the walls and ceiling.

Adele's sister came over and said they must have a lot of mice here.

I thought, "Those aren't mice; those are spirits." But I didn't say anything.

After we told her goodbye we went to the car dealer. The only car I saw they might approve us for was a little white one.

Mom asked me if I was sure. I told her yes and pointed it out because I saw Elvis Presley's spirit standing beside it.

And I said, "Look here, there's no pink in the showroom and here is a pink thread from Adele's sweater."

She gave me a weird look.

I said, "Now the man will come back in and tell us what I said."

Well, in a few minutes he came back and sure enough that was exactly what he said. My mom then blurted out that she would get that car. It was a little white Chevette. It drove okay for about a year and then started tearing up and the heater would not shut off. Luke worked on it off and on.

Well, I let it go back to the dealer.

Tom's grandmother had died and out of Tom's part of the money that was left to the grandkids, they sent Jason six hundred dollars.

So we went and put down the money on another car. It was a blue Pontiac with lifters that were kind of bad.

Luke had gone to visit his family and had said he'd be gone a couple of weeks but of course it ended up being a month this time. But he came back and fixed the lifters for me.

We got a call to come back to Alabama where we met a couple, Dr. Snow, a dentist, and his wife Sarah, who were kind people.

I had been having some pain from one of my teeth and Dr. Snow looked at it and said it would have to come out. He pulled it, and I didn't even feel it. He made me a gold tooth that included a quartz crystal to put between the other two teeth. It was cool. I wore it for a long time until all of my vibration changed and then I couldn't wear it.

After we visited and talked, Sarah said she would help me write a book. It never got made. They passed away and all the tapes I gave her disappeared.

I taught Luke how to do different types of reflexology and energy work, and also how to read cards. He got pretty good at it. Most of the girls wanted him to read because he was a cute guy. We traveled to various psychic fairs and gave readings.

At one fair, he took off with a woman for six hours for who knew what. When he came back I wanted to hurt him really bad. Everyone said he was not worth it and tried to talk me out of hurting him. I don't know why.

We worked one more fair in Ohio. His table was kind of close to mine and I was so mad at him I really didn't feel like reading for anyone. I sat there a long time and I was thinking I just wanted to go home. I started to get up and go look around at the vendors' tables and browse but I couldn't move.

I thought, "If I have to read for someone, it better not be a man."

At that time, I held a strong contempt for men because every one of them I had ever dated or lived with had cheated on me or tried to harm me. I was fed up.

Well I sat there and my eyes went to the back of the room which was really the front door where people entered. A long-haired man came in and Spirit told me he was coming to get a reading.

I thought, "No, Spirit, I don't want to read for a man. I am too angry."

Well I saw him buy some tickets and I tried to get up out of the chair but couldn't. Well, here he came, right to my table and sat down.

He presented me with two tickets, then I told him he only needed one, but he said he needed both. It was obvious he wanted a detailed reading or he had a lot of questions.

I thought, "Oh well."

I looked at his eyes and calmed down a little; I started to comment on them but then I told him I saw him doing some kind of healing work, but that it would be different from what most people do.

He said, "Let me take my shields off; you need to know some things."

Before I could say anything, he took two necklaces off and his eyes changed colors. His whole aura shifted.

And he said, "I am Ray from the planet Pagoria. I am here to tell you that you are through with him." And he pointed to Luke.

I thought, "How did he know we were together?"

He said, "Your karma is over with him. I am here to tell you that you must read the book *E.T. 101* and make a connection with the author."

As he was talking, it felt like a weird V-shaped energy was going in my head and making it hurt. I was getting angry.

"What are you?" I asked. "And what is this weird energy?"

He said, "In your Bible, in the book of Genesis, where it talks about the angels coming down from heaven and mating with human women, I am a by-product, a child of those beings."

He said angels were not the ones who mated with human women; Pagorian beings did. He said there was a lot misinformation written in the Bible as well as a lot left out of the Bible. I told him I had always felt that. By that time my head was hurting more and I told him to get that energy out of my head. He said he was probing me to tell me things.

"Well, quit!" I said. "Alien or not, you're making my head hurt. And besides, right now I'm angry at all men so it's best not to be trying anything with me."

"You will be moving two more times," he said, "and the last time you move you will move to the mountains and stay there. There will be a lot more revealed to you later."

I told him there was a woman that came to me a while back and I asked if he knew her. I told him she had something to do with the Dog Star planet. He said her name was Nacara and she and her group would contact me again. I didn't know what to do about that. But I heard the spirit world say that these beings would send shuttle ships when I traveled so I would be safe.

He had an attitude like they didn't really want to come and tell me these things but was kind of ordered, or told to. He then left and a woman dressed in black was standing beside me and said, "You must give me a reading, I am a witch."

And I thought, "Lord, what is going on?"

I looked around before she sat down to see where Ray went and he had just disappeared. I shut my eyes for a moment and saw a space ship. Luke interrupted this reading to lean over and tell me he couldn't see that man's face like the woman we met a year or so ago.

"Well, he said we were through," I said. "That's for sure."

Luke and I broke up after that, at least for eight months.

During this time, I met some people at another meditation gathering and ran into one of the guys who had been at that sweat lodge. He asked me what had really happened and I told him. I told him that Viola and Myrtle agreed that I was so sensitive that when the people were dumping their junk into the circle somehow I was taking their energy or karma on. And I told him what Gwen had also said about the Indian ways. So it could have been a combination. All I knew was, I still didn't feel like I was cleansed from all of it, or that I had been forgiven completely, because some of my powers had left me and not returned. He said maybe he could help me; his name was Todd.

He said he knew these people that would like to meet me and maybe they could help. So I went with him and this woman name Katie and Rob who lived on this mountain in Kentucky. Another woman Todd knew named Tracy came with us. They all knew each other. There was a woman and her daughter that lived over the hill on Katie and Rob's property. The daughter was blind and needed a kidney transplant. There names were Gail and Mindy.

And then in another little house were Katie's daughter and family. She had a son, Tony, that had been hurt in an automobile accident and he lived in town. She also had a vacant small trailer and a large building she did canning in, calling it a "mission house."

"I have been asking the Lord to send someone like you to help us get the healing center going," she said. "Can you come and stay? You can stay in the trailer."

I was frustrated from Spirit telling me Charlestown was going to have a tornado come through my house and that Jason needed to get away from there. I told her I would think on it and let her know.

I heard God say, "I am sending you here."

I asked for how long and He said for five months. This was to see if she would do as God asked her to do. If she didn't in five months, we were to leave.

The woman asked me if I was listening to Spirit. I told her I was listening to God. She asked me what He said, so I told her.

I went home to pack and called Luke's sister and told him to come and get his stuff. Well, he wouldn't, so I gave it away. He thought I was just saying I was moving to get him to come back.

Well, as I was packing, Jason took off with some boys who were already in trouble with the police looking for them. When they caught up with them, Jason was in the car and was taken in too. He told them he was not the Jason they were looking for but since it was Friday, and until they could clear him, he was going to jail.

Jason called me in such a panic. He said if they wouldn't let him out, he would kill himself; he was having severe tobacco withdrawals having become addicted to chewing tobacco at sixteen.

So I called a lawyer and she agreed to meet me at the courthouse; and all the way I chanted the Buddha's Chant. This one lady I had met when we moved back to Indiana from Kentucky introduced it to me.

"Nam myoho renge kyo."

It helps you to manifest what you want. When she first told me about it, and because I didn't have hardly anything, I chanted it for a week a few minutes a day and by the end of the week a series of changing events had led to my whole apartment being furnished.

I chanted all the way to the courthouse and asked for the judge to let him out on his own recognizance. And while I was in the room waiting, this other lady said the judge would end his court session and then leave the courtroom without seeing me. So I would have to wait until Monday.

I stood there and prayed for the judge to come through that room I was in. In a little while he did. The lawyer and other woman were completely surprised.

I asked the man, "Are you the judge?"

He replied that he was. I told him the story and he told me if I brought Jason back to court on Monday that I could take him home today. So he signed some papers for Jason to be released.

Even the lawyer said he had never seen him be so lenient. I told him my prayers worked.

After I took Jason back that Monday, the judge said the school wanted him to go to another school. Someone suggested a Job Corps school so he could learn a trade and get his GED.

So the judge signed papers so he could go there. It was in Pine Knot, below Summerset. Since Katie's home was not far from Pine Knot, I moved into one of her trailers so I would not be too far from him.

I tried to help the people, Katie and her family, and so did Jason, when he was on summer break. We would tend to the garden and animals. We had very little to eat. They would go to the bakery and get day-old bread and rolls and put in barrels for the hogs and she said we could eat that. I was miserable.

A few people came to get readings from time to time. Katie told them I would do them for twenty-five dollars. She said they didn't have much money and she needed a percentage of the money. She also thought her husband had money stashed. He did but she thought it was in jars in the woods and she had me going with her to different trees to dig. We never found it. I think God saw what she was really about and let her show herself. She really messed up.

One day a neighbor asked if I would take him to the next town twenty-five miles away to get some car parts. I agreed but told him we would need some gas for the trip. So we stopped at the gas station. Then we went to the car parts store. On the way I got dizzy and I felt that if I was hypoglycemic maybe I needed some sugar. So we went to McDonalds and picked up some ice cream. I ate that and then the neighbor said he wanted to go to Wal-Mart. So we went there. By that time I was getting blurry-eyed. As I walked through the store, everything appeared to be moving. I told Steve to get what he needed, that I had to go lay down. So he did. But as soon as I got on the ramp to the interstate I went blind. I barely pulled over before everything went black.

He asked me what was wrong. I told him I couldn't see and that I hurt all over. I told him he would have to drive. He helped move me over from the driver's side and into the passenger's side. When we got home Jason thought Steve had done something to me. Jason picked me up and put me in bed.

Steve went to get Katie. But she would not come to see about me. So Steve went to get his mother. I didn't have any medical insurance so I didn't think the hospital would admit me. His mother brought me some food and juice; she saw we did not have anything and brought some canned food to us. She was very upset with Katie for treating me like that.

I was blind for three weeks. I would crawl between the bathroom and bedroom. Jason would fix me something to eat. This was in August so I told Jason when he went back to school I was going to find another place to move because God said Katie was not doing what he asked of her or what she had promised to do for Him.

When I got to feeling a little better I started walking with the help of a cane.

Soon after I started using the cane, I was walking down this road picking blackberries and a voice said, "I am to introduce myself to you."

And I saw a being that look like a Hawaiian god. He wore a great feathered head dress but not like the American Indian one. He said his name was Helios and that he was a Sun God. He told me about the sun and how the energies worked.

Todd came down to visit with us and Katie took us and a few other people to a salt peter cave. It used to be a hospital in the Civil War days. I saw some of the soldiers from that era.

One of them said to me, "I have now found you once again."

I was pretty confused.

"You were my wife in Georgia," he said, "and I died here, wounded. And you died from a fever."

I told him he needed to cross over. (He later came to the trailer and I prayed him over).

My brother, Walter, came down for a visit. He was crippled and moved about in a wheel chair. Katie had someone scheduled for a reading, so I told Walter I would be right back. While I was gone the late afternoon turned into evening and then into the night time. When I returned I found Walter was very frightened.

"I'll never doubt you again," he said.

I said, "What are you talking about?"

He said, "I swear there was a whitewashed soldier at the window. I just kept praying and he finally went away."

So I told Walter now that he was seeing more it was time for him to learn about the spirit world. So I started telling him of my experiences. During this time, his guides White Water and Shamoo, came and spoke to us, and Walter started opening up more.

A psychiatrist heard about me from some people I had met at a psychic fair and gotten in touch with me through my mom, giving them Katie's phone number. Anyway, they asked me to come and do a stone layout on their son; he was failing in school and had some other issues.

So I went and they asked me how they could help people like me instead of dispensing pills. So I explained what Spirit had shared and they sent me a letter later on and said their son was doing much better and was passing in school.

Katie was getting more jealous of me and suggested she should have had Ralph take me in the woods and lose me.

Well, September came and Katie always had a gathering at that time in which she would lead all the people to this large salt peter cave. I invited some of my family to come down. Some people came from the church; and some she knew.

This one couple came in a van. But not much of my stuff would fit in it and Katie had already said she wasn't letting me have my birds, a phone or some chairs and other things. I just told her to keep it all so I could get out of there.

I returned to my mom's house, upset and hurt. After I got over my anger, I looked back on the experience as good and bad. Good because my brother began to open up and get in touch with his gifts and my son got to go to a better school and began learning a trade, masonry work.

And I started learning not to be so gullible, although I did ask God not to send me into so much danger anymore. Because when I arrived back at my mom's house in Indiana, this guy said something was leaking out of my car. It turned out the gas line had been cut and something else was wrong when they looked under the hood. I guess like before though God kept me safe.

CHAPTER 13
∞
SMOKEY AND THE OREONS

I had some more requests to come to Alabama to give clearings and readings so I traveled there a few more times. I met some other psychics. It was getting to be about late 1993 or early 1994 when I met a lady that had an herb shop; many people called her Gypsy Rose. I guess they called her that because she moved around a lot. Kind of like me. She wanted me to come over and do a trance channeling for a group of people. So I did.

She had a boyfriend that didn't believe too much of anything. He was Native American and skeptical of even natives that did different work.

He said, "If you're for real, when I take pictures something will show up on them, like ghosts or spirits."

Now, God had already told me that some unusual things would show up on someone's camera tonight. I told him to get ready because God said it would. Well, when everyone that was coming arrived I said the clearing prayer that Spirit taught me. Back then it was a fairly short one; but now it has become kind of long.

Anyway, Mafu always started coming in first, then the others. After Geronimo came in with the head dress, he told everyone to line up behind me and reach out with their hands and feel the head dress; but, they were not to touch me.

After they felt the head dress, the person would come around to the front of me and receive a spirit gift. A lot of the people said when they stood in back of me and reached out they could feel the head dress; some said they could see actually it.

When Gypsy's boyfriend had the pictures developed, they were amazed. There was a streak of white light coming toward me and one going straight through me.

Mafu said it was how they came into me and how I sometimes left.

A lady named Pat, and her friend Terrie, said she saw me leave through a green doorway. In that session I had even channeled a fairy. Then Alice told me that when each one of the beings came in, there would be a distinct change in my face, and so would my voice to a certain extent.

Different people I met wanted to bring different groups together at different times. I went to Birmingham for two or more weeks at a time. It seemed like each time I would go, Spirit would do something a little different. They told me they were upgrading the energies and bringing in a higher vibration for me and others and the planet.

It was a few weeks before Easter, around spring break, and I was still living at my mother's. I didn't have time to look for a place because I was either in Alabama or at someone's home that I knew working on things. I would help different people out with some work or get a temp job that didn't last very long. I thought when Jason got out of the Job Corps we could find a place together.

Well the next thing I knew, I got a phone call from Luke wanting all of his personal belongings from our previous apartment.

"I told you I gave it away and moved," I said. "Now I'm back. It's been over eight months. You should have answered when I called your sister's for you to come and get your stuff."

"I didn't think you would really move," he said.

I told him what happened. And he asked if he could come and see me. At first I said no, then like a fool, I said okay. In a few days he came down and said he wanted to get back together. He kept trying to persuade me. Finally he wore me down and I gave in.

At that time he was working for someone as a mechanic. So I went up to Ohio for a few weeks; but it didn't work out so well. He took me to some sort of party where this woman kept flirting with him and I told him I knew he had already been with her. He lied and said no. (I found out months later that he had - and he had even married her!)

He also told me that I needed to get rid of all my tarot cards. And I told him I didn't need them because they were only a tool and that I could read clair-voyantly. Then he told me to get rid of my guides. I told him I would never do that. At first he became mad; then he calmed down. Just like before.

I was so depressed back then. It was difficult for me to sort out a lot of things. I got a call to go back to Alabama. This was to another lady's house, named June.

When I got there, it was cold that week and her townhouse was drafty. She had traveled to all kinds of different countries and had even gone to Bali, and brought back some death masks. She explained to me that when a person dies in Bali they first bury them with this mask on and after so many days dig them up. Then they take the mask off, burn the bodies, and then place their ashes in the ocean.

I looked at the masks and said, "And you wanted these for what reason?"

She said she didn't know. I told her they were possessed.

"That's why you are here," she said. "There's something in my closet."

So I started saying my prayers and the spirits started coming out of the masks and they did not like me; one even tripped me on the stairs. There was also this little old man spirit that didn't want to cross over; he just want to stay with June.

I called on Metatron, the head of the angels and asked for the tornadoes of light to blast through the house. Well, at the time, I didn't know Luke was meditating and trying to get the spirit to cross over. When the energy came in it slung Luke's spirit through the walls too. When the angels slowed the energies down, Luke had a hard time coming back to his body. He told me to give him a warning next time.

"I didn't know you were out of your body," I said.

Luke said he almost had the spirit convinced to cross over when this white tornado looking thing slung him and the spirit man through the walls, the wood and the nails. It was weird.

I said, "Well, that lets me know it works."

"Don't get smart," he said.

A couple of days went by and some people came over and I did some readings and a couple of stone layouts. Then one night we were watching TV. I had my big blue house coat on and I was sitting in a recliner. June was sitting close to the TV, and Luke was in another chair on my left.

June said, "I don't mean to be rude but when Star Trek is on I don't talk, so don't talk to me."

We agreed. I was tired anyway and didn't have anything to say. Halfway through the show I got as hot as hot could be.

Then Smokey came in and said we have visitors.

I said, "What? Who are they?"

He told me they were okay, and neutral.

I asked what that meant.

He said not good or bad. But they were here to learn and not harm.

"I'm burning up," I said.

I started to take off my big house coat. June turned around and asked what was going on. So I told her. She said there's this glow around me. I told her all I knew was that I was hot. She asked what the spirits wanted.

Then I heard a voice say, "Are you a trance channeler?"

"Yes."

And the voice said, "I want to see how you see things and hear how you hear things."

"How can you do that?" I asked.

The voice said, "You have a built-in spirit translator and I can use that to connect."

June and Luke got up and sat right beside me. I asked June about her show. She said she had her own real show here.

I said, "Yeah, I guess so."

The next thing I knew my eyes felt like they dilated and I could see better, colors were sharper. I guess the being overshadowed my face because Luke and June were looking at me as if I had three heads or something. Then my hearing became really sharp. It sounded like the traffic was in the room with me, like everything was amplified. I was still in my body and I guess it sat in my lap or something.

Then the voice said, "Do you want to see how we see you?"

"Sure."

So I looked at June and all I could see was an outline and it looked like she was checkered, with a golden light in her chest.

Then the voice said, "We see your grid lines and soul light."

I said, "Then everybody looks the same to you?"

"No, this is how we know you, by the vibration and frequency of the soul," it said. "Each soul has its own vibration and frequency, like you identify with a fingerprint. So does your soul. And that's how we know you Sha `La. Your light tells me who and what you are and of your gifts. And we know by that you have a translator."

I said, "Okay, that's cool."

Then the voice said, "We must go now."

Then the room got cold again. All I know as a trance channeler is that when Spirit comes in to use me as an instrument, they come mostly through what is called the "Bridge of Shambala" at the back of the neck. And E.T.s come in through the throat and heart chakra.

The next night someone was blowing their car horn when Luke and I woke up. I told him someone was trying to steal our car.

He looked out the window and said, "You're right; they are!"

And he jerked his coat on over his pajamas and went outside. What had happened was that someone had gotten in the car and backed it into the road and left the doors open. Other cars couldn't pass it so they were blowing their horns to get someone's attention.

Luke always kept a picture of me on the dashboard of the car. He pulled the car back into the parking space and told me it looked like my picture was glowing.

Smokey came to me and told me they came through my picture and scared them off. I told him thanks. So I was saved by Spirit again. I say Spirit because God, Jesus, Smokey, and the other angels and guides all help or took turns helping me out.

Jason and the Gensup Weed

We traveled to Indiana and then went on to Ohio. Luke was living in the back of the mechanic's shop and the guy he was working for said he had more work for him to do.

I had a psychic fair to go to in Ohio and I had met some people there that wanted me to come to their house to do some stone layouts. One lady, named Judith, invited everyone to come to her house. We got acquainted and she said she wanted to be my student, so I told her we could work on a few things. I stayed three days and taught her about the stone layouts. She paid me and I went back to see Luke before I had to go and pick Jason up from school.

I went to get Jason so he could visit my mom and family while they had spring break. Uncle Billy Ray was raising pot belly pigs and I got one from him and took it with me when I picked Jason up. All the kids were amazed because most of them had never seen one before. It was a tiny thing that fit in the palm of my hand.

At the time, I didn't know Jason signed up for the army. As it turned out he didn't get accepted because of problems with his back and feet. But I was still really upset when I went to get him and he told me.

"Well mom, I smelled you in the dorm last week," he said.

"You did?"

"Yes, you smelled like sage or that incense you burn," he explained.

He said he felt better though because of the trouble going on there.

I told him that when I was in Alabama, a woman read for me and said that there was trouble here and that she saw some boy stealing a car and three or four boys doing drugs. And they wanted him to take the drugs also and go with them – and then she saw a car wreck. And I knew she was talking about you.

"So we lit some candles and incense and prayed for you and for them to be safe and not to do anything harmful or illegal," I told him. "Did any of that happen? Because I also called down here and told one of the teachers what the woman had seen."

"Yes," he admitted. "Let me tell you what happened. Three of the guys ran through the woods and I went with them and we went to the store and got some cigarettes, and some candy and snacks. On the way back we saw a car with some keys in it. Joe wanted to get in it and drive it and I told him he shouldn't do that, that we would all get in trouble and I wasn't going. He said he didn't care. Drake and I left the other guys and we went through the woods and came home.

"But it was the other guys, Joe and Larry, that got in the car and took off; and they got picked up and sent home. But before they were sent home, they came in all stoned and said they were seeing stuff.

"One of them said he was Superman and I tried to grab him but he climbed on the roof of this wall we had built for the new building and he jumped off.

"The other boy tried to climb the wall. And then some other boy pulled a knife out because he got scared of the first two nuts. I had to take it away from him because they had made me the head of the dorm.

"It was up to me to try and take care of these fools. Finally the instructors came and helped me out."

I waited a moment and then I asked Jason, "What were they on? Pot?"

"No," Jason said. "There was some kind of plant called Gensup weed. They said it was like pot – but more dangerous. They said it looked more like a milkweed plant; it had a pod and seeds in it and the boys ate the seeds and started hallucinating. Now the boys are in the hospital and I don't know if they will make it or not. Even if they do, they're kicked out of here."

"You better not *ever* do anything like that!" I said.

"I'm not *that* dumb," he said. "If I hadn't stopped that boy from fighting, he would have killed the other one. – I think it was meant for me to come to this school, mom, to help."

Angels on the Highway

We went to my mom's for the school break. Not much went on except visiting. Things were kind of quiet. I talked to Luke on the phone a few times. He told some people some things that had happened to us. But then one day he said something on the phone that was disturbing.

He said, "I told them you were hard to kill."

I said, "Why did you say that?"

He said, "You'll see."

Then he hung up on me. Something came to me and told me he was going to sabotage me in a lot of ways; that I needed to be careful.

I asked Spirit, "Am I a glutton for punishment or what's the deal?"

And a voice said, "It's an experiment and a test."

But I still didn't understand.

It came time to take Jason back to school. I asked my brother Walter if he wanted to ride up there with me, that it would take about five hours there and back. He said he would. I wanted to talk to him about Luke. He was tuning in to his guides by then. I needed to see from a different perspective what I needed to do.

My mom told me to take his wheel chair in case I needed it. I told her we would just go by a drive-through window and get something to eat and drink instead of getting in and out of the car.

Well I wish I had taken it. I drove around the place for a few minutes showing Walter the school area and then Jason and I got out of the car. I hugged him goodbye then I got back in the car and started home.

We had already stopped and had something to eat. Walter and I were going up this little hill through Summerset when my car just quit. There was no warning or anything. It had gotten dark and there was definitely a spooky feeling in the air.

My brother started to panic.

"Don't worry," I said. "I have been stranded before. We'll just call for help; I'll call Luke and he can come fix the car."

We were in the blue Pontiac. Trucks and cars were passing us but no one would stop. I looked around and saw a house down the hill a little ways that had a horse shoe-shaped driveway.

I told my brother that I would just push the car down there and ask to use the phone. If no one answered we would wait until daylight when they probably went to work and call then.

He agreed. Now Walt had never driven a car before and he didn't know how to drive one then. He was crippled and he was getting tired and a little scared. Well, I put one foot on the ground and had one in the car and started to push it backward, aiming for the house down the road. After about two feet, the car started rolling faster, I tried to jump in and guide it but my foot slipped and went under the car. I was still holding on trying to keep a grip on the situation.

I went in some sort of shock, because the front tire ran over my leg and my shoe came off and my heel was bleeding but I didn't feel it. Walt was shaking and screaming. I told him I was okay. Then the car started to roll from side to side. On one side there was a rock mountain; that's where it was headed. By then I had one hand on the steering wheel and one foot barely hanging in the car while my body was being dragged on the road, and I was trying to pull myself up. It was happening so fast. The next I knew the front tire was headed right toward my neck; it was coming in between my neck and shoulder and I saw my life flash real fast. But it seemed like only parts of it. The thought that went through my head was that more than that had happened to me and I guess I will die with a broken neck like my Aunt Annie did. By then I was holding on by my middle finger on my right hand and my heel was slipping on out. Then all of a sudden Walt let out the loudest and weirdest scream I ever heard. And I just said out loud, "God, help my brother!"

All of a sudden; someone, an Angel, God, or a Guide or something, picked me up and said, "Grab the wheel and put it in park."

So now I was up far enough where my left hand could grab the wheel and I put my middle finger of the right hand through the steering wheel and put it in park.

The car jerked to a stop, and Walt was still shaking and screaming and just as red faced as he could be. I thought he was going to have a heart attack.

I kept telling him, "We're okay; calm down."

He looked at me so strangely. Then I told him to breathe.

I dragged my body up and sat on the seat. The angel probably still had a hold of me.

I took Walt's hands and tried to calm him.

When he got his breath, he said, "I thought you were dead."

"I almost was," I said. "But somebody picked me up."

I looked around and saw a figure of a man walk from my rear car door around the back of the car and up to my brother's door and then disappear.

"What was that?" Walt asked.

"I don't know but I asked for God to help you and this is what happened," I said.

"They had to save you so I wouldn't die in a wreck or have a heart attack and die," Walt said. "Thank God."

Then I tried to flag somebody down. People went by us; people went around us; but no one stopped. I was hobbling and waving my hands. Finally, two young girls stopped; at first they were afraid. I yelled to them and said my car had quit and I needed someone to call 911. They saw my ankle bleeding and said that they would.

"Do you want us to take you to the hospital?" one of them asked.

"No, because my cripple brother is with me and I don't want to leave him," I said.

"Let's get your car off the road!" the other one said.

At first I was scared to move the car again but one of the girls said I needed to or a semi-truck might hit it. So I told her okay and they helped me move it to the side of the road.

In a little while an ambulance came. I told the paramedics what had happened and they just looked at each other as they wrapped my heel and ankle up.

They said they needed to get me to a hospital. I told them I couldn't go unless they took my brother too. They said they couldn't take him. So I told them to call me a wrecker and that I would deal with it.

One paramedic said, "Your leg looks broken or fractured."

"Well my brother almost had a heart attack," I said. "Why can't you take him too?"

He claimed some company policy.

Anyway, the wrecker finally came. They hauled us up in the air and I told them to take us to a hotel. I had enough money to get us a room until someone came to get us. When we got to the hotel a few guys got my brother out and took him in a room. I ask for two beds but they only gave us one. But I got Walt situated and called our mom and asked her to call Luke. She said she would get my sister and her husband or brother-in-law to come after us. I told her I didn't care who came, just send somebody.

And then the pain started setting in. I went to the desk and asked where everybody went and where my car was taken. The woman at the desk gave me the number to where they took the car. We couldn't leave it at the hotel. I told her pain was settling in my leg and foot and that I needed to go to the hospital. She told me I would have to walk there. It was a mile and a half down the road and then up a hill.

By this time, I was getting angry with everyone. I couldn't believe everybody left without seeing if we were okay or not. So I went back to the room and told my brother I had to walk to the hospital.

I set the phone where Walt could reach it. Then I took off walking. I got about a half mile down the road when a car bearing a man and his daughter pulled over. The man asked me where I was going. I told them to the hospital.

"Well I'm going there to have day surgery and we can take you," he said. So I got in the car, not even thinking whether they were telling the truth or not. But they were. So we all went to the hospital and I thanked them for helping me and he went one way and I went another.

I was in there a long time while they took x-rays and ran some tests. Finally I came out with a cast and crutches and pain pills and a prescription. My foot was fractured and some small bones were broken along with some tissue damage. I don't know how I stood it. Even the nurse said the Lord must have been watching out for me. She also said the shock was wearing off and that was why I was beginning to feeling the pain.

Then I started walking with the crutches going toward the hill to go down and back to the motel. Then the same people who picked me up before pulled up again.

"I thought you were going to have surgery," I said.

"It's too crowded in there," the man replied. "And I wanted the doctors to focus on me, not everybody else."

He said he would go back later. Then he told me to get in and they would take me back to the motel. So I did. When they let me out, I thanked them again and the man said, "Now you can say you had some southern hospitality."

They waved bye to me and as they drove down the road the car slowly faded out. So I guess God sent some other kind of angels to help me there.

The morning came and as I went in the room my brother was still talking to my mom on the phone because he was nervous. My sister came with her brother –in–law to pick us up. And a little later Luke said he would come after work with a friend to get my car.

I went back to my mom's. After three days Luke finally called and said he had the car. I was unhappy with him because he hadn't called before then. When he did call, he said some disparaging remarks to me, the kind that made me want to reach through that phone and ring his neck. I asked him several times to bring my car to me.

"When I get ready to, I will," he said. "And when I do, I don't want to see you."

He took almost three months to bring the car to me and when he finally did he dropped it of as quickly and as quietly as he could. Once it was parked, he jump in a car with someone else and took off. He just left the keys in it.

I was still in a cast and couldn't get out there in time before he took off; I guess it was for the best, because I just wanted to hurt him. I went to bed that night and Spirit showed me what he did.

Luke had fixed it just enough to get it back to me and when I drove it, or maybe started it, I would wreck. So I told my mom about it and I wound up selling it for three hundred dollars to these mechanics. Spirit said so much negativity was in it that even if I had the mechanical part fixed, it was still cursed. Spirit said to give it or sell it to someone else and the curse would be lifted. Although if I did, I would be without a car, but I didn't see any point in keeping *that* car going.

My Ferret, Maggie

I was lying in bed before I went to sleep one night and a white ferret came to me in spirit form; I could plainly see her.

The ferret said, "My name is Maggie and I am sent to you to help you get over any fear."

"I already say the Lord's prayer every night," I said.

"I will teach you more," she said. "And I am going to incarnate and be with you in that form too."

I thought to myself, "Now I really am going nuts."

The next day my Uncle Billy Ray came and said he had met the most interesting person last night at the bar and that this guy had a ferret farm.

"He had a what?" I asked.

"A ferret farm," Uncle Billy Ray said.

I asked, "Does he have a white one?"

"I was going to go up there and see them," Uncle Billy Ray said. "Do you want to go?"

"Sure."

So I got my crutches and off we went.

Some of them had just had babies that day; and the guy had brown ones and white ones.

I told the man, "Well if they aren't too much I would like to have a white one, a female."

"Okay, they'll be ready in six weeks," he said.

In four weeks, Uncle Billy Ray said that guy called him and that one of the mamas of the white ferret was killed by a dog so now he had four babies and wanted to know if I still wanted one. He said he would take a couple too.

I told Uncle Billy Ray I did.

He went and got all four of them and then brought them in the house. They still had their eyes shut. So I asked Spirit which one was supposed to be mine; which one was Maggie? When I asked that, one of the ferrets started wriggling out from the others, like it knew its name; so I took that one.

Using an eyedropper, we fed them some mothers' milk we bought at the feed store. When it came closer to the six week weaning time, a lady in Louisville called and asked if I could come over for a couple of days to do some readings. I told her I could if I could get a ride over there. I managed to find somebody to take me there and leave me for a couple of days.

While I was there Maggie started crying. I sat and talked to her and rocked her, eventually staying up all night with her; I think she had a tummy ache.

Then the next day she opened her eyes and I was the first one she saw. She snuggled up in my hand and went to sleep. I laid her down and when she woke up I said 'Maggie' and she walked over to me. So then I knew for sure that it had been her spirit that had come to me weeks ago. I took her just about everywhere I went. (My mom ended up with the pot belly pig).

Later on this one lady named Joy called me; I had met her at the Fellowship of Truth. Spirit said someone was going to speak well of me while others didn't or were confused about me.

Joy presented me with a picture she had drawn of me in armor. She told me that even though I had to walk in danger, or in the danger of the dark side, I would always come out okay.

"Barely, but I *am* still living," I remarked.

She had a gift of looking at people and seeing their guides around them and drawing them and giving the person a message from the guide. I always thought that was really neat. Anyway there was going to be a psychic fair in Evansville and she wanted to know if I would go with her. She said she would help me get a booth so I could offer readings. I said okay. So that time my mom watched Maggie for me.

I did several readings at that fair and everything was normal; until this one guy named Ed came in and started talking to me, saying he was really interested in opening up to his gifts and asking if I would be his teacher. I explained to him that I didn't have a car nor did I live around there. Then I told him a little bit about what was going on with my life. He said he lived in a remodeled warehouse that had three bedrooms and that I was welcome to come and stay there. He also said he would pay me to teach him. He told me to take his phone number and think about it. I told him I would.

On the way home, I told Joy that I see Maggie going away and I was worried. Then I heard Spirit say your mom will find her. And when I got there, sure enough, she had gotten out. Mom said she looked all over for her then started calling her name. Finally Maggie came out from under the house and mom grabbed her. She knew I would be upset if Maggie didn't come back. I said maybe she was going to go find me.

I figured out later they like to go and dig in the dirt; she also liked peppermint candy; but, she didn't want you to open it up for her, she like to do it herself. She would take candy and cookies and have her little stash in a cooking pot or bowl or something that would be her little place. She was funny. Some people said they liked shiny things, but not her; she would look in a lady's purse to see if they had candy.

About a week went by and I had my brother Walt to tune in and see if it was safe and would be okay with Spirit if I were to work with Ed. Everything and everyone said it would.

So I called Ed up and said, "If you still want me to come and be your teacher, come and get me and Maggie."

At first he called her a rat. Well, I wasn't real happy about that.

"Your first lesson is that she is not a rat," I said. "She is a ferret."

I stayed in the back bedroom of the warehouse. The next morning I woke up hearing the loudest, weirdest noise and discovered Maggie sitting beside me shaking. I got up and went through the warehouse to see what it was. As I followed the noise, I wound up at Ed's door and realized that the noise was him snoring. I had never heard anyone snore like that before. We finally got used to it. Sometimes I would just turn the radio on.

Ed took pictures of houses and put up signs for real estate people. In the evenings after supper, we would practice meditating and discussing what he experienced. And we worked with energy and the stones. I tried to get him to be more in tune with his guides.

I applied a stone layout over Ed and guided him into a past life regression; he started crying and I felt very upset. I could see his past life as if it were a movie in my head. He was King James and I was like a slave, washing clothes. I remembered that during that time in history my family was in debt and I had to pay the debt to the king for taxes.

I talked Ed through the release of negativity from that life and other lives he saw during the regression. Ed decided to get me a van to drive. We went to Birmingham in it to do the readings, and stone layouts. He had to go back home to work so I took him back and then I returned to Alabama a week later.

Sha `La, the Exorcist

During this time Rose called me and said this woman was having trouble with her son. She asked if I could help her and I told her I would try.

Soon after I agreed to help the woman with her son, Jesus came to me and said, "You are going to perform an exorcism."

"I'm going to perform a what?"

He said it again.

"I don't think I can do that," I said, "anything but that."

He said, "You are the only one who can free this boy."

I was more than a little scared.

"Don't worry," Jesus said. "I will be with you."

"I sure hope so."

When I got there I told Rose maybe she should also call a priest.

When I began, I first put the stones on the woman's son to draw the demons out; then I had him say some prayers. He said something was moving in him and hurting.

I laid three Bibles on him and lit so much white sage the whole building was saturated with the smell and the smoke.

I spoke prayer after prayer. I called to Rose and asked if she had gotten in touch with anyone to come and help.

She said they told her they didn't do that and to take him to a hospital.

I said, "What's a hospital going to do? I never heard of doctors chasing out the spirits!"

After several hours, I told the demon I would just take it on myself to get the boy out of pain.

Well, I thought Jesus would just come through me like he did when he channeled through me and would take it out of me like other things had been. I finished up and the boy went home; I told him he better be good. He said he would. I didn't know until later about his dreadful life. I got in the van to go back to Indiana.

And then I heard a laughing voice say, "You are mine."

"No way," I said. "I belong to God."

I felt weird all the way to Ed's house. I finally got to Ed's after I drove all night to get there and go to bed.

When I got there, Ed said, "Man, you look rough."

I told him what had happened. He said I had better get to bed and rest. So I took a shower and went to bed. When I woke up after having a nightmare I couldn't move. I was really sick. It felt like something was choking me and punching me.

I got a phone call from Joy and told her about it. She said there was a specialist that dealt with this kind of stuff and that she would make me an appointment. She did and Ed took me to see him. After the guy worked on me for over an hour, he said he couldn't do anything else and left the room. I thought that was strange but he didn't go into detail. He just said it was up to the Lord now. I was still choking but my side didn't hurt anymore. The guy did say it felt like my kidneys and side had been pulverized.

When we got back to Ed's house I was still choking and feeling bad. I couldn't tune in to my guides for some reason.

Three days passed and then I got a phone call from Judy. She said she had moved to Arizona; her husband had changed his job and they had moved there.

She said, "Sha `La, God came to me last night and told me you were in great danger and I needed to help you. What's wrong?"

So I told her what had happened.

She said, "You weren't supposed to take the demon on."

"I wasn't leaving the kid," I said. "And somehow I thought Jesus meant for me to take it on to save the boy. I don't know. Miscommunication I guess.

"So what do I do now?"

"Let me tune in and I will see," she said.

A few moments passed and she said, "I am going to call your spirit to me tonight while you sleep."

"I can't even sleep," I said.

"Take a sleeping pill."

I told her I would.

"I'll call you in the morning," Judy said, "and tell you what I saw and what happened."

I then thanked her for calling and helping. Later that evening, Ed gave me a sleeping pill.

The next morning I woke up and I wasn't choking any more. Ed came into the room to see if I was okay, I sat up and said to Ed, "She must have done something; I don't understand all of this."

He said, "Don't worry; it will be revealed to you."

"I sure don't want to perform any more exorcisms," I said. "I knew Jesus had the wrong person."

"Maybe not," Ed replied. "Maybe you just need some more training."

I didn't want to hear that.

Then Judy called and said, "You won't believe what happened!"

She explained she had made a space on her floor and lit a bunch of candles like Spirit had told her to do. Then she said some prayers and called for me to come to her.

"The angels brought you in," she said, "and behind them was this big black demon looking thing. I was scared and started commanding it out and it looked at me and started to come at me.

"Just then, I heard the name Metatron and this giant angel came through the doorway and took the demon out. I was exhausted. The other angels worked on you taking stuff off of you and then told me to call you back two more nights. I agreed and then the angels picked you up and took you out the door. I left the stuff on the floor and told my husband not to bother anything."

I thanked her and told her I would pay her when I got some more money.

"You're not supposed to pay me," she said. "You already did a lot for me, teaching me how to tune in to my guides. And this was a learning experience for me too.

"I'm going to bed. Now you rest and I'll call you later tonight."

We said goodbye and I hung up the phone. I told Ed about it and he said he'd fix me some breakfast. I was still weak. After breakfast, I finally got some sleep.

That night she called me again to come to her. Judy called me the next day. She said that the angels had to strip me down to my bones to purify and sanitize me and they put what looked like new skin on me.

"You're ugly without skin," Judy said.

"And I guess you'd look pretty," I said.

We laughed; I told her I felt lighter. She said they said some words over me in a different language and carried me back. She said I had one more night to go. I told her okay.

That night I felt a little stronger. Still, I couldn't figure all this out.

Out loud, I said, "I hope I am not being a guinea pig for someone to learn from."

Then I heard one of the guides say, "It's a lesson for the both of you."

Well on the third night, I went to sleep without a sleeping pill and woke up at four in the morning because I looked right at the clock. Then I saw Jesus standing at the bed.

"Now I will tell you some things," He said. "From now on, you do not take on the demons of others."

"But it wasn't leaving," I said.

"The boy had a 'contract' with the demon."

"Well, how come you didn't remove it?" I asked.

He replied, "We were bartering with the demon when you said you would take it on."

"Well I didn't know or hear that part," I said.

"You will also remain celibate until I send you someone," He said. "And you are now to have lessons from me and the elders of the Universe. Knowledge is like the ocean but you can only go so many leagues under at a time to grasp it all. You have still a lot to learn."

I told Him I did know that.

"Am I not to share or teach anything anymore?" I asked.

"You will share what you learn and one day put it in a book," He said. "When Judy calls she will tell you the same thing so you will know you are not dreaming."

"I know I am awake," I said, "and I see you and hear you."

"Then she will confirm what you have heard from me," He said. "You and she have a connection and will work together on some projects in the future. A lot will change in her life too. I will now go and talk to you later."

And then He left. But I was grateful that He even considered me to help with things; that He was willing to teach me and took the time out of his busy schedule to help me and others.

I couldn't sleep anymore but tried to because I didn't know if Judy was completely finished with me or not. I finally fell back to sleep and felt better when I woke up the next morning. I could finally go to the bathroom without any trouble.

When Judy called me she said the most wonderful things happened.

"You were glorified in some way," she said excitedly. "When the angels were through with you, you sparkled and grew wings and spoke to me and thanked me for having the courage to help you.

"But Jesus came and told you something I don't think you wanted to hear."

I told her to go on; tell me what it was.

"He told you and looked at me and told me to tell you in the morning to let you know from this day on you are to remain celibate until he sends you someone to marry," she said.

I said, "Okay...no problem."

"He also said he went to visit you at four this morning," she went on. "Do you remember that?"

I told her He had and that He had said the same things to me.

"You were to tell me again and to verify it," I said. "And so you did."

"After he talked to you a little more in Hebrew, or something that sounded like it, you stood up and spread your wings and flew away," Judy explained. "I felt better about everything for you, but I thought you would be mad about the celibacy part."

"No," I assured her. "I am done with Luke and other fools anyway. I don't care about any of that; I feel now is the time to just learn what Jesus wants to teach me and pass it on to others."

"We are to do some work together in the future," she said.

"Yes, that is what he told me too," I said. "I don't know what it is yet though."

"I guess we'll find out," she said. "Well, keep in touch."

And I said, "You do the same."

Then we said our goodbyes.

Betrayal

I got a call to come to Louisville to do another psychic fair and I met a woman there who I gave an unusual reading. Mother Mary channeled to her through me about her land and told her that she and Jesus would start appearing on two days a month. And they did.

Ed helped me place a big cement statue of an eagle and a statue of St. Francis on her property. He had made a connection up there and saw the spirit of Jesus in the sky. He was extremely tired and drenched in sweat by the time we had hauled the statues up there that hot day, but I guess Jesus and Mary were grateful. The spirits told us to bring the statues there.

Later, the woman turned on us and said the church wouldn't give her the funding to build a building on the land if I kept associating with her. What had happened was she had met another woman that supposedly channeled Mother Mary, and this woman wanted the attention. But we found out later she only read what a lady in Georgia had channeled and copied it from her.

Spirit still had me visit this place three times. I went with another friend when no one else was there. I haven't been back since then.

My Dad Passes

Ed helped me get my first massage table. We had heard from someone we met that a lady had one for sale and so we went to this bingo place and won two hundred dollars and paid on it the next day.

Ed also wanted to go out west and wanted me to go with him.

Well, some spirits had already presented themselves to me; they were earth bound out west and had asked for my help in crossing over. So, I told Ed we were to find these spirits and pray them over. He said we would fly.

At first I was afraid because I had never flown before. The plane had a lot of people and I had a fear of it weighing so much it would fall. I know it was silly, but I didn't like the flight because a lot of teenagers that had been to some sort of ball game were there and they were hopping around and yelling about their team winning. It was nerve racking.

But we landed safely in Phoenix. Ed rented a car and we drove through what seemed like the whole state. We did stop and see Judy and her husband. We visited for a day and talked about what had happened and she showed me how she did the ceremony and prayers. We read for each other and had dinner together and then we left.

Ed and I then went to the Grand Canyon and looked around. It was a beautiful place. I was dizzy though. I didn't know if it was the altitude or energies there, or just jet lag.

We did manage to help the earth bound spirits cross over. It turned out their remains were on private property, so I had to say prayers for them from the road.

Later, we drove through some of New Mexico. We found a store that would sell us some beads wholesale and Ed bought me some so I could make jewelry and sell it to make some money.

Ed said he would like to run through the desert naked, whooping and hollering. I told him to go ahead; just leave me the keys to the car. I also told him he was nuts because he would get stickers in his feet. I guess he thought about it and changed his mind. We had gotten into a couple of disagreements but we were still friends.

Finally we returned to Indiana and I got a call that my dad had died. Ed had some things fixed on the van so I could go to the funeral.

There was a girl named Amy that I had met a year prior in Knoxville at a psychic fair and she wanted to come up and visit with me. So I gave her directions to Evansville. She had been visiting for about two days when the call about my father came. She decided to follow me to Oakridge to the funeral.

They decided to have his funeral at eight that night. I wouldn't have known he had died except for a cousin who called my mom and my mom calling the funeral home, telling them they better let me see him to say goodbye.

About a month before that I did a reading on myself and it said a family member would die and I would have to forfeit an inheritance. I wasn't very close with my dad. He had been in a veterans' hospital and I had been to see him when I was with Luke but he didn't look well then either. After he and my mom divorced, he remarried and they had two children.

Anyway, Ed had given me some money to get there and for me to arrange for a hotel room for Amy and myself. On the way there, I felt a really cold energy enter the van; it was like a cold hand on my knee.

I heard a voice say, "Why aren't you at my funeral?"

Then I heard it again, and I said, "Are you Charles? Are you my dad?"

And the voice answered, "Yes, I am."

"One reason I'm not at your funeral is because no one told me that you had died until today," I said. "And I had to find a way to come down here."

"There are a few things I want to tell you," he said, "and I want to apologize to you for all the things of the past."

I told him I forgave him and not to worry, just go and be with God; that was the only thing that mattered now.

He said at least you know you can hear me even as I am now in the spirit.

"Yes, now we can talk whenever you want to connect," I said.

I told him I love him and he said the same to me. I had looked at the clock and it was about five minutes to eight.

"I must go now," he said. "They are calling me back; its time for the funeral."

"I will see you tomorrow," I said.

I felt really strange. And I cried. As I drove I called my angels and guides to be closer to me because of the experience. When we got to the town we got a hotel room. I told Amy we had to get up early and go to the funeral home because if we didn't they would bury him without me being there. I just felt it. His other children had always been reluctant to have anything to do with me.

We went to sleep and I had all kinds of weird dreams. It was like I was in the spirit world with him talking and going through the review with him. Strange.

When the alarm went off I was glad but nervous because I had a bad feeling. But I was not there to claim any of his estate; I was just there to say goodbye. Of course, they all thought I was there for his money or whatever he had.

Amy and I got to the funeral home and a man came and asked me if I was his oldest daughter.

I told him I was. So he opened the casket. When he did, here came the other kids and his ex-wife giving me a mean look.

The boy said, "If you try to claim any thing you can have all the bills too!"

I told him they could keep it all. I was only there to say goodbye. I told them my mom said he was my dad and I felt it was the proper thing to do. I told them they could have whatever he had since he didn't raise me. I didn't want anything. I also told them I already knew I wasn't getting anything.

I looked back at our dad and said my piece and for him to go to the light with Jesus and the angels, to be with God.

Then Amy and I left and went to the car to follow the line to the grave site. When we got there someone showed me a seat to sit next to my half brother. And they gave him our dad's flag. He had been in the Army. They fired the gun salute.

I looked around at the people in attendance and then I saw dad standing there in uniform looking like he did in the service when he was twenty years old. My mom had given me pictures of him in the army and he looked just like them. I thought he sure made the transition quick. So maybe that wasn't just a dream I had had that night.

My half-brother said, "You see him, don't you?"

"Yes I do."

"At least you can do that," he said.

I had read for him on one of my visits and told him of a job and a woman he would meet and he introduced her to me after the services. He said all that I told him back then had happened. I told him I hoped they were both happy.

After that Amy and I went into Knoxville to a restaurant and she introduced me to a sandwich called a falafel, which had chickpeas and some other things placed in a wrap of some sort, very tasty.

Since I was a vegetarian she thought I would like that. We talked a while then I headed back to Indiana. It didn't seem like anyone on my dad's side of the family wanted to talk to me.

(Back when I was eighteen, I went to visit him along with my aunt and uncles and cousins for a week. Since then I had visited maybe five times throughout the years. Everyone went there own way. One of the cousins wanted me to join the army with her but things kept blocking my way).

When I got back to Indiana I stopped at my mom's and told her what had happened. I stayed there for a couple of days then I went back to Ed's house and told him how things went.

He had met some more people and introduced me to them. I didn't get a good feeling from any of them. I told Ed but he didn't think I was picking up correctly. I think he found out later I was right.

But anyway, we went to the Enlightened Path Church for a special gathering. Ed got to meet them. And I think he learned a few things there that weekend too.

Then we drove to Camp Chesterfield, a wonderful spiritual retreat center where many truly gifted people lived and worked. They had these nice hotels, fellowship halls, meeting places, public walkways, an art gallery, serene gardens, and a well stocked bookstore.

I told Ed about my experience the first time I had gone there back in 1988. There were all these wonderful books, and I asked my guides which one should I buy and read first. But I heard "none of them."

"But I need to know this stuff," I said.

I heard, "No, you already know it."

I said, "How?"

Then I heard, "Your spirit knows all this and more. Go down this aisle and we will show you what you need to read now."

Well, when I walked down the aisle, out of the blue, and several shelves up, a book just jumped out of the slot it was in. Of course I know one of my spirit guides pushed it out and it fell at my feet. It was called "The Game of Life and How to Play It".

We went to a few local services and looked around. I slept in the van that night.

The next morning I heard people fussing about being kept awake all night by some loud snoring. I just laughed. I knew it was Ed. Lee had met someone and we had to go and find him.

Later, we ate breakfast and went to a service. I think the spirits gave Ed a message; then we went back to his place. I did a reading on Ed and told him about this woman that he would meet and marry. (And later he did meet her and they did marry. They moved to Roswell, near where the alien craft crashed more than fifty years ago. She didn't like Roswell like he did).

Before we left, I bought a stained glass cross that had the words on it "With God everything is possible."

I was going out to the van to put it in when a woman came up to me and said in a less than tolerant voice, "What are you doing?"

So I proudly showed her the cross and said, "I'm getting ready to hang it in my van."

She said that message meant something very different to her.

I was confused. She kept telling me that all of these negative things would happen to me. She had me so rattled, I was praying that Ed would hurry and come in from work to rescue me. I stood there for over an hour and then he finally came home and went right into the house. I told her I had to go.

"Promise me you will change your way," she said.

Then I heard Jesus come to me and He said, "Tell her you will think about it so she will leave."

And I did and she left. I went into the house all rattled. Ed asked what was wrong with me. I told him and he said to calm down. So I went in the other room and sat down and I asked Jesus to come in and talk to me. I asked what that was all about; had they sent her to change me or what?

"No," He said. "All religions will have different interpretations of the Bible and want everyone to believe what they want them too. You will be led by Me and so you will listen to Me. Just don't worry and get ready to leave tomorrow."

So I did. It was coming time for me to go and pick up Jason from the Job Corps for summer break. Ed told me to take care of the van and to keep in touch. I told him that I would.

I went to pick-up Jason and we talked and shared what had happened to each of us. I had written and told him some things that had happened and about my dad, but there was no time to go and pick him up to go with me to the funeral. That I didn't like.

When we got to my mom's, the old house across the street had come up for sale. At that time it belonged to my grandmother but two older uncles had power of attorney so they took it over, and the people that were renting it had moved.

So my mom asked her brothers if we could buy it on a land contract. They said we could but they raised the price a little. I didn't think it was fair but mom wanted us to live close by. We didn't have any heat; we had to use kerosene. We moved in there in 1995. We got some paint and did what we could to fix it up. I didn't have much money to put into it; it was over fifty years old. Every time I cleaned it, it would still look like it needed cleaning a few hours later.

During the time we were paying on it, I took Jason back to the Job Corps for his last year. And I traveled back and forth to Birmingham and up to North Carolina and Kentucky, along with several other states.

A Kirlian photo of Sha `La with her guides around her.

Sha `La was called to clear this young girl's spirit from a place of business.

Sha `La being ordained as a minister in a local church.

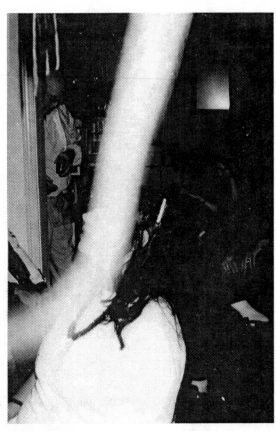

Sha `La channeled many spirits during this Birmingham session.

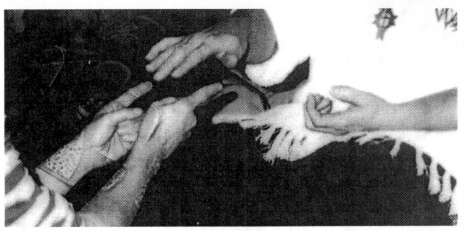

Spirit "bracelets" manifest on Debbie Hornbuckle's wrists during this channeling session.

Speaking Wind performed several drummings at Kinlock in the Bankhead National Forest of north Alabama. During this ceremony Sha ʽLa journeyed into the earth to the Ancient Ones and learned the phrase "On-Con-Ta" – which means to "return to perfection."

Sha ʽLa standing between Earth, Water and Sky as she completes the ceremony for turning the vortex in Belgium.

One of Sha `La's European hosts measuring energies at Stonehenge.

Sha `La near the top of Mount Shasta.

Samantha Robbins with God's protective light around her.

Sha `La with Maggie, her fearless ferret.

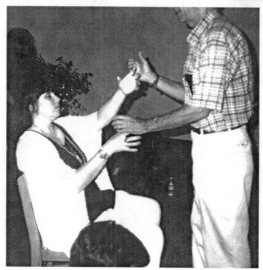

As each person honors him, they receive gifts from the spirit of Geronimo channeled through Sha `La.

White Feather, a friend who has shared adventures with Sha `La.

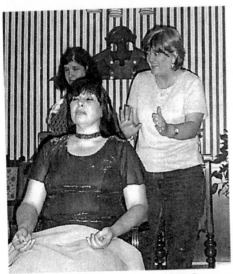

During this channel session, Laurette Turner feels the energy from the spiritual head dress of Geronimo.

Larry Turner feels the head dress energy from this session in 2003.

Sha `La channeling an eagle being. Note the eyes; in the original color photo they are gold.

A distorted energy field affects images at Souix Falls.

Sha `La Lightwolf, Led by Spirit.

CHAPTER 14
∞
NEW BEGINNINGS

God's Awakening Center

As I was traveling back and forth, I would periodically visit Myrtle's church. Finally they let me know in subtle ways that they really didn't see a need for my presence there anymore. (It's possible they were jealous that I was becoming well-known from my extensive travels). One of them even suggested that I donate half of my earnings to them. Of course, I thought that was a little unfair. I gave them some but I had to pay my debts too, plus gas for travel and sometimes hotels, and I didn't make that much. Sometimes I would get to a place and half of the people would cancel.

So I came home and went over to my mom's and she suggested I start my own church. My guides also told me to start my own church. I was uncertain and hesitant. I didn't know how to do that and I didn't know who would come or where I would start.

I did meet a lady named Meg that had gone to other churches, and she said she could help by letting me start in her living room. I guessed that was how Myrtle had also started.

We tossed around some names and I prayed to Jesus and asked him and He said give the glory to God and call it "God's Awakening Center."

I was again introduced to Todd. After I got over being upset with him, we talked for a while and I forgave him for introducing me to Katie in Kentucky. I told him about events at the earlier church; he had attended a few services but his impression was they didn't like men being there very much so he didn't go back. So Todd helped me fill out the paper work to start a new church and he, Meg and I wrote that we were going to bring this together and form "God's Awakening Center." I sent the money and paperwork in and the state registered us.

We advertised and promoted the church by word-of-mouth and people came; several different people that Meg and Todd knew and that I had met through psychic fairs. So people started attending. One man named Raymond from Germany came. He had a big house in Louisville, and he offered to let us start meeting there since he had a larger house than we did. It filled up fast. There were some people who also came from Myrtle's church; they complained they were running off all the men. It eventually evolved into an all women's church.

One of the men named Doug came over from the other church and charmed every one. Spirit told me not to trust him. We had meetings every month and then every third month. Meg decided to stop being our treasurer. So we had to do some voting for a new one. A few nominated Doug and he accepted. I did not feel good about it, but since he was voted in by the majority I had no choice.

So I thought, "God, you said you were giving everybody a chance so I guess we have to give him one too."

We all gathered together to work on increasing the size of the church congregation. But after a few months Doug started stashing money from the offering plate. I was traveling and Todd was supposed to keep up with all the paper work and files and go behind Doug to make sure all the monies were put into the bank. Both of them had ulterior motives which really upset me. And it would upset me to the point where I could not cope very well.

I let Todd take over when I was called to go out of town to do my work and the trust issues became really scattered. It was hard on me traveling back and forth. But during the time I wasn't traveling on the road I learned things from Spirit.

I was asked to do some reading at Joy's house and several women came. One lady had recently lost her son. His spirit came and told me things to tell her. She was amazed that I could hear him. I told her once a spirit finally crosses over they clear up some of their karma or baggage from down here and then they can come through a "funnel" or "doorway."

My ex-husband's spirit called it an "elevator." It was used to connect back into this dimension, and go back and forth through the funnel to recharge. I had learned by putting someone's palms together and observing if one of the fingers were out of alignment that there was an earthbound spirit hanging around them. Then I would go into a procedure of asking God and Jesus to bring in a light over that person and the spirit and we would perform a clearing prayer to release all of the Akashic records from them and the gravitation pull so the spirit could go with Jesus and the Angels to heaven.

The lady was amazed and told her daughter, Angel, to come and see me. When the daughter came she wanted to learn more so I took her on as a student. I called her Angel because all the kids said her hair look like Angel hair, long and blonde.

Angel started coming to my house at first to learn to meditate and connect with her guides. She would visit often because she was eager to learn. Once she learned how to make the connections, I started taking her on some trips with me and she would give readings. She also joined my church. Some of the people, including her, wanted to have the classes to become ordained. Once the material had been learned, Todd ordained her and a few others. I ordained some; through me Jesus would anoint them and channel through me to perform the ceremony. Everybody that came received special gifts from God.

One lady, named Louie, came and said she had been to see other psychics. She said they told her that she wasn't ready to use her healing gifts yet; that she must wait for a certain time when they would tell her. I told her hogwash. They were jealous and she had a great gift and must start using it now. So she started. It was amazing. Although I had to have her tone it down some, she would become so physically hot I was afraid she would combust.

When you are working on others you need to ask the energy to reach a level that can be managed and then let it adjust to your frequency.

Louie and some of the people in the Indiana church went with me to Alabama to teach some classes on healing energy work.

One man came that had cancer. We all were going to send him energy when the class was over but Louie started automatically heating up. She sent waves of energy to this guy and he later said he felt better.

But in the process, Louie's energy became so intense the metal in the watch of a woman standing to one side heated to the point that she had to remove it and move away from Louie. The man on the other side of Louie was chewing gum; he said her energies made it melt in his mouth. Louie wound up apologizing.

On one other occasion, Cindy and Louie and I were called to visit Bill Mc-Cowan's house. He had a problem with a vortex opening up and the spirits were coming up and a few even threw him out of bed and up against a wall.

We went up there and I asked the Light of God to come in and anchor and then asked Mother Earth to release the gravitational pull for the unseen.

Thor came in and he made my arm and hand spin around at what felt like ninety miles an hour, round and round; like it was cutting down into the earth and splitting the energy of the vortex. Then Thor used a spirit "machine" to draw the spirit entities out of the vortex and the surrounding area. They were flying up in there like a vacuum cleaner had them. One of the spirits grabbed Louie's foot and I told her to just command it off and stomp her feet. Then it left.

On another occasion, Cindy, Louie and I went to Nashville to a psychic fair to do clearing work. A woman brought her wheelchair-bound husband and the three of us started to perform energy adjustments to him.

Spirit first had me place a scarf with a leopard pattern around his shoulders. The reason was the spirit world would use certain types of energies to speed up or transform other energies. So the leopard or cheetah patterned scarf was to make his cells speed up so we could shift out the negative energies faster.

Louie stood behind him, and Cindy stood in front of him, and I did what I call my "Journey with Jesus", looking inside the man in the wheelchair.

I saw what appeared to be a twisted nerve in his back that was pinching; Jesus had me to tell him to repeat the affirmation that he "released wars and battles" since he had been wounded in the service. And he did. Then Jesus had me to have him say a few more affirmations and he did; then the man said he was burning up and sweating. His wife pointed out that he was wiping off his sweat with his hand. I told Louie to back away some and get him a tissue or something because I thought her energies were getting too hot for him.

His wife said, "You don't understand; his arm was paralyzed too."

Well, I hadn't paid attention to his arm. But it was a miracle because he finally moved his arm after all those years. Then he said his legs were tingling and I told him Jesus said that if he could soak in some Epson salt baths it would pull out more toxins and make him feel better.

"I would like to walk again," he said, "and run at least a mile a day."

I told him if he was supposed to God would allow him.

A lady from the fair called me three months later and said the same man had started walking again. I just said thanked the Lord, for we are only His instruments to work through.

Cindy invited me to her home; she had been ordained by me. Sometimes she would invite people to receive clearing sessions from me; in exchange she wanted to learn some different techniques in energy work, so I taught her what I knew. On one occasion I was channeling Metatron the Archangel and he put energy into Cindy's hand and she said it burned some; the next day she had little blisters on her feet.

I started performing some energy work on her and there were some symbols that manifested on her as if she had been branded. She meditated on the symbols and the spirit world told her that she had been anointed with them to help her with things she was to do. She now places these symbols in with the Reiki attunements she performs for people. It helps them to be stronger in their self-healing work.

At Cindy's house one day we were going to do energy work on each other. I held the energy first for her and she saw these wonderful colors and then visions. When it came my turn I lay on the table and it again felt like they were pulling chains out of my arms and the angels actually pulled my arm out of its socket and twisted it around and pulled out stuff. I must have had a lot of old programs in my arms.

"Look at that!" Cindy said pointing to my arm.

I said, "You ought to feel it; it hurts!"

After a while the angels were finished for that session and put my arm back in place. The next day, Cindy took me to this mountain were we saw orbs floating in front of us. Then I heard, "We are fairies."

I sat down to meditate and I saw myself going into this chamber where there was a big vat-like container with some people standing off to one side. I stepped beside the large open vat and a long white dress was placed on me. Then I stepped down into the vat and this gold liquid flowed all over me. I was immersed for a few moments and then after I rose up, one of the people there said, "You are now re-anointed."

Then I was sent back to my space and when I came out of the meditation it felt like I had truly been raised to another level of energy.

I would go to Cindy's house about three or four times a year. Each time was a new experience.

Learning a New Healing Energy Technique

Angel went with me to Alabama and North Carolina, and some other places on occasion. There was one occasion when this woman named Ellie wanted a session. She said all the lies some people had told her had drawn her into a little trouble. She had been very gullible. Well, we proceeded to use the stone layouts on her and we pulled and pulled the junk out of her. (When we have people to say an affirmation to let things go it looks sometimes like stringy sticky stuff or ropes). We did this for about seven hours.

She said, "You got it all but the core."

I tried and tried, and then God told me, "Tell her you are going out west to learn a new technique and you will come back and work on her again."

So I did. I didn't understand then but when I returned home Judy called me and told me she had learned something new and would like to teach me since I helped give her confidence several years before.

"And besides God told me I have to teach you this," she said. "God told me I even have to pay your way here."

At first I didn't want to go because I felt intimidated since she didn't really want to teach me; she was being made to teach me. But God's big voice said for me to accept the offer and get on the plane. So I did.

When I arrived in Arizona, I was lost; it was a big place. Finally we found each other. She had gotten a new hair style and a new husband. I was surprised. I hadn't heard from her since I had that incident at Ed's house, about three years or so ago. It was 1996 now and a lot had happened since 1993.

I stayed for about two weeks at her new house. She had learned a technique from a man that channeled information from God about how our bodies correlated with different avenues of life and even past lives. It was really very interesting. I didn't realize there was so much to learn.

Jesus came to me one night and said, "You must release past lives from knowing Tom and (other people). I will use a little different technique on you this time as an example of what to do for others."

I was a little concerned. I told Judy what Jesus had said.

She said, "I was afraid of that; now what?"

"I don't know but I guess we are getting ready to find out," I said.

She became slightly aggravated, because every time Spirit brought in some new energy or healing techniques, I had to be the "guinea pig"; but Spirit had told me, "You are just the role model."

That next morning I felt like I was having this weird heart attack. Her husband heard me and woke her up and both of them came running into the room where I was. They started running energy through me and saying prayers to balance and clear me as much as they could to return me to a calm state.

A little later the people from the class started showing up. I was a little embarrassed but I couldn't do anything except repeat affirmations from her while she tried pulling the junk out of me.

I just kept seeing all this old stuff from me and Tom, like flashes from all of these different eras. It looked and felt horrible, and it lasted for *hours*. I finally told her to go on with the class and I would just rest. But it seemed like every time she talked about something else my body would react. I was in so much pain. I know it scared her.

She didn't like dealing with the spirit world much either. But these spirits would come to me and want to cross over. I had to do it. Jesus said that was one of my jobs. But what the spirit world had me doing Judy didn't want to be a part of anymore.

When I returned home with the clearing book and information she only talked to me maybe twice and eventually said she couldn't work with me any more; she wanted no part of the next stage that I was going into.

Again I asked God and Jesus, "Are you sure you got the right person for the work you are telling me about?

I heard, "Not many will answer the full calling on what is needed but you were chosen before you were born."

"I wish I had been born with instructions," I said.

God said, "Your parents *were* given instructions but chose to ignore them. I have granted you Grace."

I didn't quite understand that but I knew that what I had learned in the physical I was now getting ready to learn more about in the spiritual. I had to switch gears again to learn what was coming up. They, God and Jesus, weren't going to let me run away. Even when I tried I just got dragged back in somehow. So I had to get ready for whatever was to come.

When I returned home, Angel came over and I ran the charts on her, page by page, easy. Then I thought, "Okay, we can do this, no problem."

Because I had learned some people had contracts with other people and other spirits out there, all we had to do was take the pendulum and shift the energy out. I asked God to help people transition through it easier and without the pain that I had experienced.

He said everyone would be different and that it was time we upgraded all of this information.

"Do I need to find out about other classes?" I asked.

He said, "Yes and no, your classes now will be with us."

I knew right then I was about to go on another roller coaster ride.

Well, God had me call Ellie.

"I think we can remove the core now," I told her.

"Come on down," she said.

"Take Angel with you," God told me. "You will need her help."

So we went to Ellie's and began our work.

I heard, "Tell Angel to monitor Ellie's heart and if there is any trouble to let you know."

"What about her heart?"

Then I heard, "Just start running the energies on the chart; you will see."

So I did, and the next thing I knew it was like I had gone into this different dimension. I saw myself and Ellie in a courtroom and Jesus was the judge; Archangel Michael was there with Him. On the other side were these ugly dark creatures. And in the back were different spirits; some I recognized and others I didn't.

I looked up and Jesus said, "You have to plead her case."

I asked, "About what?"

"Why she has this core," He said.

"Well, I learned that some people have contracts," I said, "and I think she has one and we asked that it be removed."

"Plead her case," He said.

Well, I thought I had just done that. Then it came to me that I needed to see or find out when she first had the contract, be it a past life or what. So someone brought in a screen and a projector.

"If these are her Akashic records or her review," I said, "I now need to see her past, to the beginning of the contract."

So the movie began playing backwards really fast. Then we saw her on the screen in another era, dressed slim, with long hair and holding a wine or martini glass in her hand.

So I said, "I guess she was intoxicated and didn't know any better."

"You have to do better than that," Jesus said.

"Better than that? What now?" I thought.

So I said, "She was stupid, ignorant, poisoned, tricked"...and all other kinds of words and all Jesus would say was, "You have to do better than that."

I was getting really agitated. It seemed like I went from A to Z. What else was there? Thank goodness one of the spirits in the back whispered… "*innocence.*"

"What?" I asked.

Jesus said, "What did you say?"

I said, "Innocence. We plead her innocence."

He took the gavel, struck the podium with it and the other side went nuts. He wrote on a piece of paper, rolled it up and handed it to Archangel Michael. He unrolled it revealing the word "Approved."

Archangel Michael showed it to the creatures from the dark side and they became frantic and chaotic, jumping up and down. One tried to crawl on the floor to get over to us and I saw it and told Jesus to look and He did and He made them go back.

Then He said for me to always plead their innocence; that this would get to the core of the situation. *He said they were granting all souls amnesty and pardon, because it took too long for people to get with the program to clear all of their karma.*

"They keep making more, so we are deleting the past when they come to us and removing the baggage they have been carrying around for centuries," He said. "We can only go in stages with this. It is still like the ocean of knowledge; you can only go so deep each time. But for now we have set Ellie free and she is to now focus on God."

Ellie agreed and then the next thing I knew I was back in my body and I was dizzy.

Then Ellie opened her eyes and said, "They got the core. Wasn't that something?"

"Do you remember that?" I asked.

She said, "Yes. And thank you so much for helping me."

I looked at Angel and she said I had been under for seven hours. I thought if I have to do this with every person I have a session with I will never get anything done.

She paid us and went home.

We were staying with a lady, named Hope, that had a little healing center. She let us stay there and we gave a few readings. She asked me to hold a channeling session the next day. That was taxing on me too. I used a lot of energy during those few days.

I asked Jesus if what had happened with Ellie was real.

He said, "Yes and no. In most cases, you won't have to go to court for everyone whose innocence you plead and proclaim. Some will be different but I will help guide you through them."

"I sure hope so," I said.

When we returned to Indiana, we practiced on some of the people at church. By that time some new people had started to attend.

We had a psychic fair and did pretty well considering it was our first one. Angel and a few others wanted to learn how to channel. So I began to teach them. Angel wanted to come to my house and work more. She created some transcripts for me in exchange for teaching her.

One day I was called to North Carolina. Angel wanted to go with me, so I let her. There we went to a lady's house that was from India.

I was sitting on the floor and when a spirit came in named Sai Baba. He said he was astral traveling and wanted to introduce himself to me and help me understand some other things about life and about himself.

The lady came in the room and I told her what I was hearing. She said, "Oh yes" and then handed me a book about him.

"You must be special to be honored by him," she said. "He is an avatar, a holy man."

Then she told me a little about him. I thought that it was pretty cool. He said he would visit me from time to time and help me with healing.

I also went to visit another woman while I was in North Carolina. After I had worked on her, we wound up talking in the kitchen. I happened to notice that she had a stopped up drain. She sent someone after what they call a "snake" to force the stuff out of the drain.

It was still stopped up the next morning. Jokingly, I told her I would fix it. (I am always kidding around). So I went to the sink and put my hand over it and in my most authoritative voice I said, "Release!" and the darn thing let go and drained. She looked at me with such surprise. Of course, I was also surprised, a lot. I told her it was already set to release and I just happened to do that at the same time, that it wasn't really me.

"It was just a coincidence," I said.

"No, it was you," she maintained.

She's never spoken to me since then. Years later she sent me a card saying she moved and got married. Weird.

Guided to Star - My Wolf

During my travels I would take Maggie (my fearless ferret) with me most of the time except when I had to fly somewhere or if it was too hot. She would sit on my shoulder or curl up beside me and when we got to where we were going I'd put her in her cage.

It was late summer of 1996 and I was still traveling a lot and learning from my guides about different energies. I had learned about my animal guides and totems and was connecting and becoming more acquainted with them; there were a lot of them. (Now, you should know that just like people guides, animal guides are with us to help us to learn and grow and also to protect us).

Well, I have these wolf spirits that help protect me and one of them kept insisting that they would manifest in a physical form like Maggie had. She said I would call her Star and I would find her from someone who raised wolves.

It was again time for me to go back to Alabama where I had met a lady named Lynette. She wanted me to read for some of her friends. Louie wanted to go with me, so I asked Jason if he wanted to go also, but he said he was going to work for one of our cousins for a little while.

So Louie, Maggie and I went to Alabama. While we were there I talked to Lynette about animal spirit guides and told her how I got Maggie and also about the wolf that wanted to come to me. But I didn't know anyone who raised wolves.

She said she did; one of her friends in Arkansas had some. So I asked her if she would call them and see if they had a white one because I guess I had it in my head that because Maggie came to me as a white ferret that the wolf would too.

So she called this man. And he said all of the females had just given birth and there was one white one. I asked her to have them hold it for me and I would come and look at it. They said they would.

So after we gave the readings, we, that is, Louie, Lynette, Maggie and I, went to Arkansas. On the way there a lady from Mississippi called me and asked if I ever came out that way. I told her that as a matter of fact we would go near her place on the way to Arkansas. She asked if we could stop on the way back through and do some clearing on her house and maybe herself, that there were some strange things happening there. I told her we would.

We crossed into Arkansas and took a hotel room because it was late and we couldn't see the puppies in the dark. We went to eat and when we got back to the room we did some smudging. That's where we lit some white sage and a white candle to clear the room; I took my pendulum and said a clearing prayer to send any lingering spirits to the light. There was a few there because Louie saw one in the mirror.

We finally went to sleep; I couldn't get any rest though. I was excited but also nervous about getting the wolf. I didn't know why until we went there the next morning.

This guy had over three hundred wolves. I was shocked.

I asked, "How come you have so many?"

"When I was in the hospital dying of heart failure," he said, "a friend came in to see me. I was going blind. I couldn't see what he had with him. He told me to just reach out and touch, so I did and I felt fur. But it had a strange texture. I asked him what kind of animal he had brought me, and he said a healing wolf. Wolves heal, you know. I figured if your doctors give up on you, well, there might be hope with something else.

"I felt this energy go through me and my eyesight started coming back at least halfway and I could see the wolf. Then I started feeling better. I got up in a few days and went home.

"I said from then on I would dedicate my life to rescuing wolves and wolf hybrids."

"Well, I'm interested in a full-blood wolf," I said.

He said, "I know and I had the white one for you but the other night it disappeared."

I was surprised. But he said white ones were more head strong and that I really needed a different one. Then I was disappointed.

He told me to walk around and see if I found one I liked. Well my heart wasn't in it. Louie found a cute furry black one that look like a teddy bear.

"I want this one," she said.

"Do you have a big place?" the man asked.

"Only an apartment," she replied. "Why?"

"That one has four breeds of wolf in it," he said, "and look over here at the momma."

He had this huge propane tank cut in half length-ways. When he called the mother wolf, she came out from inside the propane tank section, and looked as big as a house.

"That's how big your cub will get," he said.

I told Louie, "You won't have many visitors with it, that's for sure."

"I can't hide one that size from my landlord, can I?" she said.

"I don't think so," I said.

But she played with it while we were there. (She and I were always asking the spirit world to let us win the lottery so we could get a larger place. It hadn't happened yet).

Well, I walked around and Lynette said, "Look at these, and over here, more."

I was confused. There were so many and they were all running up to me like they were saying "Take me! Take me!"

I told the man I didn't see any that I felt was the one I was looking for, maybe next time.

He looked in my eyes for a moment then said, "I know; come over here."

"Over there is a momma wolf, and her cubs are underneath that box," he said. "Go and bring one out."

"Are you crazy?" I said. "I'm not going in there and get eaten up."

So he laughed and went in and brought out a boy and a girl cub. While we were there, a couple and their children came to buy one too. They were full-blooded Creek Indians.

The Creek husband said he would take the little boy wolf. It was light grey and white. The girl wolf was a brown and white shaded color.

"Here's the one you need," the wolf-keeper said.

"I don't know; I feel I should get a white one," I said.

"Hold her and see," he suggested.

So I took her in my arms. She was a little scared, and was trembling some. I started to ask Louie and Lynette to tune in and see if this was the one and before they could answer a light came into her and me. We both were trembling and I just started crying. It felt like "what in the world?"

Then both girls said they thought it was the one. I felt this overwhelming feeling being there; we wound up taking pictures of the place.

I told the owner I only had three hundred dollars even though he had asked for four hundred.

"If I take her, I will have to send the money to you," I offered.

He put his hand on my head and looked in my eyes and said, "You know, a lot of people tell me that and I never hear from them but I can tell you will. Go on and take her."

I said, "Give me your address."

And he did. We left and I couldn't quit shaking. I asked Louie and Lynette to take turns driving.

We finally arrived at the lady's house in Mississippi. We all went in and she told us what was going on; and even after I put my cub, Star, down, I was still shaking inside.

We took the materials out of the van that we needed to do the clearing. Louie and Lynette helped me set things up. We went outside and Star went with us; she headed toward this shed, or barn-like building, and started barking. She was only four and a half weeks old now.

The woman pointed to where the noises had been coming from and things had moved around. I guess Star had seen what it was and was letting us know.

I started calling in the light again and asking the angels to anchor it over all of the vicinity and for a several mile radius. And as I started praying more and commanding the entity to leave and go to the light, it came up to me and threw me several feet across the driveway.

We each held a staff and we were using them to hold the energies for the light so that the light could anchor to the earth and shift the negative energies and entities out.

"It's over here," Louie said.

"Just keep commanding it out," I said.

Then it went to Lynette and I told her to do the same. I got up and visualized energy coming out of my hands and I started shoving it upwards toward the light. Star was barking and running back and forth. I told the thing it wasn't going to hurt my pup.

I don't know why I started spinning but I did and the energy created a whirlwind affect and I saw the thing go up and I told God to take it. It finally went into the light. Star looked up and barked a few more times and then it was over.

The woman said she felt it leave.

I asked the angels what that was all about. They explained they were getting the rest of the entities away.

"Remember, we work as a team," they said. "You have to help too."

Star started to run down the road and I went after her. I tried to comfort her and tell her everything would be all right, and that I would protect her.

She calmed down some. We went to a hotel and got some rest – after we cleared the hotel room too. Everywhere we went we had to clear the rooms before we could go to sleep. I found out "earthbounds" and bad spirits hang out where ever they can.

Louie and I took Lynette home and we started back to Indiana. Louie lived in Kentucky. So I dropped her off at her apartment and went home with Maggie and Star. Star didn't know what to think of Maggie; but Maggie wanted to play and Star would run.

When I pulled in the driveway there was a dog chained to the fence. I went over to my mom's and took Star and Maggie with me. Jason was over there across the street with her and my brother Walt. I asked him where the dog came from. He said he had gone up to this guy's house that was one of his cousin's relatives from the other side of the family and the guy was going to shoot it.

I asked him why.

He said, "The guy had some other dogs. Two were Rottweilers and the dogs got in a fight and this one killed both of them. I couldn't let him shoot it so I told him to let me have it. Since Peaches died, I've wanted a dog."

"But I got this wolf pup for you," I said.

"She's yours," he said. "I wanted one too."

I told him, "Well, if it's a killer, don't let it be around Star."

We walked over to the house and Star jumped out of my arms and ran over to the dog. I was frantic; she laid down beside the dog and the dog just looked at her and then at me.

"If you hurt her I will whip your butt," I said.

He didn't do anything except stand there with this look on his face like "what the heck?"

Jason went and picked Star up and we went into the house.

"So what did you name it?" I asked.

"Akita," he said, "because it is part Akita mix."

"Mixed with what?"

"I think German shepherd," he said.

I guess Star missed the other wolves and took up with this one as a friend. All I know is that every time we took Star out for her daily routine she would run over to him and want to play. I would always put some food down for Star while Jason fed Akita. Of course, I also fed Maggie.

Well, not long after I got Star, I sat down with a donut and was on the phone telling somebody about her. About that time Star ran into the room and grabbed the donut out of my hand and took off with it. I was shocked, because the man I bought her from said wolves didn't eat sugar.

The next day I was eating watermelon when she came and grabbed it too. So I called the man and told him what had happened.

He said, "Oh no."

"Did you sell me a hybrid?" I asked.

"No ma'am," he said. "She is full wolf. I gave you the papers on her."

"Well, what's going on?"

He laughed and said, "When the energy came into the both of you, as you were holding her, she picked up some of you and you picked up some of her."

Because I told him my sleeping habits had changed, I would sleep with one eye almost open now and my hearing was sharper.

I said, "I guess if I turn into a werewolf person, just shoot me."

He laughed and said, "If you do that, I want you to come and live out here with us."

We both laughed; it felt a little strange.

"She will try and challenge you to see who is going to be the alpha," he added. "And she will probably win."

I was becoming more sensitive to things around me. As Star grew larger, I chained her outside for a few hours. And I don't know how she did it, but she would manage to take her chain and hook it to Akita's and she would run around the house. My uncles, and other people around us, were afraid of her because she was a wolf. But she never bothered anyone. The only time she was ever ready to attack, was when a bunch of young guys in their 20's came to the door one night and asked us where someone lived. They acted very suspicious. Jason had to hold her back.

"She may have seen a bad spirit around one of them," I said to Jason.

"No, she's sensing they are up to something evil; even I feel it," he replied.

The car circled around, going up and down the road all night. Star stared outside the window the entire time.

Some people would come over and she would play with them, while with others she would growl. She never bit anyone though. She would always want to take my food and she would sit in Jason's lap and play with him more and act like she was trying to make me jealous. I told her we must have gotten our wires crossed. She was very smart.

I went to give her some medicine one day. It might have been worm medicine or something. I thought since she always seemed to want what I had it would be easy to give it to her. But this wasn't the case. I told her to come and get some candy; she looked at me and started running. She ran around and around under the bed and then everywhere to get away from me so she wouldn't take the medicine. I wished I had a video of it; we could have put it on the funniest animal show, probably would have won. And if I could have had one outside when she would unchain herself that would have been something. I took her on some trips and she conducted herself pretty well.

Crazy Bear

Rose called me and said she had moved her herb store to Cherokee and had met a few people that were interested in my work.

I took my nephew Jo-Jo, who was about eleven years old then and on school break, with me along with Star and Maggie. We got in the van and off we went.

I started having dreams about a man and Spirit said they were going to let this man come into my life.

"What? More complications?" I said.

"No, he will want to marry you and settle down," they offered.

(Sometimes I think Spirit needs to look more into the future).

But another learning experience is what I decided they wanted me to have.

While I was at Rose's place for the third day, a guy came in and said to her, "God told me I was to come here today and find my wife."

We just looked at each other like he was crazy. He was wearing a ball cap and had his hair pulled back.

I thought, "This can't be the guy I was supposed to meet because the one I saw had long hair."

So I just ignored him.

He proceeded to tell Rose he'd been having dreams and visions of this woman.

Rose said, "It can't be me; I have a boyfriend."

"No, it's not you," he said.

"What did the woman in the vision look like?" she asked.

He described me. I just turned my head to look away from him. She had my brochure on the table and it had my glamour picture on it.

He saw it and said, "This is her."

"Are you sure?" she asked.

"Yes, this is the one in the vision," he said.

"That's Sha 'La."

Jo-Jo gave me the funniest look.

I said, "Well that's me when I have makeup on and as you see I don't have any on right now; and besides, I had visions of a man too, but you don't look like him."

"I swear to you I dreamed of you," he said.

"Take your cap off and take the little thing out of your hair," I told him.

I fell backwards; it was him. Jo-Jo's mouth fell open. We were stunned.

He and I talked for a while and he said that he had dropped off this friend of his at the Indian hospital and was going to go back and pick him up.

"I want to call you and talk more with you tonight," he said.

"Okay."

"What is Spirit getting you into?" Rose asked me.

"I don't know."

Well, he called that night and we talked for hours. I told him all about the work I did, even about the channeling and he said he was okay with it.

He and another friend of his came up the next day and we all went to the water falls. Jo-Jo said he liked it on the mountain; he wanted the two of us to move there.

"Your dad won't let you," I told him. "If my brother Ronald would let you move with me we might try living there because I also like it in the mountains."

My new suitor's Indian name was Crazy Bear. In my travels I had met several Native American people named this. He was a fancy dancer at the pow-wows from Georgia.

I went to visit him after I took Jo-Jo home, and stayed a few days. But it didn't feel right.

He and I went to a few pow-wows and I watched him dance and he came up to Indiana and went to my church.

The people in the church told me to marry him and move to Georgia and turn the church over to them. That made me very upset.

Crazy Bear and I drove up to Cherokee and had an old Indian-style wedding. Outside with the elements and swap rings, we said our vows to each other in the presence of God, so we were spiritually married.

He was supposed to help me with different things God said. But at one of the pow-wows, this one guy didn't like me and he persuaded Crazy Bear to go with him and leave me. Crazy Bear said he'd be back. I told him he wouldn't.

It was also about that time that Walter went into the hospital and I needed to return to Indiana to see him. Well, Crazy Bear wanted to keep Star.

My guide, Smokey, said, "If he keeps her, he will show her off and then sell her."

So I took her with me. And when I got to the hospital, my ring fell off my finger. I tried to put it back on but it hurt my finger badly.

"What's going on now?" I asked God.

"Your marriage has now been annulled because he has now cheated on you," He said. "You will not see him anymore."

So I meditated that night and saw him with another woman. She looked similar to me; I thought that was strange. Then I started getting phone calls from people that knew us and informed on him and they said the strange thing is she looks a little like you.

"Whatever; I was done with that loser anyway," I said.

There was this one incident where two women had a flat tire and asked him if he would help them change it but he wouldn't because they were black ladies. I made him get out and help them. One of them asked what his name was and I told her, but she kept referring to him as Lazy Bear. My brother Walter was with us and we laughed and laughed.

I said, "God, or whoever in the cosmos that sent him, I hope you got a good laugh. I have tried to obey you but this is ridiculous. I try and wear what you say is needed for the day and eat better and go and work and do what you ask, but don't send me any more men. I will stay by myself."

White Raven

A woman named White Raven came to visit me one day and, in the course of conversation, asked me about Star.

"Why do you let her take your food?"

"She just does and I can't get her to stop," I said.

"Let me teach you how to handle that," she offered.

"Well at least she keeps me on a diet," I said.

Star went up to her and White Raven said, "Now Star, Sha'la will share but you have to let her eat too."

Star looked at me and I said, "Yeah, do you want me to be skin and bones?"

Then White Raven said, "Now Sha'La, you take a bite and put your hand ou and then give her a bite."

I did and Star accepted that but I couldn't get her to eat just dog food. So we shared.

One day I took two bites and she gave me this look and made a low growl. I apologized to her and gave her two bites. It was funny in a way; everybody thought I was crazy.

In February, 1997, White Raven called and asked if she could come back up because she and her boyfriend had broken up.

I told her she could and soon after that a job opportunity opened for both of us. I had met this guy that came to the church and he said there were some openings at this place.

"All you have to do is type in orders from the government," he said.

"God, I need money so can I go and work," I pleaded.

"You can try it," He said.

So White Raven and I went to apply and we were hired. A few others from the God's Awakening Center had also applied, were accepted and started working there as well. The place had a few big rooms with row after row of computers in them.

Well, I thought since I had a hard time with machines crashing with me that I would sit in the very back at the last computer. I typed a few sentences and the darn thing quit. The supervisor came over and asked me what was wrong. I told him I didn't know. The machine wasn't a good one. So he told us to take a break so they could look at it. Of course, the girls that knew me shook their heads and grinned. Then the man said it was working and for us to come back. He showed me what keys to not touch. I said okay. I got a few more things typed on it and then it blew out everybody's computer.

"You must have a short in this room," I said.

"You just need to go home," he said.

I got to the car and it was snowing. A woman name Linda said since I lived so far away that White Raven could come to her house and stay until the weekend. I told her thanks. So I went on home. Then I started feeling sick. When certain energies clash with mine I become physically ill. I was upset too, because I didn't have any money for my bills. I had to borrow again. I was so disgusted.

The Accident

It was now February 14th, 1997. I remember this day because White Raven had just gotten a check and wanted me to take her to get it cashed. I had also bought a scratch-off lottery card with some change I had and won thirty-three dollars.

I told White Raven I needed to get Jason some valentine candy. We were on our way to the store when the light turned red, so everybody stopped. I was the fourth vehicle in line. We were talking about something, and then all of a sudden: Bam! The car behind me went right into my left back side. Its impact threw us into the dash of my vehicle and jerked us backward.

I looked over at White Raven and asked, "Are you alright?"

"I don't know," she said.

I put the vehicle in park and I looked in my side view mirror and the woman started to go around me.

"She's leaving," I said.

I took my seatbelt off and got out and told her to just get right back where she was until the police came. She had about four kids in the car with her.

"My brakes went out," she said. "And my husband said if I ever hit anyone to leave the scene."

"You have a crazy husband," I said, "and why didn't he fix your brakes? You could have killed your kids if you had hit something else."

Someone from a nearby gas station yelled over and asked if we needed the police and I said yes. Finally the police came and I told them what happened. The policeman said since no one was bleeding and I needed to go to the hospital then I should go on over there. I was so addled. I told White Raven we would go but she said to wait; that we had company coming and we could go later. I should have gone on and let the company wait because the next day I was having dizzy spells and seizure-like symptoms. I went to the doctor and he wrote down what had happened and gave me some pills.

Angel called me and I told her what had happened and how my neck was hurting and how I was having dizzy spells and passing out, and that my mind would sometimes go blank. I couldn't remember the past or even childhood things.

Some cousins came over but I couldn't remember them; they kind of got offended but I couldn't help it. Angel suggested I go to her chiropractor.

"If you think he's okay I'll ask my doctor too," I said.

I went and asked the doctor if it would be okay for me to go because the pills weren't doing much good. He said it would. So I called Angel and she came over and took me to the chiropractor.

He took some x-rays and said my brain stem had been pulled and loosened.

I was upset.

"I guess the jolt did it," I said.

He agreed.

Spirit told Angel to send energies into me when we returned home. She stayed for a couple of hours and I laid down and asked the Archangels to come in and help heal me. I felt them working on me. Spirit said it would take several sessions before I would feel better.

The chiropractor had told me to come and see him three times a week. I would get either Jason or my mom to drive me because White Raven had said she was feeling okay and had gone back to her boyfriend in Georgia. After about two weeks or so the chiropractor and my regular doctor said I would have to have surgery.

Jesus came to me and said, "Do not have surgery; there will be a slip of the knife. You may die from surgery."

"Well what do I do?" I asked.

"Tell the chiropractor to hold his hands a certain way."

And He showed me three letters that meant polarity.

He said, "Tell him I will work through him to help you."

"Yeah, right," I thought to myself. "Then they really will cart me off to the loony bin."

He said, "Tell him it's the only way you will survive."

So I went for my appointment and told him that I had to tell him something. He listened, patiently.

"I know a lot of people pray to Jesus and I do too, but I also hear Him and He told me to show you these three letters," I said, holding my hands the way God had shown me.

The chiropractor said they symbolized polarity.

"Are you sure you haven't been to another chiropractor?" he asked.

"No, I haven't," I said. "You are the only one."

He said that was the first thing they learned in chiropractic school but he didn't think it really worked.

"Well, would you let Jesus put his hands through yours and do it for me and see?" I asked.

He said, "Yes…you know my dad was a little psychic. I didn't think much of it at first. And there has been some other people come and tell me things similar to what you're saying. So…yes, I will let Jesus do the polarity through me."

I thought to myself "Thank God."

So he did. My head started feeling a little better and each time I went I felt better and the seizures started happening less and less. I told my regular doctor about it and he just said, "Keep going back and maybe it will save you from surgery."

By the third week I didn't have any more seizures. I still had headaches but he told me it would be a drawn-out process to allow the brain stem to work back in place and heal. The chiropractor said this was the first time he had done this and it worked.

"Well maybe in the future you can help someone else like this," I offered.

Each time I went to my appointment, he asked me questions; some were about what I do or if he needed any messages. Sometimes Spirit told me things to tell him. He was amazed. At different times Angel would come over and hold the energies while the healing angels would come and do healing work on me.

CHAPTER 15
∞
FOREIGN SPIRITS

Angel wanted me to train her to channel.

"Well," I said, "with all the weird things happening to me I might as well help someone to carry on the gifts."

So we proceeded to work on the channeling process. She would come to my house and we would start with a clearing prayer that Jesus had given me and then go into a meditative state. We would then set the intentions for one of her guides to come in and work with her until she felt comfortable in allowing the spirit to speak through her. We did this for about seven weeks and little by little she would allow the spirit guide to come and talk through her. I was still going to the doctor's and chiropractor at the time because my neck was still weak.

In April, Angel wanted to do a public channeling session. Since Raymond was going to downsize and sell his big house, our church, God's Awakening Center, had moved from Raymond's house and rented a room at an art gallery. One of the ladies that attended services said she had room for us, so we started meeting there in the art gallery.

We put out the message at services and on a few fliers that Angel was going to have her first public channeling session. I don't know if some of the people were a little jealous because I had worked with her more or what but they had the same opportunity to come and work also if they had wanted.

We met at the art gallery. Time was passing and no one showed up. We sat there a little longer and I know Angel grew very disappointed.

I looked at this big rug on the floor and in the designs I started seeing people that were sick and then it looked like water and I felt like I was somewhere else. At first I thought I was losing it; then I heard a voice from God.

"What you are seeing are people in other countries who are sick and need your help," He said.

I said, "Do you want me to just pray for them?"

"You will go to them and help," He said. "And I also need you to turn a vortex in Belgium."

"A what?"

He said it again.

"And how will I get over there?" I asked. "Are you going to let me win the lottery or something?"

"I promised you survival, not luxury," He said. "The luxury is in knowing me. But you will get to where you need to be when it's time."

Angel looked at me and asked, "Are you alright?"

"Well I don't know," I said, "I just heard God say..." And then I told her.

"Did I hear correctly or not?" I asked. "You tune in and see."

"No, you heard right; and I am going with you," she said.

"Well, I guess they'll let us know, huh?"

"I am hearing it will be sooner than we think," she said.

We talked a little more about it; wondering what the weather would be like and what clothes to wear, things like that. About twenty minutes went by and Raymond and his girlfriend came in.

And I said to Angel in reference to her session, "Well, two people came anyway."

He said, "Sha `La! Sha `La!" like he was excited.

"What's wrong?" I asked.

"My brother and his family are sick," he said, "and they really need your help."

"Where they are?"

"In Germany," he said.

"Are they coming to visit you?" I asked.

"No, you need to go to them," he said.

"That's our trip!" Angel said.

I told Raymond, "Well, God just said we would be going over seas."

"Good, how soon can you be ready to go?" Raymond asked.

"Well, don't you have to have a passport or some kind of paper work?" I asked.

"Yes," he said.

"Well, we haven't been out of the country before and we don't have any-thing," I explained. "How soon does he want us there?"

"Right now," Raymond replied.

"I don't have any money and don't know how to get any," I said.

Then the voice of God came and said, "Tell him to tell his brother that if he can gather more clients and collect the money up front for you and Angel to go, then you can travel there. And while you're there, you can turn that vortex in Belgium."

So I told Raymond what God had said. I asked him if Belgium was close by.

"Yes, next door to Germany," he said.

"Well, can we go there too if it's not too much trouble?"

"Let me talk to my brother and I'll call you tomorrow."
I said okay and then they left.
Angel didn't even get to channel that day.
"I guess we were just supposed to do this," I said.
"That's okay," she said. "At least I get to go with you overseas."
"Yes, since you've worked with me now you know what to do and maybe you can channel over there."
She was happy then.
The next morning Raymond called and said, "Get Angel and meet me at the post office. And bring your birth certificate with you."
We did; then he took us to have our pictures made. He told us to fill out the application and then return to the post office to mail it in. He paid for the fees. He said as soon as they came back we would leave.
Well I received a letter saying that my birth certificate was not valid. It was an old black piece of paper with white writing on in. So I had to call Nashville and get a new one with a raised seal. I sent the money and got it and then re-submitted the passport forms. I had the dates down that we were to leave the country and they sent it back quickly.
I had to go again to the doctor and the chiropractor and I told each of them about the trip. They said I had only recovered by about fifty percent and they would have to give me some paperwork so I could travel. If I was hurt or sick I was to take this one paper to the doctors over there. I prayed that I wouldn't have to do that.
Well, when I got home my guides said they were going to tell me what to take. First, I was to take certain stones and crystals; then a cloth that had an Indian print on it. Then I was to take an outfit with fringe and a painted Thunderbird on it that also had some turquoise sewn on it along with some other things. Then there was certain jewelry that had to come with me. And I was told to take some other clothes and shoes, also a little medicine pouch with some herbs in it, and some small symbols and loose fur from Star. God told me to brush her and take her fur with me, that they would use some of it to bless some places.
I was ready except now I didn't have any money, just my clothing and materials, my passport and a round trip ticket. My mom wasn't in a position at the time to help me. So I asked some of my uncles if I could borrow fifty or even twenty-five dollars. They told me no; they didn't approve of me going. Or they didn't have the money either.
A lady called and said, "Sha `La I need a reading but I only have twenty dollars. Can you do a reading for that?

"I'll do a reading for anything right now because in two days I will be on a plane to Germany," I said.

So she came over and I gave her the reading and she gave me the twenty dollars. I guess it was a test of faith. All of my life it seemed like I had to live that way, on a wing and a prayer with faith.

My son didn't work that week so he had no money to spare. We had some food I was given, so he had something to eat for a few days.

"Don't worry mom; I'll be okay," he said. "The rain will let up and then I can work some more."

I didn't want to leave him or really even go but God said, "You have orders. We work as a team and this has to get done."

So I said okay.

God said, "All will work out well; just have faith. Tonight you need to take an Epsom salt bath."

While I was in the bath, God's voice spoke to me and said, "There are two things you need to know. One is there is a demon you must fight, and the other is that one of Satan's dragons guards the vortex in Belgium."

"And what am I suppose to do?" I asked.

"You have to convince the dragon to leave and be transformed," God said. "We will guide you."

"Well, just so I receive guidance I guess it will be okay," I said.

I figured that was what I was here for. All I knew was that God had a plan and I was a part of it.

Raymond came and picked up myself and Angel and we went to the airport. On the way my guides told me that we would land in Pennsylvania and then go over to Switzerland first. And we did, but we had to stay for two hours in Pennsylvania. I took the twenty dollars and bought a coke, which then left me eighteen.

Whayne had given Angel a little money so she bought her own lunch. We then boarded the plane to Switzerland; from there Raymond would drive us by car into Germany. It was a long flight, about fourteen hours. I was reading a book so I wasn't so focused on the crowd and the hours. When we landed in Switzerland, I thought it looked beautiful, at least what I saw of it.

But when we went through the airport entrance gates the alarms went off. I had to take all my jewelry off and even my shoes. Then they scanned me. I couldn't figure it out. It was weird. They finally let me go through. We had to stay there for almost three hours.

Then it was time to go over the Alps of Switzerland and Germany. Spirit said as you travel over the Alps all three of you will pick up energies to help with the trip.

Raymond decided to first visit an old girl friend's house in southern Germany and then to drive on through Bavaria.

It was a nice place and they had an upstairs; the bedroom was really big. Angel took the bed beside the window and I was across the room. We got settled in and the next morning they had some breakfast for us. They told us we were going to be seeing a few of their friends to do some readings. I said great!

When their friends came, Angel and I took turns doing the readings but they liked Angel better. They said it wasn't my reading that they didn't like; they just felt intimidated by my presence. I didn't understand that at all. But I didn't feel very well so I didn't care.

Raymond and his friends decided to take us to see some castles and drive over to Austria. That was a strange trip too. We went looking around at the city first and then they took us to a castle that was built on top of a big mountain. You had to get in these strange elevators; they were stacked three deep. It would take the people up and down, to and from the castle. It didn't rain much while we were there so in a way I was glad of that. After we toured the castle, and prayed some ghosts over, we started down the mountain by getting in the elevator and I noticed there was a man, a woman and a boy in the one we stepped into. The elevator's capacity held far more than the six of us.

There were also several Oriental tourists there taking a lot of pictures. The elevator operator was waiting for more people to enter the elevator; the other two cars filled up but the people that looked in our car would not walk in. I had on the t-shirt that featured a Thunderbird, jeans, and braids in my hair.

"I guess they think I am an Indian that might scalp them or something," I laughed. I know it was silly, but I felt they didn't like me.

We also visited King Ludwig's Castle, Herrenchiemsee. It is located on the Herren Island in the middle of the Chiemsee Lake. It was beautiful. We got to take some pictures. I felt spirits walking with us there, so I asked the light to anchor and bless them over as well.

The tour guide said that they didn't know if King Ludwig had committed suicide or someone pushed him overboard.

His spirit was there and I asked him. He said he was tired of all the others ordering him around and was very depressed so he committed suicide. So I told him to forgive himself, that we forgave him and that he needed to go on over to the light to be with God and repent. He agreed so I asked the light to come over him and the Archangels came and took him along with some others that were hanging around. King Ludwig said some of the spirits there were his servants and were stuck too. So I asked for them to be released to go to the light with him. And I saw them leave.

Joe drove the car. He worked for Mercedes Benz and we rode in his. He drove like a hundred or so miles an hour on the autobahn. And then we went up in a parking garage to see the view of the city he also drove fast there. I was so dizzy, I felt I had hurt my neck again.

Jesus came in to me and said, "I will stay in with you during most of the trip."

All I could say was, "Thank you."

Raymond wanted to go to this festival where they had big radishes and pretzels and beer and other food. Now, I'm a vegetarian so there wasn't too much I could eat but they had dancers and everyone was dressed in these old fashion outfits. It was pretty neat. I enjoyed the shows and the radishes. For the short time we were there we saw a lot. After that we went back to the lady's house and the next day we were to go to mass at a Catholic church.

God came and told me, "Tomorrow you must face the demon. Only one Angel is allowed to help you and it is Archangel Michael."

I know a lot of people say he is their guardian angel and so I asked Archangel Michael if so many people claimed him, how could he also help me.

He said, "I can be many places in a blink of an eye and I have helpers too."

"That's good enough for me," I said.

So he sat in the room with Angel and me the entire night to protect us.

Angel had set her suitcases beside the window and in the middle of the night I heard a big thud. I woke up and thought she had fallen out of bed. But a large demon had entered through the window and kicked over the suitcases.

Archangel Michael was fighting it; he threw it out the window and went after it. I sat up and prayed. Later Archangel Michael came back.

"Are you alright?" I asked.

He said, "Yes, are you?"

"Just shook up a little," I said.

I tried to wake Angel but she just slept right through it. However, I couldn't sleep the rest of the night. I got up early and dressed. Angel said she didn't feel well and she didn't want to go. I think she just didn't want to do all that walking. But at that time she had bad knees, so I understood. They would flair up on her from time to time.

We left her there. Raymond, me, Lynn, and her new boyfriend, Joe, went to the church. When we arrived at the church, I really had to use the restroom. I asked them if there was one nearby and both of them said no.

Then my spirit said, "We will go into a trance-like state to help you hold it for a while."

It was a lucky thing too, because there was standing room only in this place. I had to suppress my personal needs for what seemed like three or four hours.

I heard Spirit say, "Just stare at the statue of Archangel Michael."

So I did, and as I was standing there God said, "When you leave, go out the back left door. That is where you will face the demon. Draw your swords and pierce the demon in the heart."

(In my etheric body I am dressed like a warrior and I had been given two swords and a breast plate from my guides).

When the service was over, I told Raymond to wait until the crowd left. And as they walked out everyone looked very strangely at me. Most of them had left when it was time for us to leave. I told the others to wait and walk out behind me.

When I stepped through the door the demon was on the rooftop of the building on the other side of the court yard. Then here it came. I drew my swords and tried to stab it in the heart area but I missed by about an inch. It almost had its claws in me when Archangel Michael took a lance and stuck it in its side, then up in the air they went.

Raymond, Joe and Lynn said they felt the wind and weird energies from it. There was no doubt that Lynn wanted to be anywhere but near me. I could feel fear all around her. As I told them what I saw, I turned around and said, "Oh my gosh! There it is! That is what I saw!"

There was a statue of Michael and the demon on the wall like they were stuck there with the lance piercing the demon. I almost passed out; I didn't know why I had to go through this. I thought I was nuts.

Jesus came to me and said, "You are not 'nuts'. You are being tested – and initiated."

"For what?" I asked.

"We must know your strengths and weaknesses," He said, "and what level your bravery is on."

At first I felt upset, but then He said, "Go to the fountain. I have something to give you."

Down the courtyard was a large five-tier water fountain.

When I got there, Jesus said, "I am now giving you a spirit peace pipe. With this you will face the dragon and offer it to him. You must convince him that he needs to take the pipe from your hands and go to the heavens and transform. If you can do that, you will have passed your test. No Angel or guide can help you; you must do this on your own."

I didn't know what to think or do. I felt abandoned but then I got angry and said I would go through the test and that whatever happens, happens. (I don't know why we are tested. All I know is if you don't pass you are given more tests until you do pass).

We looked around some more at the city and old churches. Raymond wanted me to see what I picked up from them. Then he took us to one where it was said the Devil stepped in it and left his footprint when the church was built. That place felt *really* weird.

I just told Raymond, "Well, maybe the Devil wanted to get saved. Ha-ha! That just goes to show you they hang out anywhere."

Of course, I was being kind of sarcastic. The next day we went someplace else and Angel went with us. At one point, during our walk, she felt a vortex in the middle of a sidewalk. This place had coffins in it and so we asked the light to come and escort the earthbounds over. We did that everywhere we went. I guess we were in that area four or five days. All I know is that when we woke up, and had a little to eat, then we were off to other places. Finally, we got in the rental car and headed to Raymond's brother's home.

When we got to Clyde's house, he and his wife, Erika, welcomed us. They asked their daughter to come over with a couple of friends. We had supper and I explained the technique we used with our guides and God to clear a house and how we cleared people and animals.

The daughter did the translating most of the time, either her or Raymond. I don't think Raymond told the things we said exactly or, in some cases, even correctly. Anyway, Clyde asked us to go ahead and clear the house first. His place sat on a fourteen mile long vortex and it was open and going backwards. (They are supposed to go clockwise for positive energy). So all the people went into the living room and ate cheese and snacks.

Angel and I went into the foyer. I called in the energies of the Angels and Guides. Thor came in and started sending the energies through me like a buzz saw. We split the vortex and the spirits started coming up and the entities were taken on up and away. Then Thor turned the vortex clockwise and sealed the energies.

We went through the house to make sure that all the spirits had left. Then we conducted clearings on their pet dog and then for Clyde and his wife.

When we returned to the hotel I discovered that some of my things were missing. I was upset. Clyde asked some of his friends to come over so Angel and I could channel for them the next day. We tried to settle down and get some rest. The next day we went back over to Clyde's place. We were introduced to everyone. Their little dog jumped up on us and started licking my hand; it was feeling much better.

I channeled first. My guides came through and so did Jesus. The people asked questions and I guess they were satisfied with their answers.

Then Angel channeled. She channeled some of her guides and then Mother Mary came in and spoke. Then when she came back to herself, while I was sitting there, Spirit said to me, "You and Angel are going to be given a diamond ring."

"From whom?" I asked.

"You will soon see."

Well, the people talked a little while longer and then after they left, Erika went into the kitchen and brought out a twenty-one diamond cluster ring. Her daughter was translating and said, "She wants you to take it."

"You mean she wants me to bless it," I said.

"No, she wants you to have it for healing her dog," she said.

"No, I don't want any more for helping the dog."

But the girl replied, "This dog is her baby and it got up eating and running around like a puppy, and she is so pleased."

Then she reached into the drawer and pulled out an eleven diamond cluster ring with two pearls and gave it to Angel.

Clyde came in and was shocked. I told him I didn't want to take his wife's ring.

"She wants you both to have them; just take care of them," he said.

The Belgian Dragon

We started talking about Belgium and Clyde said they would take us. First we stopped in France; Clyde wanted to show us a little bit of France. We stopped in this restaurant to eat; I was amazed they allowed their dogs in with the people.

Every time I bought a coke it was three dollars; then at the restaurant the soda was six dollars a glass. That was a shock. The glass had gold trim around it. I told the waiter he should give me the glass for that price. He went and told the boss what I had said and the boss came over to the table. So I told him what I said and then I told him this was my first time here and he should also give it to me for a souvenir. He said since I asked he would wash it and give it to me and he did. I thanked him and we finished and headed to Belgium.

Clyde was like a scientist and he had invented this gadget to measure energy. After some searching, he located the energy and we confirmed it with our guides.

Raymond was driving and getting frustrated; he asked where this place was we needed to go.

I ask God how much further it was.

"Five kilometers."

Clyde said that he felt that too. And we drove until we came to a place on the coast. Then Clyde and I said at the same time, "Here it is!"

So Raymond stopped the car and we all got out except Angel. It had been raining and cold and her knee was bothering her again. I asked Spirit if I could wear my jeans with the fringe top, because it was cold. They said it was okay.

So I gathered up my ceremonial materials and went to the spot that I was told. I drew my circle on the sand and laid my cloth down and then put the stones on the cloth. I didn't know that Raymond was taking pictures and Clyde had his gadget. When it began moving he started backing up.

"It's here," he said.

I looked up and saw the four-headed dragon. It had already started blowing smoke and fire. Then it began stomping back and forth, cursing me and telling me it was going to eat me – among other things.

I asked the peace pipe to come forward and when it did, I felt it in my hand.

I looked up at the dragon and said, "You only have two choices: take the peace pipe, go with God and transform; or, go to Hell and be beaten by Satan - *because I'm not leaving.*"

Well, it stomped around some more and finally it reached its claw in and took the pipe and flew off into the sky. The sky parted like curtains and as it went through them they closed back. Then I saw all kinds of spirits and angels in the sky applauding.

And I heard God's voice say, "Now come to the waters edge, place one foot on the land and one on the water."

So I did and I could feel the shifting of the earth; I figured they were turning the vortex.

Then the spirit of Nostradamus came to me with several long stem spirit roses and said, "Job well done. Hold out your hands."

So I reached out with my hands and arms. He laid the roses in my arms and I thanked him.

"You will do well," he said. "I will help you from time to time."

"I would like that."

Then this collective voice of all the Spirits there said, "See if they will take you to England now to Stonehenge."

I started walking back to the others and told them what I had heard and seen, and what Nostradamus had told me.

"Yes," Clyde said, "we can take a ferry to England and go on to Stonehenge."

"Wild," I thought, "I always wanted to go there."

It was getting dark and it would be three or four hours before we crossed the channel, so we took a nap on the ferry boat.

When we docked and got back in the car, we headed to Stonehenge. Along the way, we saw beautiful countryside, even a crop circle made like some sort of man, on the side of a hill.

Stonehenge

We finally reached Stonehenge. It was in the late evening and we had only a couple of hours left before they closed. I had a large size crystal with me that God had told me to bring.

"Take the crystal and hold it in front of you," God said. "We are going to send energy in through you and blast it through the rocks."

The energy looked like we were pressure washing or sandblasting the rocks and the area; it was so strong I began rocking back and forth.

Angel, and Clyde's daughter, stood in line with me while Raymond took pictures and Clyde measured energies.

After a while God said, "Now take the wolf fur and bless the circle."

So I pulled Star's fur out of my bag and said some prayers for the place and the area and threw it over the ropes. (When we were there they had a rope placed around the outside of the stones).

When we reached the other side of the circle, God said, "Here you will leave the crystal. Put it in the ground to hold the good energies."

I did what He asked. I finished blessing the stones with the wolf fur and when I completed the circle I saw Jesus on top of the stones. He put a large rainbow dome all around it.

I saw a vision of myself and some other people coming out of the rocks. I asked Spirit what I was seeing. They told me it was a past life where the stones use to be a doorway to other dimensions. They told me another race of beings came to destroy everything good and take over Earth. They also said a lot of us went through the doorway to escape. They told me I would understand the rest of the puzzle later.

Then we heard over the intercom it was time to leave. So we started to go and I looked back one more time and the dome of light Jesus had placed over Stonehenge was glowing. (I hope the good energies are still there).

It was getting late when we stopped to get a bite to eat and decide where to spend the night. Raymond wanted to stay at this bed-and-breakfast place. It was a little place, by that it looked like a small two-story cottage for the Seven Dwarfs. I had to stoop down to go through the doorway.

While Angel and I went outside to bring some of our clothes in some ghosts ran through us. They felt so cold.

"What the heck?" I said.

I heard one ghost say, "Can you hear...or see us?"

"Yes," I said. "You all need to go over to the light."

"How do we do that?"

"I will ask the angels to bring in the light," I explained. "And then I will ask the angels to take you over to Heaven."

They said that they would go, so I proceeded with the prayer. After they had gone over, it became darker and we went inside. I guess some ghosts come out in daylight and others come out in the night. As we went inside I had to step sideways to walk up the little narrow stairs. When I reached the top I couldn't stand upright. The ceiling was really very low.

I said, "I feel like Snow White."

All of a sudden I heard this cackling, then one of the doors opened and this little short woman came out. I apologized to her and she just laughed and said it was okay. She showed us to our room. Angel and I stayed in the same room; it had twin beds.

The next day we had breakfast and started back to the ferry. We talked about all that had happened. Once we returned to France we traveled through Holland. We stopped there and bought a t-shirt. There was some guy at the store who saw that we were Americans and asked us to say "Hi to Hillary".

I said, "Oh sure, as soon as I land."

They just laughed.

We took Clyde and his daughter home and then Raymond wanted to go to another part of Germany to see another one of his old girlfriends.

We wound up going to this lady's house and she showed us how to use a German washing machine. She was a wealthy person, in a wealthy town. A river ran through the town. She mostly complained about the immigrants there. We stayed there about three days. One of those days we went shopping with her. I almost jumped back when I saw the prices on things. Of course I didn't buy anything. A thin shirt was four hundred and fifty dollars and the lady paid over six hundred dollars for a pair of jeans.

"Too rich for my blood," I thought.

If I had that kind of money I could help people with homes or pay a bill or two for them, or help someone get back on their feet.

We went to one old church there that held the *Book of the Dead*. I asked God to clear that place too and Angel and I saw a light enter through the round window and fall over the book. Energies came out from the bookcase and books; it was strange looking stuff. There were even caskets stuck in the walls sideways; a rectangular hole had been cut into the wall and a casket was just sitting in the hole. Some had glass tops where you could see the corpse. Some were wrapped and others appeared rotted. We asked if their spirit hadn't crossed to please do so now.

I had just heard about a holy woman over there and I wanted to go see her. I was lying in bed and a blue elephant spirit came in and I heard a certain name.

"Welcome," she said. "I would like to meet you."

The next morning I went into the kitchen of Clyde's daughter home and she had the woman's picture and a blue elephant's picture hanging on the wall. I asked Clyde's daughter what she knew about the woman.

"She is from India and her name is Mother Maria," the girl said. "She is considered to be an avatar and can work miracles I am told. A lot of people go to her to receive a blessing."

I asked Raymond if we could travel to see her, but he just kept saying we didn't have time.

"We would if you quit playing around with old girlfriends," I said.

Returning Home

It came time to return to the states. It was a very long flight. I was tired and had to sit by two guys that drank alcohol the whole way back. During the flight, I experienced an anxiety attack. The pilot said we were two thousand feet from landing. Well, I thought that was close enough so I just grabbed my jacket and was ready to run off the plane. I could not relax for anything. Then we had to go through customs, which took a long time. We finally got home. I was glad to see Jason, Star, Akita and Maggie and of course, my family.

That whole trip had taken place during May of 1997; we had traveled through, and seen parts of, seven countries in fifteen days. It sure seemed a lot longer. I guess I had jet lag. I must have slept for about two days straight after that.

And when I got back I found that Star was pregnant. Apparently she had gotten loose and ran outside where she and Akita became more than just friends.

I went back to the chiropractor and told him about the trip. He, and my general practitioner, thought it was amazing and just said, "that's nice." He didn't believe in what I did so he just chose to say I gave lectures.

UFOs, Orbs and Puppies

It was getting to be about mid-summer 1997 and I was called back to Alabama. I shared my story with those people, and gave a few clearings and readings. And some of the people like Cindy and a few others said I needed to set a booth up to give readings at an UFO conference. So they help me do that and we went together. I also did a channeling session and several people came.

I met one lady that said she had some friends in Mobile and asked if I would come there some time and channel and do clearings. I told her to just set it up and I would come. She told Cindy the next day that she had never seen anyone channel like me and she couldn't sleep all night. The energies she felt were extremely strong in the headdress.

The next night we all went to the beach. A lot of orbs were out in the atmosphere and we saw a triangle-shaped space ship exit from the water and take off. They didn't beam us up or anything like that. Guess they were there for other reasons. Probably didn't want to deal with a bunch of alien hunters anyway.

A few weeks later in July the lady from Mobile called me and I went down and we became more acquainted. Her name was Dana. And Dana had a sister in Birmingham who was a hair dresser who had her own salon in this big building downstairs. The upstairs had been turned into apartments. One of the apartments became available and when I went to Alabama I would rent it from her. It worked out okay for a while. I was going back and forth about every two months.

At the end of July, Star had her cubs. Jason and I had to help deliver them. I was shocked at the number; she had eleven! There was one that was a lighter color and Jason picked that one to keep and named him Thor after Thor the

Thunder God that helps me with the turning of the vortices. (He said he was honored to have the pup named after him).

All the pups were different colors but definitely had the wolf look and color and texture of fur. I started telling people about them and most of them were taken at seven or eight weeks old. One was given to Walter; he wouldn't answer to any name.

One day it was raining and I had the door open and stood there in it wondering what to name him. He was black with a few light markings; he look more like a Siberian husky dog. I kept hearing the name Rambo.

So I said Rambo out loud. His ears perked up and he came over to me. So I guess either his spirit told me or something. I took him over to my mom's and whispered to Walt to call him Rambo to see if he would come to him. He did and the pup walked over to Walter and sat down beside his wheelchair. So he kept him for a while. I kept feeling he would make a great cadaver dog.

We had one more pup left, a reddish colored female. Jason named her Foxy Lady and she answered to it.

It was my mother who told a man about the pup and he came and took up with him right away. I thought it was funny; the man asked, "She's not pregnant by the male is she?"

And Jason said, "I told him no because they were brother and sister. Then he gave me a funny look. But he said he would take her and then he gave me fifty dollars."

The fall season came and the leaves began turning color once again. I loved the fall of the year for some reason. I guess the temperature was always just right for me.

A lady that was an airline hostess from North Carolina named Madge, called me and wanted me to come to her house and provide some readings and perform a couple of clearings. She made arrangements for me to fly and meet her. So I did.

When I arrived she had several people scheduled for readings and I read for three. But then suddenly all but one cancelled; and she was scheduled for the next day. I said that was okay. So she showed me where to sleep and I went to bed.

I said my prayers and Spirit said, "Tomorrow will be a rough day; get your rest."

CHAPTER 16
∞
WHITE FEATHER AND SCARE CROW

The next morning, about nine o'clock, the lady came for the clearing. I had just had a cup of coffee and no breakfast yet. I figured I'd eat later. Well, the woman came in and I felt all kinds of spirits around her. I told her first we would check her hands like I do everyone's and sure enough they were out of alignment. I explained to her I would ask the light to come over her and them and help them to cross over.

Then I heard a voice say, "No, we are waiting on her and she is to come with us."

I responded to the spirit with, "She has a lot of life left and she needs to stay in her body for a while longer."

The woman then said, "Eight of my family members died of cancer and I feel them wanting me to have the cancer so I can be with them."

So I told her – and them – that in the future she could go with them when it was her time, not then.

Well that made the spirits angry. (I hadn't had to deal with such angry family spirits before).

"Then we will give *you* the cancer!" they said.

And before I could say anything or do anything, the spirits jumped in me. I started praying and praying and it seemed like my guides were throwing them out of me and sending them on to the light, because I had said to take them on over so they won't bother her (the woman). But they left their cancer in me.

(How that happens is when a person dies and doesn't shed a disease when departing from the body, the spirit can carry the disease with it, or the "memory" of it. And they can carry this until they are cleared from that energy on the other side, or somewhere else, as in the way they deposited it in me because they were angry. Because cancer can be a manifestation of suppressed anger).

Well, all of a sudden, I started vomiting and Madge gave me the garbage can and I threw up over a half a can and it stunk like a body dying from cancer.

God said, "If you don't get this out of you in forty-eight hours, you'll die."

"Why didn't you stop them?" I asked.

And He said, "We all had our hands full because other spirits and negative entities were swarming around here. We did our best to get them out of here and the others out of you. We have taken out some of the deposit but the fast growing cancer hit your weak cells and is spreading."

I was about to freak out.

"I can't leave Jason behind yet!" I cried.

I *happened* to look over at a thin magazine and noticed there was a seminar in Baltimore.

Spirit said, "Go there and see this man and listen to what he says. He will help you."

I asked Madge about it and she said it was only two hours away.

"I know I didn't make much money but would you accept what I made for gas to take me there?" I asked her.

"Yes," she said. "In the meantime though let me call Jewel and channel some Reiki energy to you."

"Please!"

Well she did and even though they both ran Reiki on me, I still didn't feel any better. In fact, I started burning up. I took four showers in cool water. Then I could barely sleep I was burning up so much and then freezing. I knew the healing angels were trying to get the stuff out of me, and then I would throw up again.

When daylight came I was extremely weak. Madge had a cane and let me use it to walk with; I was all bent over. So Madge and Jewel helped me into the pickup truck that she had and off we went to Baltimore.

When we arrived at the place where the seminar was there were people that had tables selling things. I said we have an hour before the guy speaks and I sense I am to go over here and see what they have.

Madge asked, "Which aisle?"

I heard "the back third one" and so we walked down there and there was a lady that I knew from previous psychic fairs selling diodes.

She looked at me and said, "What happened to you?"

I told her the story and she said, "Quick, put this diode on you."

Immediately I started shaking; it was starting to shake the stuff out of me. I felt a little better. I thought maybe that's what Spirit meant, to just come here and I would see Sally and receive a diode and be okay. I heard "that is one reason but you must listen to this man's talk as well."

I said, "Okay."

So she let me take the diode and told me I could pay her later. I thanked her and left to hear the man speak. We sat in the first row and he started talking about cell rejuvenation. My body started shaking so hard I almost fell off the seat. I knew the people in there must have thought I had some weird reaction or Parkinson's disease. I couldn't control it and the girls just looked over at me in amazement or shock, I don't know which.

The man saw me too but he kept on talking. Close to the end of the talk I finally slowed down and began to feel much better. After his talk he asked for a couple of volunteers to help him with his things and to carry them back to his booth that he had set up. He was also an artist and had drawn a few very nice pictures.

So Madge and Jewel volunteered. I followed them. There was a woman with the man dressed in a Native American, or southwest, looking outfit. She was carrying a few little things. He had an easel and some pictures and the girls helped carry them. I didn't carry anything. I felt that I didn't want to touch anybody's personal items until I was completely cleared.

While we were walking to their booth, Spirit told me, "You are to connect with these people."

So I went and the people started to gather around this man, named Scare Crow.

I found a chair and waited until I could talk with him. The girls said they would look around at other peoples' merchandise and come back in an hour or so. I said okay. While they were gone, the woman came over and started talking to me. She said her name was White Feather.

"I saw you shaking in the meeting. Are you okay?" she asked.

I told her the story and what I was about. I also told her about how my guides told me to be there and connect with them for some reason. She leaned back and said, "I know why you are here; it is for me, I have been praying for a teacher."

"Really?" I asked.

She said, "Yes, I have studied different books and talked to different people about metaphysics but there is so much to learn and understand. And I asked my angels and guides to send me a teacher that can teach me more.

"Take my card and give me one of yours and we'll keep in touch. Scare Crow is having a workshop in the spring and I will tell people about you and your work. You can come out to Arizona and stay with us and teach me some things."

"Okay, that sounds great," I said.

So she hugged me and the girls came back by and we left. I spent the night and I called my brother Walt and asked him what else I was supposed to do while I was here, because Madge and I felt we weren't suppose to leave yet.

He described a store that sold stones and books and metaphysical objects and Madge said she knew where the store was.

"All I am hearing is a place," I said. "Is there a place called Chichen Itza, or something like that?"

"Yes, near Cancun, Mexico," Madge replied.

I thought, "I don't have the money to go there."

Then I heard Spirit say, "Go to this store and ask if you can do any readings there."

So we went to the metaphysical store and the woman there said, "Yes, I will call a few of my customers and see if they are interested."

We left and she called back later in the day and said she had three people.

Madge was checking on how cheap she could get us on standby. It was like one hundred and sixty-nine dollars, which included her discount.

"It doesn't look like we can do it this time," I told her.

My readings back then were only thirty-five dollars a piece and three people were not even going to pay for the ticket, let alone pay for hotel, food and a bus trip to the pyramids.

When the first person came for the reading it was a man and he liked his readings so he gave me an extra five dollars. The second person came and did the same.

"Well, I still need more money than this," I thought.

Then the third one came, a lady, and she sat down and noticed my jewelry and said, "Wow! I love the jaguar around your neck. You know there is a tribe at Chichen Itza known as the Jaguar people and I resonate with that energy!"

I told her, "Spirit said I needed to go there and do some energy work but I haven't made enough money yet to afford to go."

She asked, "How much do you need?"

So I said, "Well, we have this amount and we need at least this much more to go and eat and have lodging for two days."

"You can do all of this in two days?" she asked.

I said, "That's what Spirit said."

"Well go ahead and read for me," she said.

And of course I did and afterward she looked in her purse and said, "I don't have enough money. Do you trust me to go to the bank and get some?"

I said, "Sure."

I thought, "If she doesn't come back, oh well."

We waited around the store talking to the owner a little longer and the lady came back and handed me an envelope and told the shop owner to give her the two Zuni frogs that were in the case. She did and the lady told a story about them.

She said, "You will go to the pyramids and take one of these and it will keep you safe."

So I picked one out.

Then she said, "Now let me pay for it; you two must be on your way. I put a note and my phone number in the envelope. Call me when you come back in town."

I said that I would and we thanked the shop owner and I thanked the lady for the frog and Madge and I left. We got down the road and I opened the envelope found that she had put four hundred dollars in it.

"I guess we are supposed to go," I said.

When we got back to Madge's house I called Walt and explained to him what had happened. Then I told him I'd be gone a few more days; that we were going to Mexico.

We got on the plane the next day and flew to Cancun. Then we rented a taxi and went straight to a hotel. It was evening so we couldn't go to the pyramids until the next morning. So we settled in and went out to a restaurant to eat. We were guided by Spirit to one a few blocks down the street. After we ordered, the waitress came over and started talking with us. Madge told her we were going to the pyramids the following morning.

The waitress said we would love it but asked if we had someone else to go with us. We told her no. She said she felt things too and she thought she needed to go with us. We said we appreciated that; she went and told her parents that owned the restaurant and they said that they were okay with the plan. She told us her parents were from Argentina and would probably return there soon. She said the people there knew there were going to be earthquakes there in Mexico and she felt we could do something to hold the earthquakes back so they could make arrangements to leave and go back home. She knew it would be safer there so I guess she was also in tune.

I told Madge there were many reasons why Spirit sends us places and the unusual ways to get to where we need to be. She said she realized that now.

"Just by being with you this week I have learned a lot," she said.

I laughed and said, "Yeah, me too."

The next morning we took our showers and Madge managed just fine with it. But when it became my turn, the rods that held the curtain up fell on my head. It was a miracle I didn't get a brain concussion.

I finally dressed and we went to meet the lady at the restaurant. She said her name was Castaneda. We found a bus that was going to the pyramids and paid for our way there.

On the bus we mostly looked out the window but I didn't like a lot that I saw. One guy had hogs on poles cooking them right there on the side of the road. People lived very poorly there. The houses looked worse than mine. I gave thanks at that time that at least mine had electricity and city water. Theirs didn't even have that. People were carrying water in jugs and it looked dirty. As we rode on it took several hours to get to our destination and by that time I had to go to the bathroom.

But my spirit guides came and said, "We are going to give you some symbols for earth, air, water, and fire."

I thought that was cool; I could share them with Jan when I returned home. Jan had introduced me to Reiki and attuned me to it when I came back from overseas.

So I saw in my mind what the symbols looked like and drew them on a piece of paper I had in my purse.

When we arrived at the pyramids I was glad they had restrooms. We went there first of course, and then went in towards the pyramid. People were selling tourist knick-knacks there and I bought something small to take home to Jason. And then I bought something that Spirit said to buy, a small statue of a jaguar.

We decided to climb up to the top of the pyramid and as I walked up the steps I became dizzy. We reached the top and all I could see were past lives of me, or of someone. I saw peoples' heads being cut off and rolling down the pyramid and blood and fighting. It made me sick; I sat down and started to throw up.

Madge and Castaneda came over and started telling me to breathe deep and they sent Reiki energy to me. I started feeling a little better. They had to help me in getting down from there. Then we went into this small opening where there was a jaguar statue and a person was there telling a story about it. Then we went and saw another section where they had played some sort of games, but the winner had their head cut off. I wondered who had made up that stupid rule. Anyway there were earthbound spirits there and I asked God and the Angels to cross them over.

Then I heard a voice say, "Go to the different ruins and have the symbols of the earth, air, fire, and water placed in you."

So I went and stood where they told me and at each place I felt different energy. When I got to the place where the fire symbol was, some guy told me I had to get away from that place. But I think I stood there long enough to receive the energy; at least it felt like I did.

In my jewelry I had a wrapped stone that Bill McCowan had given me. He said a year or so ago he had come here and found the stone and he was told he had to cut it into four pieces and I was to receive one. I finally remembered he had told me he had found it here and then I started looking for more.

Some people came up to me and said what a beautiful stone, where did I get it. And I told them a friend found it over there on the ground and gave me a piece of it. They said there was no stone around there that looked like that.

"It must have fallen from the sky," one of them said.

Then a couple of them asked if they could trade for the stone and the jaguar pendant. I felt I should say no, so I did. I said it had sentimental value and I felt I needed to keep them.

We finally got back on the bus to go back to the hotel. It was getting dark, a long strange day. Of course, during all of my days something strange happens; at least that is what people say who are around me long enough.

The next morning we got a taxi to go back to the airport. We had exchanged phone numbers with Castaneda and when we got back to Madge's house she called Castaneda and let her know we made it okay. Madge then put me back on a plane to go home.

When I landed in Kentucky I wasn't feeling very good. I went home and slept for a while then shared my experiences with my family and called a few people. I talked about the trip with a lot of folks and also with the congregation at church.

The holidays came, Christmas and New Years. It was pretty normal. Sometimes I bought things throughout the year so I would have a present to give at Christmas; although Jason also had a birthday the same month. This Christmas he wanted a pair of jeans and I didn't have any money.

Spirit said, "Scrape up some change and buy a scratch-off lottery ticket."

I did and won thirty-three dollars. I bought the jeans with that. I was thankful at least I had that for him.

CHAPTER 17
∞
TRANSITIONS

How Singing Fawn's Body Really Works

I still did some traveling back and forth to Alabama to different peoples' houses to do some readings and clearings.

One woman name Rena wanted me to help her cross over the spirit of an ex-boyfriend. He kept bothering her and she said he wanted us to come to the graveyard to help him over. I asked my guides and God and they agreed. So we went and his spirit was sitting on this tombstone. His name was Doug. So we talked to him for a few minutes and they said their goodbyes and I asked God to anchor the light over some trees in the graveyard and it came through and I guess it woke some of the other spirits up.

Some came up from the ground and saw the light and started to go to the tree.

I said, "Wow, I didn't know so many had a belief system where they thought they were suppose to stay in the ground until some signal, like the Angels blowing their trumpets or horns."

But I looked up in the sky and that is exactly what I saw. I asked God if it was the end of time.

He said, "No, but it is the end of *their* time to just wait in cemeteries and be dormant. There are many interpretations in the Bible about the end of time including Judgment Day. As I have told you before I am granting all souls pardon and amnesty in my way so each one now has a chance to start a new life whether they are in the body or in the spirit form. I know a lot of people are not going to agree but there is vast knowledge in the Universe. It is time for people to wake up and know more of the truth."

"Good enough for me boss," I said.

He said, "People have to wake up out of the dark ages that they set themselves up for in history."

After that Rena said she knew of some more cemeteries that needed help. So we went to another one and we asked the trees there if it was okay to anchor the light so any remaining spirits could go on and cross over and I received a "yes." So I said the prayer and the light was anchored; some of the spirits were confused. They thought it was the end and Judgment Day too.

I just said, "You don't have to wait to be with God."

Some of them went into the light and some went back in the ground. I asked God what that was about. He said some had issues and some were so deep in the memory program that they were supposed to wait until a certain time to cross over.

I asked, "Couldn't you just take them on up anyway?"

He said, "That's the way the free will program works. If they want to wait then it is their choice. And all have to respect that."

I said I understood. I explained it to Rena because she didn't know how it worked either.

Then she said, "There is one more down the road but it's kind of spooky."

"What's wrong with it?" I asked.

"I don't know," she answered.

I asked God if He wanted us to go there.

He said, "You can try but after this one, don't go to any unless I let you know which ones are safe."

I forgot to ask Him if this one was safe. Now I always ask because when we got there it had a very strange energy about it. And when we left the car and walked onto the property I noticed this old log shack of a place; it was built up off the ground on creek rock, so I figured it must have been there for a very long time.

I tuned in and saw what looked like mangy dogs underneath it. I didn't know they were hounds from Hell. I heard them growling and so did Rena.

"I'm scared," she said.

"Well animals get stuck here too sometimes and they need to be prayed over to the animal kingdom for their evolutionary growth," I said.

Then I felt I needed to take my cornmeal, cinnamon and salt mixture out and sprinkle it around the building to purify the energies.

I told Rena to hold my staff but she said, "Hold my hand."

I looked at her and said, "You chicken. I have to sprinkle this around and I can't hold your hand and do this too."

"Look, I'll hold on to your shirt, okay?" she asked.

I agreed. As we walked onto the cemetery grounds, I heard, "You have entered an unholy place."

I thought, "We better anchor the light now and change it."

I asked and prayed for the Light of God to come through and I could see it coming down, but just then I also saw a dark energy come up from the ground and it started pushing the light away from the place. I had not seen anything like that before. I kept praying and so did Rena and we walked on up and I sprinkled the cornmeal mix around the building and then prayed that the energies be transformed into love and light. I heard inside me that the mixture was going to act like black powder and to draw the line away from the building and ask the fire spirit of light to come and ignite it so the darkness would be transformed or take it to where it needed to go.

The next thing we knew it felt like a swarm of bees had attacked us and these things came after us and I heard, "Leave now!"

And I could see the darkness would not let the light anchor. Rena was shaking like a leaf.

I said, "Okay, we're leaving."

And then I heard, "Don't come back!"

We got in the car and as we drove down the road we started smelling something rotten and stinking. Rena was driving and something took the wheel and tried to make us wreck.

"Pull over; I'll drive!" I yelled.

"It won't let me!" Rena cried out.

I turned around and saw two nasty decaying spirits sitting in the back seat. I started commanding them out.

One said, "We don't want your kind around us."

"Then why are you with us?" I asked.

"To teach you a lesson," it said. "There are places on the Earth that don't belong to your God and we don't want you or Him to come and try to save us, you goody two-shoes."

"Turn the steering wheel loose," I said, "and let her drive and we won't go back to your place."

And it did. Rena was swerving all over the road. I saw a gas station and told her to pull over there. We stopped and she got out shaking all over.

I still saw the two spirits in back and I said, "You leave this car now and I mean it! If we can't come to help with your place then you have to leave ours and take that smell with you."

And they did.

Rena and I changed places and I drove the rest of the way to her house.

She said, "That was like that scary movie Pet Cemetery."

"Yeah, I didn't know we couldn't change everything," I said.

Rena said she wouldn't go to anymore grave yards.

"I wouldn't go to anymore either unless God said we had a plan to transform it or change it," I said.

I went home and shared the story with the congregation in Indiana. The lady that let us use the art gallery was now going to sell it. So I told the people the only place I knew to go to now until we saved enough money to get a different place was my house. I had an extra spare room and it could be fixed to seat twenty-five or thirty people. Or we could purchase a big tent and set it up in the yard.

Springtime arrived and I had the first service in my yard complete with a table full of food and drinks. Even some of my relatives came.

I thought, "That's neat; Maybe some folks are waking up and going to help me with this."

On the days it rained we held services in the room I fixed up. But people who attended also had issues about having to drive twenty-five miles to my place.

I thought to myself, "Now here I have been willing to drive the distance back and forth to Alabama and Georgia without complaining; but they can't get themselves up twenty minutes early and come to where I am."

I grew very sad and depressed. But that was just the start of my depression. I went to the bank to see how much money our church had built up and if it would be enough to start renting a place in the middle to balance the distance for everyone. When I got there the teller told me, "You only have $49.00 in the account."

"Excuse me?"

She said it again.

"It must be a mistake," I said in disbelief.

"No," she said, looking at her terminal again.

And then she told me about the last deposit. When I was going in and out of town, Doug was supposed to have put the offering money in the bank and the money we had made from the psychic fair which I knew was over eight hundred dollars.

I became very upset. I called Doug. And I called a meeting. But Doug didn't show; and, everyone was very disheartened when they found out. I called Doug several times and he kept giving me excuses and the run-around. I felt very betrayed. It was one of the worst feelings I had ever had, and I was upset with myself because Spirit had told me not to trust him.

But when you are in a group where you have to vote people into office for anything you run that risk, and like I had said, he had everybody buffaloed. After that, almost no one continued to attend. Maybe ten did, but if there was only one I was going to have the services on Sunday. So when people from other places wanted me to come and do some work or teach I said fine, but I had to be home on Sundays. And unless something weird happened that prevented me from being home on Sunday, I would be there. Or I would let Angel conduct the services. I felt I could trust her with the money.

I called the state attorney general and even the prosecutor on Doug, but because he had moved they couldn't find him. They were going to charge him with theft by deception.

I found out from a former girlfriend in Alabama that he had taken the money and bought her some gifts and himself a new car. She said he had called her and asked for the gifts back; that he was going to break up with her. I told her to keep the gifts. They were not paid out of his pocket; they were the church's and therefore it wasn't his to begin with.

I was scheduled to go to Ohio to do a psychic fair. While I was there I decided to have a reading for myself from someone who didn't know me. The person started to read me and said, "I am hearing that you started a church or something and that it would falter but it was not your fault. People are not ready. But the next one will be a success."

"I still don't understand," I said. "There are other metaphysical churches and they are surviving."

"All I know is God now has other plans for you," she said.

I went home and the other ten were arguing about irrelevant things so I said, "We will all be evangelist ministers. I will still hold some services here but only one Sunday of the month, until I know what's next."

I asked God why he even had me start a church.

And He said, "I wanted you to do your ministry and give others an opportunity to unfold and assist themselves in the development of their spiritual gifts. Sometimes people are not ready when they think they are or the fear sets in and it creates jealousy and other negative reactions."

There were some people who had come to test me. They had been studying a popular method of mind control. I certainly didn't like that. And I told my guides that if one of them tried to get in my head then please have them feel like they were surrounded by a swarm of bees.

Well about two weeks after I had said that, I was driving down the road and I had to pull over because my head felt really strange. I called on God and Smokey, I always called on them first thing, and I asked what the heck was wrong with me.

And Smokey said, "You said if anyone tried to get in your head you'd make them feel as if they were in a swarm of bees."

"Yeah, but I didn't want to have to feel it too," I said.

"But the only way that they could feel the sensation," he said, "was if you felt it too."

"Well, cancel clear that and get my head straight so I can drive," I said.

In about ten minutes I started feeling normal again, well, normal for me anyway.

Then I asked, "Show me who was doing this to me."

And I saw two women who had been attending the church.

Then I said, "What was their reaction?"

He said, "They were frustrated and wondered how you could function."

"Maybe they won't mess with me anymore," I said.

Of course they quit coming to church.

Teaching Relatives about Their Guides

A few of my nieces and nephews came over and visited with me and I baptized them. Jo-Jo and Kristy came over and we started cleaning up the place. Well, we were cleaning and moving things around when one of them yelled out. I went running into a bedroom and they said, "Look at that!" pointing to the blue curtains. It looked like water was running down the curtain. I heard it was "Tears of Christ" and after it had slowed down it looked more like the face of Jesus. Well, we took the curtain down and showed it to my brothers that were next door at my mom's. After that little incident, Ron, Jo-Jo and Kristy's dad, wouldn't let them come over very often. I guess he was scared.

My sister Sandra's kids would come over when she came up to visit Samantha and Billy; they wanted to learn a few things. Samantha told me she was seeing different things.

I asked her, "Do you know what your spirit guide's name is?"

"I was going to ask you," she said.

I said the name of her guide and she looked surprised.

She said, "I have been hearing that name in my head for quite a while now."

So I sat with her and showed her how to communicate with her guide. She wanted to learn how to perform healing energy work and I worked with her on that.

I was doing some energy work on this one woman, when Samantha, my mom, my sister and a couple of my visiting cousins came over. Each one was complaining of pain so I told them to lie down on the table but none of them would.

But Samantha did.

"Well my back really hurts," she said. "And I have no problem lying down so you can help me."

Since she was so small framed, I could put my fingers on each side of her spine and the bones would pop back into place. She did have some scoliosis and she would visit when she could, asking me to help heal her back as she was growing.

I told the grown ups, "Aren't you ashamed to be afraid when this little girl has more courage than any one of you? Is there any one of you now who would like for me to do some energy work on you?"

And they all walked out the door and left. You know even Jesus wasn't recognized for his gift in his own home town. Oh well. Most of my family didn't believe in anything I did growing up so I didn't know why I thought they would start now.

I would go and help my brother Walter to clear energies and help him through the years. Even toward the end of my stepfather's life, he asked me to do some work on him. It helped a little. His name was William and he even knew when he was going to pass away. He asked me to preach at his funeral. I spoke at the funeral along with another preacher.

But my mom never let me work on her except for once, at a later time. She let Louie do some work on her when she fell and broke her hip. She could feel her energies better. Sometimes, depending on the circumstances, it takes a different person to help heal another.

Myrtle always said I would be frustrated because nine times out of ten I could not help my family or close friends. And she was right on that. If your family never believed in you, most likely they never would unless there was some miracle, but for the most part they stay closed minded.

White Raven and Allen

It was later in the spring of 1998 and I had gotten a letter from White Feather. She invited me to come to their workshop in Arizona in June. I wrote and told her I would try.

I was invited back to Alabama to do some classes and I went and then White Raven called wanting me to come to Georgia. She and her boyfriend were breaking up again and she wanted me to rescue her – again. She said he had put some weird spell on her to the point where she could hardly move. So I went over there and did the clearing on her and asked Jesus to take the knotted spell out of her, and He did.

The boyfriend came home from work and looked at me and said, "What did you do?"

"All I did was ask Jesus to help her. *I* didn't do anything," I said.

He said, "I have been working with energy all my life but no one has ever broken any of the spells."

"That's because you put fear in them," I said, "and I am not afraid of you or your spells. And God and Jesus and the Angels help me and they do the work. I just hold the energies."

White Raven glared at her former boyfriend and said, "Yes and you can't hold or hurt me any longer, so get out!"

I was led to show her some protection techniques. And then I left for a psychic fair and then to a person's house in Chattanooga, also to work on some people there.

White Raven came to the fair to do some readings. She told me that her former boyfriend Allen was very afraid of me. She said she tried to tell him he needed to turn to the light, adding that he would be here in a little while.

"I'll attempt to talk with him about it," I said.

After I did some readings I saw Allen come through the door and I asked him to come over and sit down a minute. He did, reluctantly. I explained to him that God wasn't going to hurt him and He wanted Allen to turn his darkness into light. And I was only taking orders from God to help people to heal on any level that they needed it. And that's what I was about. And I explained the clearing method in a little bit more detail to him.

He said he'd think about it, then he got up and left. The fair was for two days and the next day he came over and apologized to me for being so rude and he would give God a chance in his life. He said that all he had ever known was some sort of abuse in his life and he didn't understand why God had allowed it to happen.

It was then that I began telling him about Free Will.

Since the beginning of time, when a handful of people decided that they really needed God, God started lifting negative energies off the planet for a good while. And I had learned during the period called the Dark Ages (and it went back further than it is recorded in history books) the dark side didn't want God convincing people that they needed him; that they could do anything they wanted to have fun. So they started energetically creating parallel lives and energy vortices so the Light could not shine through.

God sent some of the ancient Light Workers back to the planet to help peel the parallel dimensions away but he needed us to count on him to assist us. We are the anchors to bring the Light through to help in removing the layers of darkness off the Earth and to awaken the people so this earth can be more positive and easier to live in. But the other side wants to use people to keep the darkness here.

I said God was going to win in the end but actually there would be no end, just new beginnings. And different people would help with the transformation in different ways. So it would be good, I told him, if he could walk away from the snares of the dark and Hell's energies and work for God. And God did forgive him. Allen said he'd work on it and start reading the Bible and meditating. I told him that was a good start.

I went to the home of my hosts after the fair and they invited some of their friends over to have readings and receive energy work. Then my mom called and said she needed some money to pay the last payment on the land she had purchased on a land contract. If she didn't have it in a few days she would lose the property. So I told the man and his friend that I was staying with about it. They gathered enough people together for readings and energy work so that I was able to make enough to help her and to get back home on.

Later, I was asked to return to North Carolina to provide some work and this gave me enough to begin my trip to Arizona.

Then I got another call from White Raven. She said she wanted to leave and go out west and asked if I would go with her, that she had been guided to ask me.

I told her I had been asked to come to this workshop and if we could stop in Alabama once more, we would have enough gas money to drive out there. Maybe we could find some work out west to return on, or maybe even enough to consider moving out there. I really didn't know.

So I told Jason that I was going on the road to Arizona to check it out and that we might move out there. He said it was okay but for us to be careful.

When I went back to Alabama, I told some of the people about the workshop out west and one lady wanted to go. Her name was Leta. She had a health food store and provided me the opportunity to work with several people there. I gave her White Feather's phone number and Leta called her to make arrangements to come out there.

In the meantime I met with White Raven. She had packed all of her stones and most of her clothes and belongings.

"I'm ready for a new start," she said, "and if I find a place then I can send for my son and Allen. Leave your van here. You can pick it up later."

Spirit said, "No. Leave it at Jan's house."

And so she followed me to Jan's house where I left it.

White Raven then informed me, "I need to go to Florida, to the Everglades, to see someone before we go out west. We might be able to make a little more money for the trip."

So we did. But when we arrived, the woman wasn't home and she had left word that she would be out of town for a while. I wasn't happy about that.

But White Raven said, "I think we will have enough. Let's go to the alligator farm."

"I have no desire to do this," I told her.

She kept insisting, so we went; but I didn't like it at all. Some of those things were huge and not in a fenced area and if the alligators were hungry you could have been dinner.

White Raven walked over to this guy who was letting people hold the little ones.

"You go ahead and I'll take the pictures," I said.

So she did. While she was posing, I noticed the attendant had a bandage around one of his hands and forearm.

"I bet that mama bit you, didn't she?" I asked.

"Yes she did," he said, "just two weeks ago. But I still want to work with her and the others."

I thought, "Yeah and one day you'll be eaten for lunch or something."

We finally left. I was glad to get on the road. I told White Raven we could stop and see Ed and his wife in Roswell for a night or two and do some energy work on them for staying there so we could rest. She agreed.

Well, when we got to Roswell, White Raven copped an attitude and I barely got to spend a day with them. We were traveling in her little van and she wouldn't let me help drive which I thought that was strange. She kept driving slowly on the left lane, which drove me nuts. People were passing by us blowing their horns and I told her to please drive in the correct lane. But she said she would just do as she pleased. I wanted to smack her, but I didn't. It was then I realized one of the gator spirits had jumped into her.

We had driven a little further down the road when she began swerving. I suggested we get a hotel room and rest. She finally agreed but she didn't sleep much at all. We got up and went on into Arizona the next morning. I was exhausted; I just wanted to sleep for a day or two straight, but I didn't.

White Feather had been to a women's seminar working with some people from California and they wanted her to do some promotion work for them. I soon wished I hadn't come.

White Raven told White Feather that my energies and her energies were clashing and she didn't want to share a room with me, that she would sleep on the couch. I didn't care. White Feather told me there were three people who wanted to have a reading from me and that we had to go into Phoenix to see them. White Feather took me over there and White Raven went with us.

I had been running out of money so what I made there helped in buying food. We went into Sedona to make some connections there to do some work at some of the metaphysical shops. We left them our brochures and phone numbers. A week went by but there were no calls. We went up to the rock formations in the national park and did some energy clearing on them.

While we were there these little Volkswagen bus vehicles started coming in packed full of people, like sardines.

The park rangers were there, guiding them in. The tourists looked like a bunch of old hippies from the sixties or something. While they were getting out of the buses, some of the people started taking off their tops, men *and* women, and I told the park ranger what they were doing. He said that the neighbors had complained too. I asked if it was against the law for them to do that but he said in a public park like this one, no. I was shocked. So White Feather and I left.

On the way out though I asked one of the guys why they were all here. And he said every year at this time they come here and celebrate the Earth and give their energies to the stones.

I thought, "That's why the stones were crying out and we had to go and clear them."

I told White Feather in a few days, after these people left, we would go and clear them again. In the meantime, Scare Crow was getting his class together and only a few people had called to say they were coming. I didn't have a good feeling about him. In fact, I wasn't having a good feeling from being out there in general. I didn't do well in the desert; it was starting to get to me and it became hard to breathe. At least, I thought it was the desert.

White Feather began to open up and admitted to me how odd Scare Crow had been acting. I told her if he wasn't feeling well maybe he'd let us give him a clearing. She had already received one.

Then she blurted out, "I think he is having an affair with his secretary."

I just looked at her, nodding.

"She'll be here today; I'd be interested to see what you sense from her," she said.

I said I would. The woman who came, Michelle, was attractive. She came in and was introduced to me and White Raven. White Raven talked to her more than I did.

I felt that the woman was definitely being more than a sales associate; the way she was flirting with Scare Crow it was obvious. But just to be sure, I asked Spirit also and they confirmed it.

I really didn't want to tell White Feather so I showed her a method that would allow her to know for herself. She carried out the method and came into the room very frightened. She told me what she had seen.

"Well, did he agree to a clearing?" I asked.

"No," she said, "but I'm going to make him."

"He will tell you that he will do it for you," I said, "but he doesn't like me so there will be no way of telling what's going on until I can see for myself when we perform the clearing."

White Raven agreed to assist in the clearing. She was curious too. He came into the room, and laid down on the massage table. We started out with some prayers, then the affirmations. I kept seeing talons. White Raven saw them too. In fact, I kept referring to them as claws. And as we went to the top of the body, in his head was a big snake.

"So you have revealed my secret," he said during the clearing.

I didn't know whether to run or hide or what.

So I told him, "Hey, it's your business."

"I don't want to change," he said. "I have almost transformed my spirit and energies into an eagle."

"Well you were complaining about your legs hurting," I said, "and I'd say this is part of it."

"Yes, but if I can get my spirit to change into the eagle instead of my true self, I can go back to the Indian reservations and get them to accept me," he explained.

"Well good luck," I offered.

I didn't know what else to say, so I figured I better play along to get out of there safely.

He looked at all three of us and said, "Just don't interfere."

"It's your body, not mine and it's your life; so like I said, good luck," I said, trying to sound as neutral as I could.

We did what we could to complete the clearing.

White Raven wanted to stay and meet people out there and I just wanted to go home. The workshop was to take place the next week and Lena was coming out. I thought if I could get by until then, I could just go home when she went. I pretended like it didn't bother me.

He kind of backed off of the threatening energies and went to bed. He looked at White Feather and asked her, "Are you coming to bed?"

She was so shocked she couldn't speak. She went; and while she was walking toward the bedroom, I whispered it would be okay. I knew then I had to get her out of there.

The next morning Spirit said, "Watch what you eat and drink around here."

"Yeah, he will probably try to take me out; I feel it," I said.

Scare Crow left for a while and then returned with some weird people he had met at the river. An older man said he would like for me to help him get rid of some spirits that jumped in him, and so White Raven and I did a clearing on him.

"What were you doing to attract these spirits?" I asked.

He said, "I tried to clear two houses and a church and these things started dropping from the sky. I was told since there were so many holes in the ozone, it left an opening for the incubus and succubus spirits to come into Earth's atmosphere. And I could feel them sucking the life out of me."

So I started commanding them out into the light that we had called in. That was the first time I had seen that type of spirit creatures, or whatever they were. Jesus came in and said there were many on the earth and I would have to help shift them out.

"I need you to tell me of the others and what to do," I said.

"I will," He said. "And Smokey and you will need to talk about how to go to the four corners area and Mount Shasta."

"Where are those places?" I asked.

"Ask White Feather," He said. "She will take you there."

So I asked her.

"Why?" she asked.

I told her Jesus said I needed to go there and shift some energies or vortices.

She said they were a good distance away.

And I thought to myself, "Well heck, I don't have any money for gas or anything."

Then she said, "I'll ask Scare Crow if we can go. He owes me some money and we can use it and my gas card to travel on."

Then a woman called me while I was there who had heard of me and my work from another person who had met me. She lived in California and said, "If you are ever out here, call or come by and I will line up some people for readings."

"Well, as a matter of fact," I said, "we are going to Mount Shasta."

She said, "That's great! My place is on the way."

I told her a little about the situation and she told me to call her when we started in that direction. I agreed.

Scare Crow said we could use the RV to go to the four corners area, so we all went, including White Feather's cat Mickey, and Beau, her golden retriever.

When we got to the area, I told White Feather, "I am hearing to go down the road to a certain place."

She said, "Are you sure you haven't been here before?"

I said, "Spirit tells me where to go and I just try and follow directions."

So we went and performed a ceremony for the Earth Mother. White Feather had a tent and White Raven and Michelle slept in it. White Feather and Scare Crow slept in the RV. He said in the morning we could go and stand in the circle where the four states intersected.

When morning came, we had some breakfast and went over to the area where the corners of the four states met. We spoke prayers in each direction. There were some Native Americans there selling jewelry and other things, in each direction. It was different.

We walked down the road and Scare Crow said there was a legend that the Anasazi Indians came to this place and disappeared when they were told that the white man would come and take over the land.

He took some little stones from the ground for souvenirs. There were some orbs floating around and I wondered if maybe they were spirits of the Anasazi. Soon after Spirit said they are of the Ancient Ones. We thanked them and prayed they would be well in their world and at peace and then we left.

We also went to another place. I forgot where it was but I stayed in the RV and the rest rode into the canyons. Spirit told me not to go. When they got back they said it was a rough ride in the jeep and they almost fell out.

On the way back, Michelle did a card reading on me and said, "I see you in some very difficult situations."

I agreed.

"And when you get back, you will hear of a niece being pregnant," she said.

"I only have two," I said. "One is nine and the other is fifteen. I pray you are wrong."

When we got back, White Feather said, "I want to take you up to a place I like to go to meditate."

She called it the muggy ol'rim. It was like a forest on top of a mountain; and the valley was a desert. I told her she needed to tune in to nature more and see what she felt and maybe heard.

"Well I hug a tree every now and then," she said.

"That's good," I said. "It will help ground you."

When we got to the place she liked the most, we took some of the lawn chairs out of the car and sat and stared out over the rim. It was beautiful.

Then I felt a pain on my arm. I checked my hands to see if it was a spirit and my hands and fingers were even. But I kept feeling it.

I thought, "What the heck?"

Something turned my head toward some trees and then pushed my chin up and I saw something sticking out of the tree. I got up and went over to it and saw a big black ice pick in the tree.

"Look at this," I said.

White Feather came over to see.

"I wonder how that got there," I said.

And then I heard a voice say, "An angry old man stuck it in me."

I thought, "Okay."

Then I said, "Well little tree, I'll pull it out of you."

And the tree said, "Thank you."

I had to tippy-toe and stretch to get the thing. Then I sent Reiki into the tree and it was like a sigh came from it. Then all the trees started swaying and they said, "Thank you Sha `La!"

"How do you all know me?" I asked.

And they said, "We know you from the past."

I guessed from a past life. I blessed them and then it started to get dark. We were headed back down the mountain when a big elk crossed in front of us. I thought it was a giant deer because I had seen deer as large as horses before. White Feather said it was an elk. We blessed it and went on.

While we were driving, I told her of the shaman man named Speaking Wind and described the drummings that he performed. I told of how I had taken a group to a place called Kinlock, in Alabama. I remembered lying on this great rock and how Smokey took my spirit through the rock. That was when I saw the Elders in the earth and I learned the phrase "**On Con Ta**" which means to "*return to perfection.*"

So we shared different things that had happened to us in life.

In a few days, the people that had come to Scare Crow's and White Feather's house came back and a young man from another group started flirting with White Raven. They went off to talk; she decided that she would go with them and travel and sleep in her van by the river. I was disappointed in her.

She said to me, "You will have to fin for yourself and go home the best way you can."

"I already knew that," I said. "So you don't want to try and get a job and share an apartment like we started out to do?"

"I need a man," she said, "and I'm going with him."

"Well, good luck," I said.

I had hoped for better from her but Spirit had told me that she would do that. Before they left, she, Scare Crow and the others sat around the patio table and ate and drank.

Scare Crow was showing off this strange amulet that had some weird energy with it. He told the story about some family that had a farm and how a space ship had landed there years ago. Apparently, the farmer told the authorities and they took the ship and told the man not to ever speak of it again. Then one day another ship landed and it made another hole in the earth. When it hit the earth, most of the ship shattered and the man told his sons to find what they could, put it in the hole and bury it. Years later when the boys grew up they dug into the hole and the only thing remaining was an object that might have been a motor and they took it and melted it down and made pieces of jewelry out of it.

Scare Crow said, "Here Sha `La, feel it and see what type of being you see landing here."

I barely put my hand toward it when I started getting sick.

I said, "You already know."

It was reptilian. I figured he could stand to wear it because his spirit was one himself. I became sick and had to throw up.

White Feather came in to see if I was okay. Scare Crow was outside laughing with the others because I had gotten sick.

I told Smokey I saw a grocery store that had closed down and beside the building were some old carts. I was going to go and get one and put my clothes in it and start walking.

He said, "You won't get far. Wait and go to Mount Shasta and then we will get you out of here."

I thought maybe I had to go with Lena but I tried to call her to see if she had left yet and to warn her of these strange people but I could not reach her by phone. I think Scare Crow could read my mind sometimes and blocked me. I had already heard from Spirit that he was going to try and do me in.

White Raven held the metal piece and since she didn't get sick from it I just assumed it was because she had held that alligator in Florida, and still had the energy in her from doing that. I know she started acting stranger after that.

White Feather came to me, while Scare Crow went to the store, and said, "I looked into the mirror again because I didn't want to believe that all of this was happening. It's so bizarre. But you are telling the truth and we are in danger. He wants to kill me too."

"This is why Spirit sent me here," I said, "to help you escape. I just wish they would have told me before I got here so I could have been more prepared."

"If you had known though something else would have stopped you," she said.

I heard, "Yes, it would have been more difficult."

"We have three days before the workshop," she said. "Let's go to Mount Shasta and then leave after the workshop, although I don't have anywhere to go."

"You can come and stay with me if you want," I offered. "I live in an old house but it will be safe until you figure out what you want to do."

She said that would be fine.

"He is reading your mind too," I told her. "And be careful what you are thinking."

"He kind of said this morning that he could do that," she said. "I was thinking about how to leave and he just looked at me and said I wasn't going anywhere."

"I was just thinking about how I could leave and take you to Mount Shasta and back before the workshop started," she said. "All he did was just look at me.

"Call that lady," she continued, "and we will use my gas card to go and buy food on it. I'll call the woman that wants me to work for her in California. Maybe that is where I will end up going."

"Okay," I said. "If we're going to do it, then we need to do it now."

White Raven paired up with the man that was staying on the river. I asked her if she forgot why she came out there. And I asked her if she had forgotten about her son and Allen. And all she said was that they could care for themselves.

As it turned out, Scare Crow didn't have very many people to sign up for the workshop so he told them they could take the workshop for free.

Mount Shasta and the Escape

The lady that White Feather knew said for us to stop in at her house on our way to Mount Shasta so we could perform a clearing on her and her son. We could also spend the night or rest before we continued on up the road.

We made it there and did the work. But she didn't pay us *anything*.

"We feel better," she said, "but I don't have any money and you need to go on now. I have to go somewhere."

So she turned out to be a big liar. She also told White Feather that she changed her mind about her working for her. I told White Feather not to put too much stock in what she was telling her. I felt she was a user and a liar anyway; White Feather was much better off not working for her.

"Everybody can't be like that, can they?" she asked.

"Everybody isn't," I said, "but you have to discern everyone to see who is and who is not."

That was a big wake-up call for her.

Leaving disappointed, we went on to the other lady's home. She had two readings for us and we told her what had happened. She gave us some groceries to take with us.

She said, "I only have fifty dollars to give you but I will pray you get back east safely."

She told us to be careful. We thanked her and left to go on to Mount Shasta. When we left it was getting dark but we took the fifty dollars and drove as far as we could and got a room so we could rest. The next morning, as we traveled, we ate some tuna sandwiches on the way.

White Feather asked, "Do you know where we are going?"

"No, just like at the four corners area, they will tell us when we get there," I said. "The only thing I see right now is a dirt road and as we go down it I know there will be a clearing with a big tree and a creek. I know we are to perform a ceremony there and then go up a mountain or hill."

She just looked at me.

"What?" I asked.

"I don't know how you can just live on faith," she said.

"That is all I have and whatever I am on the planet to do, I have to try and get it done or I get sick," I said. "And I don't want to have to reincarnate and do it again. It's too hard now."

So as we drove on up the road, Spirit said, "Turn here."

And I told White Feather and she said, "Are you sure?"

Then, before I could answer she said, "Never mind."

Then she turned to me and I said, "They are telling me we are going to go three miles and then for us to turn left."

So we did and there was the tree, the clearing and a creek.

Again she said, "You've been here before."

I just said, "One day you will believe me."

We got out of her little truck and I put some stones in a circle and said my prayers for the Earth Mother and the area and blessed the trees.

Then I said, "Now we have to go..."

I turned around and saw this big mountain and said, "...up there."

"How do we get up there?" White Feather asked.

"We just get into the truck and they will tell us."

So we went and discovered there was a festival in town. She wanted to stop and look around a little and go to the rest room, so we did. She asked someone how to get up the mountain and they told her. She was getting a little spooked I think. We went up, all the way to the top. Even though this was July, there was plenty of snow at that altitude and we couldn't go any further.

I said, "Now we will find a place to sit and meditate."

White Feather found her a spot and I found mine. I heard the mountain spirits and they told me of earth changes that were coming and that there were beings in the mountains that were not from this earth. But they were okay.

"One day you will meet them," the voice said.

They thanked me for coming to the earth (being born) to help in the changes. My conscious mind still didn't comprehend everything but I guess it didn't matter.

I said, "I am hearing we are to stop one more place and then go back."

She agreed.

She said, "My guidance was telling me that I am to go home with you and get away from Scare Crow; that I wouldn't survive and you have a lot to teach me. I guess I never knew that there was so much out there I didn't understand or know about."

We went down the mountain and found this store where the people were all dressed in orange and they had pyramids and gadgets that were to be used as energy wands. We didn't have enough money to purchase them but they were really fun to try out.

I was guided to this tapestry on the wall and I kept staring at it and the woman told White Feather that she had only seen one person look at it the way I did.

I told her what I saw and she was amazed.

"You must have special gifts," she said.

White Feather told her some things about me, how I lived on faith and how Spirit told me where to go to do ceremonies for the Earth Mother.

The woman looked at me and said, "I feel you need to relax in the pyramid."

"I don't have enough money."

"Go ahead; with your talents, be my guest."

So I laid down on this little mattress and she played some music and I just felt like I was spinning. I didn't know what happened next but I knew I felt better after it stopped. When I was able to get out of the pyramid, White Feather said I had been lying there for over an hour. I told her about the things I had seen and about the spinning sensation.

The lady said, "You must have astral traveled to Katmandu."

"Where is that?"

She said it was a holy place overseas. And the holy man that lived there was very special and told me some things about him.

I said, "Maybe one day Spirit will send us there."

We began the trip back to White Feather's house. She knew a person in Los Angeles who also traveled; he could make music with his mouth and hands. We went there to rest and she wanted to see what he thought about something that was happening. I told her I would sleep in the truck and watch over our gear. There were cars that kept circling around and around the block and I felt they were going to try and steal our belongings that were under the tarp. This one man circled around all night long and saw that I was not going to go to sleep. Finally, when daylight came, I went in and told White Feather what happened and that it was time to go.

But somehow we went the wrong way and ended up where the movie stars had imprinted their hands and feet in concrete. We went ahead and took some pictures while we were there. Some guy said he would give us five dollars a piece to be stand-ins.

"Hey, let's do it," I said excited by the prospect.

"No, we have to get back," she said.

So we made our way back to White Feather's. Smokey told me not to go in the house until he came back, that Scare Crow had a trap for us and he had to go in and defuse it.

White Feather asked what was going on now. And I told her I saw a "watcher" in the cactus lamp and so then I had to explain to her what a watcher was.

A Watcher is an energy being that a person can create with their energy by building the energy between their hands and programming it to do as the person asks. And then they place it into an object to bring it to life, so to speak. But these things are dangerous.

I told her about this thing that was at a friend of mine's house, that one of the people at the church had sent it there to watch me. It would not leave unless it was satisfied with some information to take back to the one that created it. And so I told it some kind of malarkey so it would have something to report back to the sender.

She said, "I didn't know Scare Crow knew how to do these things."

"There is a lot more you don't know," I said. "But for now you don't need to know. That way he won't be able to know what you found out. You will know later. If Lena doesn't take me back, I am going to go into town and get a basket cart and load my things in it and leave."

"I'm going to leave too," she said.

About twenty-five minutes later, Smokey came to me and said, "I have taken care of the watcher; now it is safe to enter."

So we slowly got out of the truck and went in. Scare Crow came in about ten minutes later with a grin and then the grin dropped; he couldn't figure out what had happened to his watcher. He went and got a "boom box" and started to play some weird music to the cactus lamp. I just ignored him.

Some people started to show up for the workshop; they had brought watermelon and different snacks. Scare Crow started insisting that White Feather and I attend the workshop and I kept hearing Smokey say no.

I went to the sink to cut a piece of watermelon but the knife slipped in a strange way and cut the artery in my hand; the bleeding would not stop and Scare Crow started laughing. White Feather gave him a look and called an ambulance. The paramedics came and said I would need stitches.

White Feather looked at Scare Crow and said, "I guess you will go on without us."

He was not happy.

So we got into the ambulance and went to the hospital. They put about nine stitches in my hand.

The paramedics then took us back to her house while I tried to figure out how to leave. Lena had arrived but she had flown in and used an airport rental car to get to the house. I took her outside and told her some of what was happening.

I said, "If you can loan me some money, when I get to Alabama I will pay you back."

"I only have a few dollars and some credit cards," she said. "Meet me in the morning and I will get a U-Haul to go on the back of her truck and fill up her gas tank."

"Yes, great; that'll work," I said.

The next morning while Scare Crow went to Flagstaff to have a tire changed, we met with Lena. And she did what she had said. Then she went to the airport to go home while White Feather and I went to the house to load up.

She didn't get to take all of her stuff because the U-Haul was kind of small and she had a lot of books that she wanted to take. While we were getting what we could, I heard a voice in a heavy east European accent say, "Tell White Feather to push button and go like hell."

I stopped and told her what I heard. She said that was her grandfather.

Then I heard him say, "You only have twelve minutes."

I told her and we hurried as fast as we could go. Then the darn cat decided to hide. We had to find her. We did and then she decided to go to the post office to check the mail.

"Hurry," I said, "because I feel him coming."

"I will."

She came out and someone started to ask her what she was doing and she said she was helping me to go home. As we were getting ready to turn onto the main road out of town, here he came. He started shaking his fist and screaming at us.

"Don't look back and do what your grandfather said!" I yelled to her. "And if you stop he will kill both of us! This is what Spirit said!"

She started accelerating and crying at the same time.

"I can't believe I am leaving my beautiful home," she said.

"You know what he's about now and what his intentions are," I said.

"How could I not see that before?"

"What would you have done if you had?" I asked.

"I don't know."

The Gargoyle Spirit

We stopped in New Mexico. It was the Fourth of July because we could see fireworks in the town at a distance. I had forgotten what day it was.

"I keep feeling I have to give him a courtesy call," White Feather said.

"He is projecting that to you so he can get into your head."

She insisted.

"If you want to, go ahead," I said.

"But I told you I'd take you home," she replied.

"Just tell him you are taking me to Alabama and you will be back. If I can get there, or most of the way there, someone will meet us and pick me up."

When she called him, he said he wanted to talk to Beau the dog. I shook my head no at her. I told her earlier that he would put something in him or on him.

I had to pray over the dog. He started getting sick all of a sudden, then I took him outside.

"No, he wasn't feeling well," White Feather said speaking to Scare Crow on the phone.

I told her to believe what she wanted to but she had to make her own decision.

She told him that she knew he was having an affair and didn't want to be in that situation. The woman, Michelle, had confessed to White Feather before we left.

White Feather was very confused. I told her to rest; that I was going out to straighten up the U-Haul because we just threw our things into it.

We drove on to Santa Fe. I was told by Spirit to stop at the Loreto Chapel and gather some energy to help us. I told her about it and we went and asked people where it was. Once we received directions, we found it easily, parked and went inside.

Spirit said to walk to the front and sit down. I did and White Feather followed me.

Saint Joseph came to me and said, "We have some spirit gifts for you."

I saw Mother Mary and she put a blue spirit shawl around me. Then Jesus sent a blue and silver light to me.

White Feather said she was feeling energy come to her as well.

Then Saint Joseph said, "Do you want to know more about the spiral stair case?"

"Sure I do," I said.

He said, "I was the one that appeared to the nuns and I built it with light. This is another lesson for you in alchemy. I asked the light from the heavens to come and form through the wood so it would take its shape and then I asked for four pillows of light to stabilize it and make it sturdy, and it did. In a few moments, go over and look into it and reach out and feel the pillow of light."

I did and I could see it.

"It is similar to the way your spirit holds substance together in your body," he said, "so you can be a life source in what is called physical life in embodiment."

Then I looked up at the top of the stairs. I saw Jesus standing there and He said He was blessing us for a safe journey. We sure needed it.

I thanked them and then we left and walked around town for a little while and went to see some statues. We saw St. Francis of Assisi and asked him to bless the animals.

We stayed the night in a hotel where there was a family next door. White Feather had Beau getting ready for his evening walk when this boy about nine or ten years old came out from the other door and looked at Beau.

"He won't hurt you," White Feather said. "Would you like to pet him?"

"No, I'd like to cut his throat," the boy said.

White Feather was horrified and yelled for me.

"What kind of kid is this?" she asked me.

I heard "a reptilian species" and I repeated this to White Feather.

"What?" she asked confused.

I said, "Let me walk Beau; just sit down. Now you have some more learning to do."

So I walked Beau and went inside. White Feather was still upset and couldn't believe what this little blonde-haired, blue-eyed boy had said. She wanted to address this to his parents.

I said, "It's best you just settle down. We'll leave here in a short while."

It took her a while to get use to all the things I was telling her.

I said, "You said you wanted a teacher so I guess God figured you were ready to go to the next level of understanding. Always watch what you ask for."

Of course, it still was kind of hard for her to swallow. It was hard for me too when I started to learn these things but I had to, to survive.

We got back on the road. I decided to lay in the back of the truck with Beau for a while on top of the tarp which had some suitcases in it. I needed some fresh air.

We had been traveling for a while when I looked up and saw this gargoyle looking spirit jump off the overpass and onto the truck, and Beau saw it too. It made the truck drop down some and I started commanding it off. I asked for the Angels and Guides to help. Beau was barking and finally they took it off.

White Feather had the little window open and asked what all the commotion was about, and I told her.

We finally got into Texas somewhere. She had a Citgo gas card so we had to fuel up at those places. She was able to get us some food on the card too, which I thought was strange. She said those guys in there looked dirty, spitting tobacco into a coffee can and dressed in weird clothes.

"Are they what I have heard called 'good old boys'?" she asked.

I said, "Those 'weird clothes' are called overalls. Haven't you ever been in the south?"

"I was told to stay out of the south; that they would shoot Yankees," she said.

I just started laughing.

"Those good old boys might save your life one day," I said, "and they are not going to shoot you unless you make them really mad."

She was nervous and scared. I never had seen the like. She asked if I wanted to drive. I said sure. So she helped me understand the truck.

It was a stick shift and a little different from the big rigs I had driven. I was used to the automatics. But I drove for a while and we finally made it to Alabama. She felt at one point that all of this was just her imagination, or that I was just cuckoo.

We finally got a hotel and I left her and the animals in the room so I could go to Cindy's house to do some work and make some money.

I tried calling the hotel but there was no answer. Finally we went on over there and found that she was so exhausted she had gone into a deep sleep. When I finally woke her up so she could answer the door, she said she was hungry and asked if I would go and get her something to eat.

"Right there is the restaurant; how come you didn't go over there?"

I had given her some money that Cindy had given me in advance and then I paid Cindy back after the people paid me for the clearing.

Again she said, "I was afraid that they would know I was from the north and hurt me."

Cindy laughed and said we were more civilized now, and don't do that.

"All you have to do is say you're with me," I said. "And since you look Native American they won't hurt you."

I asked her what she would like to eat and went and got it for her. Though I told her if she decided to leave and go back to let me know so I could get my belongings from her truck. Cindy could take me to get my van in Tennessee.

"What are you going to do?" she asked.

"I have some more people to see tomorrow and I'll go and pay for another night's stay for you," I said.

She agreed and we gave her Cindy's number. I stayed with Cindy that night because the first person was coming over early.

I finally got in touch with Lena and she ask me to balance her body's energy in exchange for the money she loaned me.

"When I left you, I felt something had come over me," she said, "and I was really dizzy and almost wrecked. I almost didn't get to the airport in time for my plane."

I agreed to the terms and she came to where I was and I said, "I owe you more than this."

And she said, "When you come to town, just work on me again."

"Okay," I said and thanked her for her help.

White Feather finally called and Cindy took me to meet her. She said she decided to go on to my house and stay for a while.

We went to Jan's house to pick up my van. I said I would drive. We got there at night and Jan said we could spend the night. So we did. The next day she and her husband went to work. I started to get up and go but this skunk came into the driveway and its scent was staggering. I didn't know if it was just sick from the heat or had rabies. So I called animal control because it passed out right beside my van. I felt bad and was going to go out to see about it when White Feather kept insisting not too, so I didn't.

When Jan and her husband came home we got our things situated. I had taken some of my clothes out of the U-Haul and put them in the van. I had air conditioning back then so I told her to let Beau ride with me. I knew I had put the pad lock on the back of the U-Haul and locked it. At least I thought I had.

And when we left, Kelso said he had fixed something in my van and I thanked him. He had looked everything over before we left. And I even thought he was the one that had helped me shut the U-Haul door and locked it.

Anyway, we headed down the road, and she followed me. We went up and down little hills and around a lot of curves and even went up a big hill. People started blowing their horns and yelling, "Your door is open!"

Something made me look at my gas gauge and I saw it was on empty. I pulled into the next gas station. A couple of cars pulled in behind White Feather. I got out of the van and she got out of the truck and she said, "What's all the hollering about?"

I told White Feather all I had heard was "your door is open" but mine were all shut.

We looked at each other and walked behind the U-Haul and one of the people who had been driving behind us was standing in amazement. The rear door was open all the way and everything appeared to be suspended in air. I was shocked because we had just climbed a really big hill and by the law of gravity it should have all fallen out. I grinned and shut the door.

Spirit said, "We sent Fred to help hold all your things in."

"Who is Fred?" I asked.

Then I saw an octopus spirit spread out over the back of the U-haul.

That was when God said, "I can send any of the spirits to assist when need-ed."

I just said, "Thank you so much, because if all of that stuff had fallen out it would have been such a mess and maybe have caused a wreck."

When I explained it to White Feather, she said, "If I hadn't seen it with my own eyes I probably would not have believed you."

"Me too."

We finally arrived at the house in Indiana; I could tell she didn't like it.

I said, "I don't either but it's all I've got and can afford right now."

So I introduced her to Jason and my mom and then the other family members as they came over. I told her she was welcome to stay if she wanted to and as long as she needed too.

She said, "I guess I have no other choice right now."

A few days went by and she called her cousin in New York. The cousin said that she could come stay there for a while. So she went there for a few weeks and then called me and said it wasn't working out and asked if she could come back to my house. I told her yes, so she did.

She had a hard time adjusting to things. But that can be expected going through the trauma of having to run from someone you thought was a good person at one time, especially a mate.

The weekend came and my Uncle Billy Ray drove over with some things he had bought from the flea market. He had some shorts and tops and some of it looked like they had Native American designs on them.

He took one look at White Feather and said, "She's mine; you brought her here for me."

I told him that he was nuts. He had recently had shoulder surgery and said his arm had been hurting.

"You want me to do any energy work on you?" I asked.

"Only if she helps," he said.

She said she would and we took him in the next room where I had the massage table set up and we both sent him energy to try and ease the pain. He said he felt something. And he told White Feather that she had healing hands and asked if she would go on a date with him. At first she said she didn't want to date right away after having to leave Scare Crow; but Uncle Billy Ray kept coming over almost every day until she finally gave in.

I tried to teach her some things I knew. Some were overwhelming for her. I guess she went on the date to break the monotony and get back to some sense of a normal life.

She found a job and worked for a group home at first. Then that got to be too much so she found a job working for an older woman who needed help and moved in with her for a while. White Feather had been a paramedic and had worked for an elderly woman in Arizona at one time, so the work was familiar. She also had worked for a group home in Connecticut at one time.

She and Billy Ray dated for a while, and then there were some complications. She moved back in with me and Jason, and found a job as a waitress. Christmas came and went; I had ordered some things from a catalog on credit.

Receiving My Eagle Staff

In 1998, White Feather and I were asked to go and help these people in Cherokee, North Carolina. So we went there to do a clearing for a man, a woman and a piece of land. Some people were trying to prevent them from building a house on the land. They needed us to shift the energies there. After the clearings, the man asked his wife to retrieve an Eagle staff that he had carved while in the Merchant Marines. She didn't want to part with it, but he said I would be the one using it and that I would need it to work with the Earth Mother in the future. So I accepted the staff and we thanked them and left. As we proceeded down the mountain toward the Pigeon Forge area, halfway down the truck just stopped working. Some people pulled over to help us and we were able to make it to a hotel. We used the money we earned from the clearing to pay for the hotel and the mechanic's bill.

Seeing Fairies

We returned home to Indiana. We arrived about four o'clock in the morning and looked up at the safety light in the yard where we saw what we thought at first was a great moth. Looking closer, we saw that it was a small pale-yellow tinted little woman with wings. In other words, she was a fairy! Also up in the sky we saw what looked like a navy blue rectangular doorway with different colored fairies flying in and out of it. We watched them flying around for a few hours and then as daylight started to break, they all flew into the doorway and it closed. We were excited! We had actually seen fairies!

Moving to Alabama

Because of all the traveling, I decided to move to Alabama. I think I was there about six months. White Feather stayed at the house in Indiana and had it organized pretty well.

Jason came down and we rented an apartment over the top of a beauty parlor. Dana had set it up for me. Jason took a job at the oldest hotel in downtown Birmingham. He was a custodian. But he had to do all kinds of work, even park cars for them. He didn't like it very much.

"Mom, there are ghosts in that place," he said.

"Probably a lot of them," I said. "Well, keep working until you can find something else."

"I will, but I need to get out of there," he said.

A trip to Mobile with Dana had come up for me. One of her friends there wanted me to do some work on them. So we went, Jason kept the van and took Thor with him to work and left him in the van, because with both of us gone he would howl all night. Jason worked the night shift and Thor would have kept the neighbors up. Of course, during his break he would go sit with Thor in the van.

I had a cat named Kitty Cat, that's all he would answer to; and, Maggie, my ferret. I would take Maggie with me in a little carrying cage. One night Thor tore up all the seats that were left in the van, and chewed the seat belts off.

While I was in Mobile for a few days, I had this one client that was experiencing a lot of pain and I saw babies around him, five of them.

I thought, "What's this all about?"

Spirit said, "Ask him if he has been with any woman that had a miscarriage or abortion, or still birth."

I did and the man said, "Yes, five of them."

I asked Spirit why the babies were with him. And before any would answer, the man said all of the women had had abortions and he hadn't wanted them to do that.

He said, "I wanted to marry the women and have a family but they didn't."

I asked Spirit, "So the spirits of the babies are here because the man wanted them but the women did not?"

And they said yes.

I asked Mother Mary to bring in the midwives of the heavens and take the babies back to heaven to go somewhere else and be born. I had the man pray with me on this matter and forgive the women and himself. The babies started leaving.

There was a lot of energy during this time because Dana could feel it and also see what was happening. Even her shoes turned colors, a silver appearance. I think they were normally black or a much darker color. She freaked out.

"Well that's different," I thought.

"What kind of power was *that*?" she asked.

"I don't know but it was different," I said.

"I don't know about you Sha `La," she said.

"It wasn't me; it was the energy and the spirit world," I said. "I like the new color better. Are you okay?"

"I feel strange," she said.

"Well sit down."

"I have to go smoke a cigarette," she said. "While you are with your next client, I'll just wait in the lobby."

"Okay."

It was more than she could take in. The next day we had to go to a person's house and help a child, a little boy, about eight or nine. He was born with something wrong with his lungs and he had never cried. The parents were taking him back and forth to the hospital about once a week.

The child curled up on the couch in the fetal position facing the back of the couch. Jesus had me kneel down and hold my hands out and pray for him. While I was doing that Jesus stepped in me and I looked like I was solid gold in my aura.

Jesus said, "I am going to take something from you that he needs."

"Don't I need it?" I asked.

He said, "I will fill your void with pure light and yours will grow back."

"Well what is it that the child needs?" I asked.

"The lining of your lungs."

And as He said that, it felt like he ripped skin off me and it *hurt*. I was literally *feeling* the pain. So I tried taking some deep breaths. In a few minutes, the boy started breathing deeper and then he started crying. I told Dana to come and ground his energies, because I was buzzing so high I couldn't come down right then.

His mother grabbed him and he started to suck on her face. After Dana held some of the energies, he leveled out. Finally I came back down into the grounding space. My chest was sore but in a few days I felt better.

A Friend from India

A doctor named Gama, from India, came and talked with me about the gurus and swamis and the deities that they worshiped and worked with. He asked me if the clearings could raise his vibration and I answered yes. He wanted to come to me at least twice a week but I told him twice a month to start out. (This was what I heard Spirit say). So he came and he also sent a friend to have a clearing.

One day I was watching television and there was a story about another tomb that had been discovered in the pyramids in Egypt. Then I heard Spirit say its time for another upgrade.

"I don't understand," I said.

God said, "This work with the human body is correlated with the information and secrets of the pyramids in Egypt."

CHAPTER 18
∞
THE YEAR 1999

The building where we were living in Birmingham was haunted too. I would say prayers every night. I think there were day spirits or ghosts and night spirits or ghosts. It was quieter in the day than at night.

One night Jason went to work as I was getting ready to go to bed when Thor began barking and jumping up in the air. I started calling in the light and saying my prayers. The next thing I knew Thor was on the floor not breathing and even though the Angels and Guides were winning the battle, I began to be knocked about. Before I blacked out I prayed that at least one of us would be alive when Jason came home. I asked for it to be Thor if I had to pass away but later I woke up with Thor licking my hand.

Jason came home and told me about nearly being electrocuted and seeing more ghosts and then he added, "I've had enough of this; I'm going back to Indiana."

I told him I understood. And I prayed that he'd be safe. So the next day Jason took his things and Thor and moved back to the house in Indiana. I didn't go; I felt I was needed to keep the energies shifted around there to help the people. I was told by Spirit to stay for a while longer.

Kitty Cat and Maggie stayed with me. And I did well until some of the people started turning on me. People would call the phone at Dana's when she and I would go out of town. Her ex-husband answered the phone while we were gone and told clients or potential clients that I didn't live there anymore or that I didn't provide healing work anymore. Then some of the same people who had called would see me in town at the store and ask why I quit reading or doing healing work. I would tell them I didn't and ask them why. And they would tell me that Dana's husband told them I had left orders for him to tell people that.

I talked to Dana about it when he had left for a few weeks to go on some kind of job. I had a few more clients to come and they ask me to keep living there.

As it turned out, there was a triple vortex in Birmingham; it was hard to keep them moving in the proper direction because of the level of activity in the city.

When Dana's husband came back he told her he was not going to put up with people calling there for me. At first though I tried to find another place to rent but I didn't find anything I could afford. So I also decided to move back to Indiana.

I called White Feather and she came to get me. Then my grandmother died and I was trying to get back in time for the funeral but didn't make it. When White Feather arrived, we started loading her van; she had traded her truck for a van because her truck was in constant need of repair. She also said she was returning the favor to me for letting her stay at the house for free and even for helping her get away from Scare Crow.

We packed all we could that night and decided to finish up and travel the next day. The following morning came and White Feather wanted to get a bath before we finished loading the van with the rest of my things. I was in the kitchen washing the dishes from breakfast. After I let the water out, I finished packing them in boxes. As I went to the sink to get something, a loud growling sound came up out of the sink and said something to me. I was stunned.

I went to the other room and in a few minutes White Feather came out of the bathroom and she looked at me and said, "You're grey; what happened?"

I told her and she started saying the clearing prayers with me and then said, "We are now going to see this thing shrivel up into a small ball and disappear."

So we did and it went away. We grabbed Maggie and Kitty Cat and left. I think I slept for almost two days when I got back to Indiana.

I had heard about another psychic fair; this one was in Evansville. I met a few people that seemed interested in my readings and the clearings that I did with Spirit.

It was at this time that I met Lionel and Ellen. They came to me for a reading; and afterwards, they asked me to be their teacher. So I asked them what they wanted to learn because they already gave readings to others. In fact, they were already giving readings at that fair.

They wanted to know how to turn the vortices and perform the clearing work on people, animals, buildings and land. So I told them that I would teach them what I could so they could go other places and help others. I told them what I could and took them on some of the jobs that Spirit led me too.

Lionel was the host of a radio program and he invited me to be on one of the shows. The listeners who called in said that what I had told them helped them with some issues that they were having.

There was another man who hosted a local television show who also invited me to be a guest on his show. Angel went with me to this show so the host asked both of us to channel the spirit guides on the show, and we agreed.

I channeled Mafu and Angel channeled Mary, Mother of Jesus. In the taping we heard doves cooing. On one of the shows we demonstrated how the clearings worked. We also told viewers how to check their hands to see if they had any negative spirits or earth bounds attached to them. We told the people to say the prayer with us.

Then the show's host said, "Sha `La is leaving town for a few weeks and if anyone out there needs a clearing call me, and since I see how she does it, I can do it for you."

This caught me off-guard.

"There is a lot more to it," I explained to him when we were off-the-air.

"It can't be that hard," he said.

"You don't know what you're doing," I said.

"Whatever," he said and then left.

Now here was an example of people needing help and others using their ego to say they knew what they are doing. People really need to discern who they deal with. Just as it says in the Bible; you have to discern the charlatans from the ones who really walk the talk. I try to do my best at walking my talk everyday.

Going Back to Alabama

I was now asked to come back to Birmingham and channel at the house of a lady named Irene. During the channeling session, Spirit told us to watch certain movies; that the movies would bring a certain energy we needed to assist us in shifting our energies.

I spent a few days at Irene's house and we watched the movies; and as we were watching them, we all saw lights and symbols floating in the air. We felt like we were being downloaded with some special information. We watched one show called "The Visitor."

I heard Spirit say, "Hold your hands out and receive."

We did and it looked like different colored crystals in our hands. Then we heard that the media was going to put information out so the general public could receive on different levels. It would come through different programs and the information would be input through our brain waves to help us on a subconscious level so that when the hard times came we would know what to do. Although the information was accurate, it might come through in the form of science fiction because a lot of people wouldn't believe it right now. So it had to be presented in a way that would reach the masses on multiple levels.

A good example of this was the movie "The Fifth Element" where the four elements of earth, wind, water and fire were connected with the fifth one: Love.

Irene felt that because our society was based on fear and violence through the masculine energy it was now time on Earth to return to the feminine vibration which carried more love. Considering the world was based on male power, that is, it was based on large ego and negativity or control, it should now return to the female power that is based on soul and heart. This is needed so things may be resolved through understanding instead of depression and oppression. Love comes more from the heart and things can be resolved far more easily and quickly through the Love vibration.

And speaking of love and gratitude, we all need to tap into our inner source to our own potential of knowledge and capabilities to bring forth our true selves because we all have these capabilities on some level or another.

Meditation is a valuable and valid energy we all need to practice to help tap into our own capabilities and spiritual gifts, our brain power and other levels of self that are seeking expansion. Our conscious is the connector between the Divine element of self and the ego self. One must be willing to accept themselves on all of these levels to attain their true self.

Irene helped me to connect with some other folks. One man was ill and while we worked on him in a class-like setting, Irene, myself, and some of the others, sensed he was being poisoned by his wife.

One of the students said, "Now that we are making you aware of the situation, it is up to you if you proceed by following up with some medical tests."

Then it was suggested that he look further into the situation because his wife had just taken out a large insurance policy on him. We reminded him that he had free will on whether to follow up on this or not.

A lot of U.F.O. investigators were coming to Birmingham at that time and it seemed like there was a lot of activity. We all felt that the extraterrestrials were using the statue Vulcan as a signal point.

Irene became interested in her past lives. She wanted to know why she had this karma with ex-husbands. She and one of her ex-husbands shared a previous life where he saw her bring a goose back to life. Believing her to be a witch, he had her burned at the stake. Because he misjudged her, and because she had actually been an innocent and a healer, he was to work out that karma with her in this life.

We all come together for many reasons. Some come in for balancing a lot of karma, others come here to correct and balance being misjudged or misinterpreted for whatever reason. It is up to each individual to bring forth the truth in all situations and then call it like it is.

In the clearing with Irene we had her to release the past lives with her husbands and the reasons they had done what they had.

When the memory is deleted the individual can move on and not feel guilty or embarrassed any longer.

In another lady's session she had to release multiple life times with this one other lady; it seemed in her records she kept repeating the same pattern. In other words, she didn't learn the lesson. So once we had her to state a series of affirmations then the program or "broken record" was removed and she felt a great deal better. She reported to us a while later that she saw the lady she had had trouble with throughout the years in this life and since the clearing they had begun talking again and even had a pleasant lunch together.

So once a root connector is dissolved through an energy clearing it can also be felt by the other person. And peace can come in between the people or situation, or even an animal.

I had a message from Spirit that Pat needed another clearing. She had received them before but sometimes things happen over a period of time that suggest or even require someone to have another one. I call them "upgrades" or "tune-ups." Anyway, she said she had had this pain in her right hip for a while and that was what I might have been picking up on. So we proceeded with the clearing and it appeared to me that she had energy that looked like hooks in her. I was hearing from my guides that some one stuck this in her and was draining her energies and that these "hooks" also had an attachment, like some sort of entity. All of a sudden this big entity came out and I ask her how that felt to her.

"Did you not hear that?" she asked. "It was like a big growl."

"Yes."

"What was that?" she asked.

I gave her a description of the big hairy entity. I told her Metatron, the Archangel took it. She then confirmed the pain had left. She said the growl had started at her pelvic area and came out of her mouth.

The Angels and guides finished up and she was better.

"Why didn't you tell me about the pain before now?" I asked.

"I just thought it was a pain from the car wreck," she said. "I've had the pain for over a year and a half."

Seeing the Dalai Lama

I returned to Indiana. White Feather and Jason were getting along but it seemed that when I was there the energy would change and there would be difficulties. I don't know if there were too many females in one house or what.

At the time, I wished I had money to get a motor home, or something where I didn't have to be there. But then my van started messing up and Jason was having a hard time getting work and even if he found some work he didn't have a way to travel back and forth.

White Feather made some remark about him needing to get out and walk to a job.

"Are you crazy?" I said. "He already has problems with his back and we live twenty miles from the nearest factory."

The day before she had also asked me to go see the Dalai Lama. I didn't want to go at that point. I started feeling sick and Jason came in and asked if I wanted him to carry out some Reiki on me. I told him he could.

"I call on all your guides," he said and then started naming them.

I was surprised that he remembered them all. I was proud of him. In a little while White Feather came in and apologized to us for her statements. She and Jason took me in the other room where I had my massage table set up and Jason helped me get on it and lay down. Both of them started praying for me. It took almost an hour before I began to feel better.

Jason suggested that I go on to Bloomington with White Feather to see the Dalai Lama.

Well, she and I went and as we walked down this path toward this huge white tent, I heard Spirit say, "You are walking the path of all religions."

I could see them in my mind's eye and it was strange. I told White Feather what I saw. She asked me what I was supposed to do once we arrived.

I asked Spirit and God said, "We are shifting the energies through time because there will be another war and it will start in New York City.

"A great devastation will take place; many people will die. All religions will come together at that time. Only then will more people come closer to me."

I said, "Why don't people wake up and just come closer to you instead of having to have something devastating happen?"

God said, "I wish they would; it would be better for all if they did. But the people are in the United States now and will soon attack."

I said, "Is that why I have been feeling that they have also placed bombs in the fault lines?"

"Yes," He said. "But this will be in the air and tall buildings will fall to the ground."

"Is there any way I can stop it?" I asked.

"You can call and warn certain people but they will not listen to you," He said. "Do not worry; we are preparing for this moment and you will have to go to New York and pray for their souls to be released."

"When?" I asked.

"When I tell you."

White Feather and I walked on into the tent and sat down. I told her maybe something would happen that would change what I heard. Maybe the Dalai Lama could.

I heard, "He's been told many things from God and even his words would not help. Because people listen for only a few moments and if they don't feel the impact they won't follow through because they feel like they still have time or it won't happen in their time. But it will; you and others will soon see what I am talking about."

"I believe you," I said. "Why did I need to come here to see or hear the Dalai Lama?"

God replied, "I sent you because I needed your energies to shift the path for the people."

"Okay, I'll be glad to," I said.

And God said, "I will use you for many shiftings for the earth."

"If people don't listen to this famous holy man, then who will they listen to?" I asked.

Then I heard, "Actions speak louder than words, sometimes."

We drove back home and a week later Jason and White Feather got in some sort of argument; she wanted to leave but had no place to go.

I prayed that God would help her find a suitable place that was inexpensive or a job where she could live with the people and also make some money.

Later that night a man from Alabama called me and said, "Sha `La I need your help. I have three boys and I need someone to come and help me with them while I work. Will you pray with me to find someone?"

"I have already prayed," I said, "and it looks like two prayers will be answered."

I told him about White Feather and her background of caring for people and how she needed a change of scenery from here.

"Would you like to talk to her?" I asked.

"Yes."

I took the phone into her room and she asked, "Who is that?"

"Your new boss," I said. "He needs someone to help with his children and you need a new location, so here, talk to him."

I gave her the phone and they talked. I went to watch TV while they were on the phone. She came back and told me that she would be leaving the next day.

"Well okay; be careful," I said.

The next day I helped her load up her van. She called me when she reached his home. She said the energies there were strange and asked what she should do. I told her how to go about clearing the place.

"Tell me what happens," I said.

Later she called and told me the next day the man's ex-wife drove by and saw her spreading a line of sacred corn meal around the place and called the police.

I started laughing.

"What did you say?" I asked.

"I just told them that I was doing a Native American ceremony to bless the land since I had just moved here," she said. "And they said okay, and drove on."

She sounded like she was a little panicky. I told her I would pray that she would be okay and she was. She worked for a few months there and then things began to change in the man's life so White Feather took a couple of jobs as a waitress and moved into an apartment with another person that I had met before. So she was satisfied.

It seemed like three or four times a year I would go to Alabama and each time I went I would meet new people. And Spirit would upgrade the energies of the clearing work and raise the vibrations and frequencies. Alabama had a key vibration within the earth so the energies would always need to shift there.

As I performed the work through different towns and states, each time it would seem a little more intense. I asked God with all the shifting would we ever be able to accomplish the goal of the transformation.

He said, "I have others doing similar work but on different scales and I feel it will be done as long as I have you and the others to anchor the light and do your part. Each has a part in the scheme of things."

"Kind of like an assembly line in a way," I said.
"Kind of, but more than that."

CHAPTER 19
∞
THE POWER OF THE SPOKEN WORD

God and the Universe take things literally; or maybe mankind set it up that way in order to learn. I know one of my lessons when Jesus came to teach was the power of the spoken word. It's in the Bible and in my personal lesson.

Jesus told me, "Today's lesson is the Power of the Spoken Word."

"I thought that meant it's for people who preach or do public speaking," I said.

"Wrong; it's everyday language," He said. "There is one word you have to quit using and it is the word *sorry*."

"Why?" I asked.

"Look at people's lives," He said, "Words can hold negative consequences and negative vibrations. *Everything you say 'I AM' to, you become.* The cellular memory is like a computer or tape recorder. People are confused a lot because they give themselves mixed signals. One day you may say 'I am worthy to have this or that' and the next day you will say 'I am worthless'. So your body asks 'What Am I?' and becomes depressed because of the confusion over the words you are choosing to use that apply yourself.

"Do not use the phrase 'I love so-and-so or this-or-that object to death'. If you do, you have just placed a negative energy on that person or pet or object or thing. Leave the word 'death' out of it. Please."

"What do we do when we accidentally use the word sorry or another negative?" I asked.

And Jesus said, "Say '***cancel clear***' right afterwards so it will be erased in the memory banks. ***Then replace it with a positive.***"

So he had me write down a long list of positive words and "I AM" affirmations and I said them every day and it began working. I tested it in different ways. When I was growing up everyone used to say I was ugly, so I felt - *and always thought* - I was ugly.

So I started saying I was beautiful and one day I met a stranger who remarked, "Now you're a pretty lady."

Then I ran into three men at a dance club and they had always thought I was ugly and I thought," I'll ask them to dance and see what they say."

They didn't know me at first, and then one of them said, "Hey, you know, when we were in school I thought you were pretty ugly; but now I think you're just plain pretty."

I laughed about that one.

I think if we are programmed to be a certain way then others will pick up on how or what we think of ourselves and *react the way we think*. I started noticing that more and more with people. So whatever we program, we receive, *so be very clear of what you want to convey to other people – and to your self.*

When I was working with people in God's Awakening Center, some of the people were calling me "mom" because I was the founder. And I would say "okay children." It wasn't long before my body started reacting. Because mothers nurture, my breasts started leaking milk. It was wild, so I had to talk to my body and ask people to stop calling me mom. I had to reprogram my body to be a teacher, not a "mom."

When you say "no" or "I don't want" be careful how you word that energy too. Because you can also receive what you really do not want. For instance, one day I was making a statement to this woman who was riding with me somewhere, and we were talking about men.

I said, "Well I surely don't want a man whose wife died and he's not over her yet or still grieving. And I don't want one that is going through some weird divorce."

I should have kept my mouth shut, because the first man who came into my life after that was the one with the wife that had died. That was a horrible nightmare. Then several months later I met a man going through the weird divorce.

So on this note watch what you say, and when you "order" something or someone up from the Universe be very specific. When you ask the Universe for a mate and don't want a smoker for instance, or any other "don't wants", you have to word it like this:

"I prefer a non-smoker (or non-whatever)."

This will keep your desires accurate instead of getting a potential mate that you don't really want. However, if the person has most of the qualities you are looking for, then say you would like someone who is willing to quit smoking (or whatever the case maybe) easily and that they have an easy time changing or stopping the habit.

Practice on yourself and see the difference in how you feel and how others see you or feel about you. Do not let others put you down; don't accept it. Always say "I am better than that."

Misery loves company and if a person is not willing to change their habits than they don't want you to change your habits either. So find people that are more positive or ask the Universe to place you in a more positive place and around more positive people. Remember, God grants people survival. And one way to survive is to use the proper words to continue to survive – or better yet, thrive!

I was in a nightmare relationship for several weeks and one day I just asked God, "Do you want me to survive?"

"Yes," He said. "Now have you learned your lesson?"

"Yes."

"Abandon the project and leave," He said. "Even though I offered help to this person, some people refuse to accept the help; they prefer to live on drama and wish to drag others down with them."

Jesus said, "Sometimes you just have to wipe your feet and move on because there are other people out there that will need your help and will accept it."

So I called White Feather, and while we talked, she said, "I am hearing I need to come and get you so you can get away for a little while."

So she came from Alabama, this time to get me from Indiana. It was wild; we were always rescuing each other. As soon as I stepped out of her van in Alabama, I found a seven leaf clover.

"Maybe now my luck will improve," I thought.

I was there a couple of weeks when I called some people to see if anyone needed any readings or clearings. One night I gave a channeling session.

And one man who came to the session said, "You know I am a dragon spirit."

"Oh really?" I asked.

Well, I knew there were a lot of different species of spirits that lived in the design of the human body. And I could see his spirit. Now, I have encountered many beings. It's like living in a Star Wars movie. And they are out there. Jesus showed me this several years ago. Because of our relatively simple design, I guess it's easier for the spirits of alien species to enter the human body.

Another man came and asked for a clearing. I will describe the clearing process a little more now.

Every cell in the body holds memory, from the time the spirit was first a spirit or soul in the beginning. Through different incarnations the spirit holds memory of each one that he or she needs to work out karma. Karma can be with self or with another or many.

The body has gene pool programs. For instance, if diabetes are in the family history, it may be that a certain cell says, "Okay at age fifty, the body will pro-

duce diabetes." And this will set up a series of events that will lead to death in this dimension, unless it is changed by prayer or intent; or, it may be changed by a series of energies that the person may seek out to change that outcome, maybe to live a little longer so they can work on their ascension process, or to complete unfinished business that they had set up.

Once the body and spirit meet up with each other it becomes a package deal. So you now have a combination of things to work through.

When God told me to do the clearings, he said everyone had a chance to clear the karma before their death so they could live longer or be more productive. In this way, some people nearing the end of their life now have the opportunity to have a clearing to settle a karmic debt from the past in any issue.

He said, "I will grant people pardon and amnesty for past sin. Sin is what you do to harm self or another."

So God really wants everyone to ascend. Ascension is working with the self to produce a happier and healthier body and live a more productive life and lifestyle, to shed the worries, doubt and fears that are set up on this dimension and become more positive and productive long term. God said there is hope for everyone.

So in the procedure of what I call the Clearing, through prayer and affirmations, we can help the person shed some or a large amount of the excess baggage, and or spirits that may be attached.

I put the hands together in a prayer position and if one or more of the fingers are uneven than they have a spirit attachment that needs to be prayed over. Or if someone has a pain that moves, it's a negative spirit. And then we have found that some like to hide and we have to run them out on another level.

I start my prayer by calling on God, Goddess, Jesus, Archangels and Guides, and especially Mother Earth, who I call Singing Fawn. She said that is one of her names. I know some people call her Gaia and other names, but Singing Fawn is one too.

After I call on all of them to come in, I start the clearing prayer. The prayer is spoken this way:

"Father, Mother God, Infinite Intelligence, Master Jesus, Archangels, Healing Angels and Guides, I ask for the Light to come in over this area (a vicinity or a variable radius, depending on the size that Spirit tells me) and over this person, (if I have a person or animal on the table, or by their name).

I then ask Singing Fawn (Mother Earth) to release the gravitational pull for the unseen.

Then I have the person to repeat after me:

"From my Higher Self, Christ Light, earth body of my being, I declare my freedom and free will now. All earth bound entities, demonic and satanic forces, negative thought forms, negative space and earth beings, poltergeists, ghouls, watchers, astral beings, multiple souls, dementers, incubus, succubus, separates, goblins, gargoyles, linamese, hillibees, sillibbees, nillibees, quillibees, millibees, trillibbess, reptilians, all species, ranks and serial numbers, vampires, were-wolves, animals, insects, amphibians, all ocean urchins and creatures, harpies, banshees, juggernauts, jackals, monsters of all natures all other seen and un-seen, labeled and unlabeled with all hexes, spells, curses, voodoo, black magic, santeria, hoodoo, and any other form of negative wishes sent against me, I com-mand you and banish you out of my plane of existence now and forever in the name of the Father, Son, Holy Spirit and the I Am of my Self. So be it, Amen."

Then we proceed in the area of the feet which represent Laws and Judgment over self, then the knees, which represent bending, bowing, begging, pleading, crying, crawling, and being drug through the dirt.

Then I move to the first chakra, which is the root, and represents root causes. The root chakra also represents all laws and judgment over sexuality, sensuality, procreation, and survival.

Then the second charka; it corresponds to the spleen, fears, doubts, worry, and insecurity.

Then the third charka which corresponds to the solar plexus and is tied to all emotional baggage and career issues.

Then it is on to the fourth charka, or the area of the heart. The area of the heart symbolizes all heart emotion, the releasing of people, places, things, ani-mals, etc, that have bothered or hindered them from positive expression, or has caused them wrong for any reason. They go through the forgiveness process and forgive self for holding on to the emotion.

I proceed to the fifth charka. This covers the throat, communication, expres-sion, and bottled-up levels of speaking on different levels.

At the sixth charka, I work with the Third Eye, the all-seeing. This deals with seeing the future, forgiving the past and moving forward.

The seventh charka is the crown chakra. It represents the all-knowing, the con-nection to God or Higher Self and the Universe, Angels, and Guides.

After we go through the basic affirmations, we address the issues of the per-son. And we start releasing personal issues, while the Angels and I look into the different levels of the bodies, to see where "programs" are stuck or spirits are hiding.

The body is vibrating extremely fast when the person's spirit is lifted up and put into a light cylinder and another vibration of light is placed around the body clearing both energies at different speeds and on different frequencies.

One of my gifts is to see inter-dimensionally, on the many levels of etheric bodies and other levels beyond the physical. Throughout the clearing many symbols cover the body. First in the geometric system is the shape of the pyramid, after that is cleared, then other shapes appear over the body, like circles, stars, mountains and oceans.

We have grid lines, geometric symbols, and so many layers that programs can get stuck on many of them. When a person goes through a clearing it's like peeling an onion.

As I watch the spirit "time machine" and the different energies that God has the Angels work with, it is so amazing.

I ask the people what they are feeling and some just say they're relaxed and lighter and others that are more sensitive say they feel tingling, warm, cool, and some have felt other sensations.

But after the Angels have taken all that the body will allow at that point in time then the energies start slowing down and the new vibrations are put in place, sort of like a sound system, except in this case cylinders of light that make up sound, grids, transformers, circuits, batteries, and wires are put into place. Or you could view it as a computer being upgraded.

I then clear the adrenals, the lymphatic system and then balance the chakras and meridians.

Then the spirit is placed back into the body renewed and restored for that session. It is up to the person to perform self-maintenance and work to stay positive so that negative programs do not re-enter and stay.

And then I say a closing prayer.

God has upgraded the body so much by now, I am amazed every time.

White Feather Returns to Indiana

White Feather's roommate had moved and later she received a phone call that her former roommate was coming back, except this time with more friends. That didn't sit well with White Feather.

I told her she could come back to my house and get a job where she could save some money to get an apartment. We had apologized to each other for the stress and outburst before she moved. I helped her load up her van and off we went.

Jason had taken a job requiring a little traveling with a small company that built cabinets.

I asked Spirit if it was okay for me to receive some job training and what I should take.

Spirit said, "Go over to the training facility and we will help set it up for you."

So I did and the lady named off several different jobs and I thought about going back to cosmetology school, but then she said, "Hypnosis."

And out of my mouth came, "That's it! Hypnosis."

I said silently to Spirit, "Are you sure?" and they said, "Yes, trust us."

"Okay," I said and told her to sign me up, and she did.

I told White Feather about it and she asked how much it would cost.

So we called to find out and they told us and said we could make payments if we needed.

I had mine set up but White Feather didn't. But they went ahead and made arrangements for both of us to go at the same time. It was offered over six to eight weekends and was a class I would never forget.

Because of the clearing work, I had been investigating more of the human anatomy and seeing through different levels how and where the body stored things. And even when I channeled, Spirit only used a certain part of my brain, and brain waves.

But when we practiced hypnosis the energy would go and enter different sections and corridors of the brain, like it was deep in the middle.

It was also a place to release more old memories of past lives. My body would go through different shifts in class; it was embarrassing but I couldn't help it.

Some woman went to the teacher about me, asking, "Is she having seizures?"

"I understand Sha `La has different reactions to things," he said. "She'll be fine."

Not too many people will ever understand me. My body had control, not my consciousness.

One weekend the teacher asked me, "Could your guides control it a little bit more? These other people are becoming nervous."

I said, "I asked them and they said I had to process and release some more past issues."

And my body just went in to automatic shifting. I apologized; that's all I could do.

Some grew accustomed to me but I never knew what would happen next. The teacher did give us a weight loss program and I dropped back down to a size eleven. So that was a good thing.

Meeting Peter

About this same time, Spirit told me – insisted actually – to go out dancing; so I called up Angel to see if she wanted to go, and then I called White Feather to see if she wanted to join us. So we all met at this night club. At first no one asked us to dance although I thought at least someone would have danced with Angel by then. But no one asked either one of us.

The music changed to a much faster beat and suddenly this man walked up and asked Angel to dance.

"I don't dance to this music very well, but she does," she said pointing to me.

So he asked if I wanted to dance. I thought what the heck, I might as well. So I danced with him, and then Angel slow danced with him, and then when White Feather joined us, she danced with him too. So the rest of the night he took turns dancing with all three of us. He said his name was Peter, it was his birthday and he was going through a divorce.

I thought, "Oh no! Is this why you wanted me to come out tonight Spirit?"

And of course they said, "Yes."

Although he seemed more interested in the other two, Spirit said he would end up with me.

"Does he have to?" I asked.

They said, "No, but he will."

"Whatever," was all I thought.

It came time for me to dance with him again. The song ended and we stayed on the dance floor for the next dance. Suddenly Peter collapsed and fell to the floor; he said that his legs gave out because of his back problems. It was around one o'clock in the morning. I helped him up off the dance floor and made him sit down. While we were sitting and talking, Spirit told me to tell him I studied massage and to tell him that I would give him a massage.

I asked, "Do what?"

They said it again.

So I told Peter, and asked if he wanted a massage. He asked me how much it was going to cost him. I told him I would do it for his birthday and because he was nice enough to dance with all of us. As we were leaving Spirit "told" me to hand Peter a business card. I gave him my business card and asked him to call me.

"I'll set aside some time to give you a massage for your back."

He took the card and said he would call to set up a time for the massage. I was embarrassed again because I thought that he thought I was coming on to him.

I thought to myself, "Well Spirit, you've got me in a pickle now."

"He will need you in the future," they said.

"Whatever."

We all went our separate ways and I just forgot about it. Three weeks later I was called again to go out of town to work when Peter called. I told him to call back in a few days and we would set up a time. When he called back we told him to come on over because all three of us was there at the same time.

While we worked on his back, White Feather and Angel held the energies for the other part of the clearing. He said it actually helped.

As it turned out, he was living with one of his brothers and trying to reunite with his wife before the divorce went through; he also had two children. And he wanted the marriage to work because of them. But despite the circumstances, his wife didn't really want him.

I told him I would do what I could in prayer to see if she would change her mind to take him back. But she misunderstood our involvement and thought we were his new girlfriends. He wanted us to counsel her as well. I told him we would make the effort but when it came time to meet she changed her mind and missed the appointment.

One day Peter and White Feather went to lunch and he shared what was happening with his life. When he returned to my house, Angel and I told him we would be his friends and that way he could have some people to talk with. He agreed to just being friends.

We prayed for him and his wife to get back together because that is what he wanted. So then I figured that Spirit just wanted us to help him in that way, to be listeners and give him advice as time when on. And since we did that and he knew how to work on cars, that maybe in exchange he would be our mechanic. That was okay then with me.

But as time progressed the situation became worse for both of them. So Peter would ask to come visit and talk. If I wasn't busy or needed something done that I couldn't do without help, then he would come over and talk or fix something, whether it was the van or something in the house.

I asked him one day if he wanted to go with me to a house that had some ghosts that needed to be crossed over and he said he would take me. He didn't say much more.

Then I needed to go to Alabama and he said, "If you fly down, I can come and get you. Since you're having a channeling session I would like to see that."

Well, he arrived there just in time; and I think the session scared him a little. Again he didn't say much afterwards.

And even though we were only friends, I still wanted him to know something of the work that I did. Besides, I figured he must need to know something about the spirit world since they told me to be his friend.

I told him about his angels and guides and explained the things to him the best I could of what I knew about the spirit world.

I was to go from Alabama to Cherokee, North Carolina, the place I had received an eagle staff and perform some more work after that, so he took me up there.

I said to him, "Hold on to this while I perform this other part of the prayer."

He couldn't believe the energy that ran through it.

"This feels like electricity," he said, "and it's strong."

"Oh yes, just stand there then since Spirit is using you for this part instead of me," I told him.

"I don't know if I can hold on or not," he said.

"It will be over with soon," I told him.

After that he was truly amazed. I figured if that didn't scare him nothing would. But he kept calling me. Maybe no one else was willing to listen to his complaints about the ex-wife.

One evening I became bored and I told him we needed to go play bingo. He agreed and so we began playing bingo once a week if we had the money. I told him at least he was getting out and doing something.

When White Feather was there she would talk to him because I was beginning to tire more easily. I wasn't feeling well.

Some things were pending with Uncle Billy Ray and after they were cleared up, he and White Feather started dating again. Soon after, Uncle Billy Ray moved in with us and then he and White Feather began looking for an apartment.

Peter was over that night and I became very sick. So I went to the hospital. Jason was out of town working; that was in December of 2000.

The doctor gave me a prescription and in January, when I went in for a physical, he gave me some other medicine that caused me to have an allergic reaction. I had to go to the hospital again; except this time I stayed for a few days. Jason came home a nervous wreck because he thought I was dying.

Since we didn't have normal heat for that old house, we had to use kerosene and electric heaters which made the electric bill very high. I guess the fumes had been making me sick. I had a rough winter. During that time, Pete brought me a vapor machine and that helped some.

I began to feel a little better and then one evening he said, "Let's get out and go to bingo or a movie."

By this time, his ex-wife-to-be was not budging to let him come back but she did want him to come and cut the grass and perform chores.

My mom had asked us to go out that evening so we met her at a club. After we had danced a few times Pete looked in my eyes and kissed me.

"What are you doing?" I asked.

"I don't know but I am feeling closer to you," he said.

"Let's not get carried away," I warned.

One of his uncles sold rugs and blankets on the side of the road and he had told Peter if he ever needed money he would let him sell some of the rugs. So Pete asked me to help him, and we picked-up some of the rugs and traveled to a different spot to sell them. I didn't care for it much, mainly because some people tried to steal them from us. We did that for a few months and I finally told him it wasn't worth it, so we quit.

A woman I knew that used to come to the church called me and said she had met a lady in North Carolina. She wanted me to meet this woman because she felt that we had several things in common.

"I told her about you," she said, "and she said she could arrange for some clients if you came to her home and the two of you became acquainted."

I told her that would be fine. So I called the woman, her name was Lilu, and we made arrangements for Peter and I to go and meet her and her husband.

When we arrived, we found she had about five people gathered there. We shared a lot about how we worked with the spirit world. She asked me if I could attune her to Reiki and teach her how to perform the clearing. I told her I could. Peter and I visited there a couple of times during a two month period.

Not long after that, Peter's brother's girlfriend asked Peter to leave their home and give them some space. So I let him bring over his little truck that had a camper on it and park it in my driveway. He would sleep in it and then come in the house to eat and take a shower.

I was called to Kentucky to clear a house and Peter and I went. During the clearing, the ghost man refused to leave the house. I did everything I could think of and then the woman said, "Tell him that if he quits scaring my cat then he can stay."

"I have done too many things to go over and be judged," the ghost man said. "All of you here will have a day when Black Tuesday will come soon and you will be busy with a lot of things. I am the least of your worries. This world will change and everyone better start looking into more than just themselves."

"What do you mean?" I asked.

"You already know it is coming, you just don't know when," he said.

"Do you?"

"Yes," he said, "the third world war will start in New York City. The murderers are already here and you won't be able to stop them.

"First they will bomb a place and then there will be large buildings side-by-side to fall and many people will die. Then the world will change for a while but it will continue until the end of time."

I told the people there what the spirit had said.

"If any of you know anyone that is in charge of things warn them," I said. "We can at least tell the Army people."

We mentioned it to some sergeants and other people with higher ranks but they thought I was on drugs or something.

Getting Bear

Peter and I were sitting at the kitchen table talking over learning about Black Tuesday from the ghost man when we heard whimpering at the door. My mom's dogs had pups and there were two left. They were at the door wanting something to eat. I tried to get them to come in but they wouldn't, so I gave them something to eat and drink outside. The next day they were sitting in my mom's driveway looking at me so I took them something.

The next evening we heard a scream and we ran outside and discovered that a truck had hit the little brown one. We went to get it out of the road and the truck had spun away. I wrapped it in a towel and took it into my mom's and we said some prayers. I didn't have any money for a veterinarian.

My mom said to just leave the pup and see how it was in the morning. That night I saw the pup's spirit leaving; it was rising up and I saw wings so I knew it was dying.

I told Peter and he said, "All I have is a little money left on a credit card."

"What should we do?" I asked.

He said, "Go and get him and we'll take him to the vet."

So we did but the vet acted ignorant; she wanted to do all this exploratory surgery on him. Peter told her not to. She wound up charging Peter several hundred dollars for a few injections for pain.

Peter called his uncle and the uncle told him to take the pup to his veterinarian in Kentucky. So we called the vet and took him there. He said he had a broken leg and pelvis, and that his hip joint had pulled away.

So first they put a cast on him, then a month later they performed surgery and only charged three hundred dollars.

My nephew Brian said he had claimed the pup but that we could keep him. He also said his name was Bear. We put some pads down on the floor and he used them to drag himself to the door to go outside.

I tried to get the little female pup to stay in the house with him because I felt like he was scared, but she wouldn't stay. Then my mom gave her to one of her friends. I don't know what ever happened to the pup. And then later, when my mom gave the father away, the mother dog ran away. It was really strange. The father was the terrier that had been in the big flood but swam to safety and was returned to my mom.

Peter said, "Well Bear, I guess you're ours."

When we traveled, I would tell Bear he was now a traveling dog and he was going to be okay and that I needed for him to be quiet when we were in the hotel rooms. And he was. I would wrap him in a blanket to carry him into a hotel.

Once a female security guard asked if she could see my baby and I said, "Well he's sick and has a broken leg."

So she said she understood.

He was quiet and still the whole time. I thanked him; and then I fixed a pallet for him in the floor with the blanket. He was, and still is, a good dog.

He would get in between me and Peter during disagreements and whimper because he didn't want us to argue.

When I drove with Bear in the car, I would sing along with the radio and he would sing with me. He also wanted to wear the seatbelt. No one told him he had to have one. He just let you know to put one on him too. He would shake and push his body up to the back of the seat and nudge at the seat belt. When I put it around him and buckled him in he would relax like he knew everything was okay.

Once, God told me that I needed to move to Tennessee. And I told Peter about it and he said after his divorce was final we would go there and buy a trailer. I agreed to wait on the move. We did visit the Smokey Mountains and I really wanted to move there but it was too expensive.

About this time, I wasn't feeling well, and I heard Spirit say "Jefferson City." I thought they said Jeffersonville which is a town in Indiana. But Peter turned off the exit while I was lying down and when I asked him where he was going he said Jefferson City. (I thought I must have dropped off to sleep and slept far longer than I realized because I thought we were back in Indiana).

He said, "No, we're still in Tennessee."

So I tried to sit up.

"I'm going to see if we can go ahead and get something to live in and move there," he said.

I said, "Spirit said a man that wears a cross would help us find a place."

And sure enough, we met a man who told Peter to bring him back some paperwork and he'd help him get a mobile home. He didn't have enough credit to buy any land so we had to rent a spot. We were told it would take three or four weeks to get everything processed and to put the trailer in the park.

We were now entering September of 2001.

Moving and 9/11

I awoke as I heard God say, "Today is Black Tuesday."

"What can I do?" I asked.

"Nothing," He said. "It is destiny."

About half an hour later my friend Pat called me and said, "Do you have the television on?"

"No."

"Turn it on," she said. "They just ran an airplane into one of the twin towers."

I hadn't even reached the television when she said, "Oh my God! Another one is going to hit! They say there are three."

"No, four," I said. "But it won't hit. Something is going to intervene."

And of course the people did.

God said, "People will have to come to me now. That's the only way many will survive."

Peter called me from Indiana; he was a sergeant in the reserves.

"I have to stay here all night," he said. "Everything is on red alert."

"Okay, but be careful," I said.

So our move to the mobile home was also delayed because he had to be there every day instead of just the once a month weekend.

October came, and Lilu got in touch with me to come back to North Carolina. There was a man that came for a clearing. Lilu was helping me at that time and she was seeing different things and I saw what look like pieces of spirits, like they were shattered.

"I see these energies and pieces of spirit," I told her. "I am hearing a name… and another name…and another name."

The man who came for the clearing started crying.

"The name you just spoke is my friend that was killed in the first tower building that was hit in nine-eleven," he said. "We had just finished brunch when he went into the building. I just saw dust and pieces of the building coming down and I ran and I ran until I found a place to get between two other buildings; it was awful. – My friend was killed."

I gave him a tissue.

"Okay God, what's the deal with this?" I asked.

"This is why I want you to go to New York in December," He said. "And be there on the eleventh. You will ask Lilu to go with you and pray the other ones that became splintered over to this side."

When the two planes collided they broke the "sound barrier" of the souls, and spirits of the people flew everywhere.

"Some of the psychics said that they went there and the Angels had already carried the spirits over to the light."

"Not all did as you can see," He said.

"I see," I said. "So where will I go there to do the work?"

He said, "You will take what I tell you and stand in Times Square on the point. We will use the old clock and the new clock to shift time so we can call all the pieces to the light."

We finished with the man's clearing and Lilu helped me with a couple of others and then I left. I returned to Indiana and Peter and I loaded up my van and his truck and proceeded to move to Tennessee. It was a little difficult. Jason finally moved down with us.

Jason didn't stay but a few months and then he went back to Indiana. But before he left, he watched the cat and Thor while we went to New York. White Feather offered us the use of her van.

So God had me travel to Alabama and do a little work to get the money to go to New York; then Peter and I went to North Carolina and picked up Lilu and then we left on our mission.

On the way, some spirit from the dark side jumped in the van and attacked me; I had to pull over and Lilu had to help get it off me and then it went to her. Finally, we expelled it from the van. Peter started driving then so we could keep the prayers going until we got to New Jersey and got a room; then we had to clear the room. We then went to a Japanese restaurant.

The next morning we got up early and headed to Times Square. The people were so busy; taxies pulling in and out in front us. I felt like I was suffocating because of all of the concrete; everywhere I looked I couldn't see anything but concrete.

Peter and Lilu were okay.

"I could live here," Lilu said.

"Not me," I said. "I have to have my trees."

We finally found a parking place around seven or eight blocks away from the point where we were to stand. We gathered up our stuff and started walking and we went through a subway station and street after street.

I thought, "These are awfully long blocks."

I became tired, especially since I had a hard time breathing. I also think it was partially caused by the energies there, particularly after what had happened and since I was so sensitive to energy anyway.

We finally reached Times Square and saw several people putting up a tall Christmas tree.

I said, "Thank God, I can focus on that and breathe."

Finally my lungs quit hurting. We drew our circle to stand in and placed the Bible and other things God told me to bring inside the circle. I couldn't see the old clock anywhere that had been in my vision. That was the first time I had ever been somewhere and didn't know what to expect.

So I saw the new type clock where the statue of the man was. We faced that direction first and started saying our prayers for the fragments of the souls, spirits and others that might be earth bound there for whatever timeframe to come so they could go to the light and be with God.

We said a long prayer and after a while each of us heard at the same time to "turn around" and we looked at each other to make sure we heard it together and we had, so we all three turned around and then I saw the big clock diagonally across from the new one. So in a different way they lined up.

And as we continued praying, I saw Jesus in the sky and he parted the sky like curtains; then I saw the spirits and pieces of spirits go toward him but they looked like swarms of bees or something.

Peter said, "I hear crying and screaming."

We had a tape recorder on the ground but we wouldn't know until later that it had captured sounds of the crying and screaming.

Lilu could see the spirits and hear them too. As I stood there watching what was going on in the spirit world I didn't pay attention to what was going on around me with other physical people.

I felt a rumbling under my feet but Peter said it was probably a subway train. It felt like an earthquake. After a while, I think just a few hours, I heard "End the Prayer" and we did. Then I came back to the physical realm and I saw people putting lights on the Christmas tree.

We asked a woman if she would take our picture. She said yes and we gave her our cameras. We told them we were doing a Native American ceremony for the people that died and she thought that was nice.

One guy asked me if my staff was a shaman healing staff and I said it was. He said he honored it and bowed and then thanked us for coming and praying.

I didn't know that other people were saying prayers at Ground Zero around the same time. I guess God coordinated it that way. We then were told by Spirit it was time for us to go, so we blessed the place and left. I hadn't even noticed that some people were on the street watching us.

When I am in the spirit world watching things I don't see or hear the realm of what we call our physical world.

We went into this restaurant that Lilu wanted to go to and had something to drink. Then we went to another one that was a little less expensive to buy some sandwiches to go. On the way back to the van we took some pictures of the area and in front of some places; I remember seeing a woman with green hair and she had a hair band made like rabbit ears on her head. I thought she was in the wrong season.

We were now going to Ground Zero. On the way we felt pain and sorrow, a lot of emotion. When we got there, Lilu got sick; I was in the back seat and Lilu was in the front and Peter was driving. I pulled the side van door open and saw the sight between the buildings. It was awful.

God told me to leave a couple of things on the ground so they could use them to anchor the light through the threads of the earth. I left a couple of pieces of jewelry with stones in them. Sometimes Spirit will use stones and things to reinforce the light through for the different vibration that is needed for the different layers and dimensions of a place that needs to be cleared.

As we left, we said more prayers for the people's families and friends to help them to adjust and cope with all that had happened.

We got back on the road and Peter wanted to go to Oneida to see his mom since we were already up that way. So we started and somewhere in New Jersey we were pulled over by the police. Peter had been speeding a little. He had a beard and they thought at first he might be a terrorist. The policeman asked Peter to step out of the car and get in his.

Then the policeman came back and asked us if we knew Peter and what we were doing up that way. So I told him. He asked Lilu her name and if she really knew Peter. She said she did. Peter had his food on the console and she had hers in her hand. The policeman then asked Lilu where she was from.

She said, "Hungary."

The policeman gave her a funny look and then said, "Yes ma'am, I see you are; go ahead and eat."

I got tickled. He asked me to open my door and asked me if I knew Peter and I said yes and I told him what we were doing in New York, and that we were on our way to his mother's.

He said Peter's license was suspended in New York and that I would have to drive if I had a driver's license. I told him I did and then I showed him.

"You must be proud of your heritage," he said.

"Yes, I am," I said.

Then he said, "Well, drive safe, but don't let him drive."

"Yes, officer."

Then he left and Peter came around and got in my seat. I was telling him what had happened and then it hit me about him thinking Lilu wanted to eat instead of telling him where she was from, but she really had been telling him where she was from. We all started laughing; I laughed so hard all my make-up ran down my face.

We finally got to Peter's mom's apartment and stayed the night and shared with her what we did. We turned the tape on to see if anything was on it and that's when we realized that we were hearing the screams and crying of the peoples' spirits and souls. It was hurting my ears.

Peter said, "See, I knew I heard them. And Lilu said she did too."

"I am hearing we need to burn it," she said.

I did too; I really don't know why but we did. We said some more prayers and sent the energy to the light. We went to the store to get our pictures developed and when we looked through them we saw that this giant orb had been following us. We felt it was our guides protecting us. In one picture a big gold light was with us; and another photo featured a lot of red. We felt it was the negativity and anger that was still in the air there.

Going Home

Peter's mom wanted to come and stay with us for Christmas so he helped her drive while I drove Lilu home. I finally got home and Peter, his mom and I went to Indiana and picked up his daughter. I took White Feather's van back to her and shared with everyone about the trip and what had happened.

We spent our first Christmas in the trailer: Peter, Peter's daughter, his mom, Jason, Thor, Kitty Cat, Bear and me.

Jason wanted a pack of cigarettes and I went to the store to get him some, and Bear went with me. On the way, I saw a cigarette outlet and stopped and went in. The young woman behind the counter looked at me and noticed the crystal I had on and out of the blue she asked, "Do you give readings?"

"Yes; why?"

"My friend and I have been looking for someone to give us a reading."

I said, "I'll bring you a brochure with my phone number; it lists the services that I provide."

"Great!"

So I went to the car and got my brochure and gave it to her.

Bear and I then went to the grocery store and I bought a few things including a treat for Bear. He was leaning over the side of my seat. When I got in the vehicle he looked around me and then I saw there were men standing around staring at me.

"Are you married?" one of them asked.

"Yes."

"Well you sure are pretty."

"Well...thanks," I said.

He started moving closer to the vehicle and Bear pushed his head around mine and began growling.

"Don't come any closer," I warned, "He'll bite. What do you want?"

"I just want to talk to you," he said.

"I have to go home."

He kept coming closer and I was trying to get my other foot in the vehicle and get the thing started. Then Bear got in my lap and started growling louder.

"You better back off," I said. "He *will* bite."

He was slowly coming closer and I felt he wanted to harm me. I finally got the door locked and started the vehicle. The man kept walking towards me in slow motion then he had this strange look on his face and about a foot from the vehicle he stopped. And I left.

I just said, "Thank you Bear, for saving me."

That was a strange thing, but I am glad I had taken Bear with me.

2002

Jason returned to Indiana for a couple of months; but he didn't find any work so he came back down to Tennessee. There, he found a job in a furniture factory. Four months later he got his first new Saturn car. It only had three miles on it; that was in 2002.

A woman who wanted a reading called and said someone else she knew also wanted one. I set up an appointment with her. She sold products made by Melaleuca. I was guided to order some and they helped me feel better. The t-waves of my heart rhythm were inverted and I believe the herb helped to relieve this condition.

I still traveled the road to different places to perform clearings and give readings. Peter still went back and forth to Indiana to the reserves and to visit his children every month.

White Feather and Uncle Billy Ray decided to move to Tennessee. They managed a motel in Indiana. Eventually they grew tired of it and moved to Kodak, Tennessee. White Feather found employment at a hotel. Uncle Billy Ray did odd jobs. White Feather went on a few jobs with me when she had a few days off from her other work.

The year 2003 was spent about the same as the year before, traveling and working. White Feather and Uncle Billy Ray moved on to Moorsburg, by Cherokee Lake. They liked it there and she began working at Sears.

Peter spent a week in the reserves and while he was putting up a tent the tent pole fell on his head; I didn't hear from him for three days. I was really worried. He finally came to and had someone call me. After a few more days he came home.

A lady called me to invite me to a class on hospice so White Feather and I went and met some new people. Some were okay and others I didn't care for. But one introduced me to a woman that had an herb shop in Morristown. So she and I became acquainted and I worked there a little when she had someone that needed a clearing. White Feather filled in for her a few times when she went out of town.

CHAPTER 20

∞

ADVENTURES OUT WEST

Different things began to happen in 2004. I started teaching some classes at the herb shop. One particular morning that I was supposed to hold one, I was awakened by God saying, "Get up."

"What?" I said, trying to open my eyes.

I heard again, "Get up; there is an earthquake you need to do something about."

"Where is it?" I asked.

"California," God said.

"They have them all the time out there," I said.

"Not an eleven point nine," God said. "You have to shift it to a lower vibration to save some of the innocents out there."

"When am I going?"

"Soon."

"Where is the money coming from?"

"You find out soon."

"Okay."

I told Peter about it and when I went to class that night one of the women said, "I can confirm it because they discovered that there are large caverns filling up with lava from Yellow Stone to the Golden Gate Bridge. The geysers are draining."

"Holy cow," I said.

"We can't cause a panic," she said. "I don't know what they are going to do, except maybe to monitor them."

"Call me when I get on the road and let me know what is going on, okay?" I asked.

She said she would.

The next day I got a call from Alabama and people there needed me to do some clearing work.

God said, "There is your money to go."

"Okay."

So Peter and I went to Alabama.

I told the people in Alabama about it and one of the young men there said, "I want to go with you. My family is out that way and I have a friend in Oakland. You could spend the night at her house."

So we said that would be fine. We came back home and I had a few more people to see in Tennessee. One man there had so much negative energy my massage table broke. I couldn't fix it. Peter made several attempts. Nothing.

In the meantime, a woman from Arizona wanted me to come out and do a workshop and I told her what God wanted me to do and why.

"I guess God wants you to work here for the money to return on because I woke up and heard that you are to come here in two weeks and conduct a workshop," she said.

"Okay," I said. "I have to figure out how to get a new massage table though."

"Maybe you can order one and have it shipped here and it will be here when you arrive," she suggested.

"Let me see what I can do," I said.

The next phone call I received was from a lady in Tennessee who said, "Sha `La, my friend needs a clearing but she doesn't have any money; she wants to know if you could trade with her for a new massage table she owns."

I laughed and quickly said, "Bring it on."

Thank You God.

So the next day they came over. I asked her if she was sure about the massage table because if she needed it I could wait on the money.

"I'm sure," she said. "You need it more than I do and if I need one later I can order one. I had gotten this one but decided not to use it."

"Well, you can be the first one to lay on it," I offered, "and receive the first clearing on it."

I told her what had happened to the other one.

The next day I told Jason, along with the pets, that I loved him and we loaded up White Feather's van. She had loaned it to me once again.

God said, "You need to seed crystals along the way."

I had some but needed more so we stopped in Nashville and purchased some from a lady that collected them and sold them as a second business. I picked out the ones God said He wanted. I paid the lady and off the four of us went, Bear, Alex, Peter and myself.

We were guided to put the crystals around rest areas and train tracks, pay phones and water ways, for the flow and communication connections.

We went through terrible storms but we kept going until we couldn't drive any more and then found a hotel room. We stopped in Arizona at the home of a lady, named Bonnie, who was setting up the workshop. She let us stay there overnight then we got up and went on because we were on a deadline. We had to be there by a specific day and a time.

We finally reached Oakland and God said, "You have time to shower and change and be at the Golden Gate Bridge by six this morning."

It was already four a.m. Alex's friend told us how to get to the Golden Gate Bridge. We finally got on the road and were there at that precise time. I had purchased an eight-inch crystal and had it stuck in my belt. As soon as I took three steps toward the destination point it broke into two pieces.

"Oh no," I thought.

I felt it was either too late or there was so much negative energy in the area the crystal took it instead of me.

Alex stayed with his friend and it was Bear, Peter, and I, and of course, God, Jesus, Angels, guides and space beings that help with things like this.

We proceeded on to the area under and close to the bridge. We were dressed in certain white colors and there were people jogging by and others standing along a pier.

One said, "Oh look, a wedding ceremony."

So we let them think whatever they wanted. We even had to cut a lock of our hair to represent the male energy and the female energy of people and throw a few crystals into the water. We prayed for the people to be safe and for those who needed to live longer to be safe and if they need to move to another area that they get the message somehow to do so. We prayed there for about two hours.

When we left we could feel the energy changing.

And God said, "Job well done."

So I knew we were through and the earthquake would be less on the Richter scale. On the way back we saw Alcatraz from the shore but Peter didn't think that it was that.

"Yes, it is," I said. "I'll ask someone what place it is and see what they say."

So we drove just a few feet and a woman was sitting on this step of some sort.

I said, "Excuse me."

And she came over to the van.

"Can you tell me what that is over there?" I asked pointing towards the island in the bay.

"That's Alcatraz," she said.

I looked over at Peter and said, "See, I told you."

I looked back to the lady and said, "Thank you."

She looked at the video camera in my lap and said, "If you need a tour guide I can do it after I meet my friends. We do crack, do you have any?"

"No way," I said. "I don't even smoke cigarettes, and no thanks; we don't need a tour guide."

I told Peter to leave. She had her hand on the van and I told her, "You need to back up."

"I'm from Russia and I have drunk antifreeze and did (she named several dangerous drugs) and I am still living, but I need money," she said.

"You need a place to go and get off that stuff," I said.

"I can't," she said.

"I'm not going to give you any money for drugs," I said.

Bear started to growl and she lifted her hand off the van and backed up.

I told Peter, "Go; now."

And we went. We finally found our way back to the girl's apartment and went to sleep for a few hours. While we were sleeping, Alex woke up, turned on the computer and began surfing the internet. He discovered that some Native Americans out west also knew about the lava building pressure, and had felt the changes in the earth, and had started building giant medicine wheels to help prevent or minimize coming earthquakes. So, there were many kinds of people that played a part in slowing down or stopping the eleven-point-nine quake.

We knew we needed to leave when we woke up because they were planning some sort of party and said, "You can stay if you want to."

I looked at Peter and said, "Let's just get out of here."

I offered the girl some money for sleeping there and a clearing but she refused both. So we prepared to leave. We headed down the beach to seed some more crystals.

We were guided all the way from San Francisco to San Diego. Peter's nephew was in the Air Force there and we stopped and saw him for about an hour. We took him to a restaurant then we headed back across the mountains toward Arizona.

Finally, we arrived at Bonnie's house and got a good night's rest. The next day we started the three-day workshop. On the second day Bonnie and her daughter went and bought me a very nice, and very expensive, dress.

When I wore it to the workshop the next day, Jesus channeled through me and when the people touched the hem of the "garment" they could feel a lot of energy coming through.

Bonnie channeled one of her guides and almost passed out. We had to catch her. It was wild. We stayed a few more days and did a few private readings and clearings.

While we were there Bonnie took us to Mexico where God had us to seed some crystals there as well. God also had us buy a few things before we started home. He said we had to go seed some crystals at the Grand Canyon and the Four Corners area. We said our goodbyes and headed to the Grand Canyon. The energies there were not feeling right either. So Peter and I said prayers and placed the crystals where God told me to.

After that we started toward the Four Corners where we encountered the worse wind storm I had ever seen. There were a lot of dirt tornadoes and it felt like sand had gotten into my lungs. I was tasting sand for days. We finally got there and I walked to each direction and buried a crystal and said prayers in every direction while the wind was whipping my long hair all over the place. It felt awful. We finally got back on the road. We stopped at a country store and Peter bought a flute and a couple of necklaces for me.

When we could get in range with the cell phone I called Jason to see how he was doing. He had received some money from his grandmother so he could purchase some land and put in a septic system. Well, it turned out the people next door had stolen over five thousand dollars, his video game console, some games, some videos and trinkets from him and us – and the cops wouldn't do anything. I was so angry.

When we returned, Jason was a mess. Before we had traveled west, Kitty Cat had been sick with thyroid problems and losing weight. Jason told us Kitty Cat had died. I was so sad; I cried and cried.

"Pray his spirit over to the animal kingdom," I said.

And he said it with me over the phone. While we were praying, Kitty Cat opened his eyes and Jason freaked out.

"He's alive!" he yelled.

"Give him some water in a eye dropper," I told him.

He meowed and it sounded like he said, "Help me, Help me".

"I'll take him to the vet," Jason offered.

"Just sit with him and see if you can get him to eat a little soft food," I said. "Okay."

But the next day, Jason said he went ahead and crossed over.

"I said the prayer," he said.

He buried him in the back yard, so then we were left with Thor and Bear.

As for the people in the neighborhood, they only received two days in jail before the woman's boyfriend bailed her out. The police came over and I told them that our "neighbors" would sit on the steps smoking crack and doing other things out in the open; what made the situation so bad was that they had little children around them the entire time.

The only thing the police officer could say was, "We know about these people and we can't do much about it. And don't go inviting trouble or asking her to come into the yard."

I told the policeman, "If she comes over here on her own, I'll whip her tail."

He recommended I have a witness that she started it or I would end up in jail.

The next day, when the drug heads were out there smoking their stuff, I took my rattlers and sage and feathers and walked around our trailer shaking the rattlers and letting the sage burn really well and saying prayers out loud. And loudly enough so that they could hear me, I called on God to make all evil ones pay for what they did and to take them away from here.

In about four or five weeks they moved but only because they hadn't paid the rent or electric or water bill for a couple of months. But they did have the nerve to ask my son for money.

I spoke my mind to them face to face and they finally left. Later, several people told me that those people usually burned down other peoples' homes.

"Let them try; they haven't messed with someone like me," I said. "They will not get away with it."

I always prayed Jason would be safe.

He and I had been traveling one day when he looked over at me said, "Mom, I wish God would send me a woman that was tall and could love me for me."

On his birthday a lady called and said, "My name is Patsy. I heard about Jason from someone else I had met and I was wondering if I could meet him."

"Well…you can meet him," I said. "It's his birthday today; why don't you come over to his house for the party?"

She agreed and arrived at Jason's soon after. I introduced myself to her. Peter and Uncle Billy Ray were there. White Feather had to work. And a neighbor was there who had met Patsy through the same person who knew her and Jason. Everyone helped themselves to cake and soft drinks.

Well, Jason was kind of shocked by Patsy because I hadn't gotten a chance to tell him she was coming over. It was a great surprise; she couldn't have been more of who he was looking for if he had placed an order from a catalog. They started dating and after a while, I started hearing that they would be married in three months. And I told Jason, but he just kept saying, "You're crazy."

"I know what the spirits keep saying," I said.

He said Patsy had told him that they would talk about getting married in a year if they were still together.

"Well I say you will get married sooner than you think," I said.

And they were; in three months they were married, on March 25, 2005. I took pictures and cried the whole time. I don't know why I cried so much. It was like my baby was leaving me and I couldn't do anything about it. It was a strange feeling; I just felt overwhelmed. It took me a while to work through these strange and new emotions.

She moved in after they were married. I stayed with Peter. I missed Jason a great deal. I have adjusted to everything now though, although Jason did take Thor with him.

But I welcome my daughter-in-law and pray for both of them every night to be safe and happy.

White Feather and Uncle Billy Ray rescued this pup that came to their door in the middle of the night. She was looking up information on the internet when she heard this whimpering at the door. She opened it and saw this little hound pup.

They tried to find out who it belonged to but know one knew. Since they already had two dogs, a cat and four birds, the landlord said they couldn't have any more animals, so she brought it to me.

God said, "This will be your dog and you are to name her Amoria."

And so I did and we accepted her. At first, she was really shy, then she finally started playing with Bear. During this time I had given some readings and performed a clearing on this one man and his partner. Then one day he asked me to come and clear his house. So I did and during the course of the visit, I discovered he had these adorable dogs, several Yorkies and one four-month-old Lhasa Apso. I had always wanted a Lhasa Apso and she came right to me.

The mother Yorkie had had trouble giving birth so I did a clearing on her and I told him she would have pups again and be okay.

A few weeks later, I was driving home from the store and I heard God say, "Andy is going to offer you a pup."

"Should I take it?" I asked.

I heard, "Yes."

It was about half an hour later when he called and said, "Sha `La, would you like a pup?"

"What pup?"

He said, "Mattie."

"Mattie?"

"Yes," he said. "She and Mimi aren't getting along and I want Mimi to have her pups and I'd like to give Mattie to you."

"Why me?" I asked.

"I talked it over with Dennis," he said, "and we agreed you were the one to have her because she went to you and she didn't really connect with any of the others."

"How much?" I asked.

"Nothing," he said. "Just come and get her and I will give you the papers too."

"Is she registered?" I asked.

"Oh yes."

So I accepted Mattie and took her home. Peter was jealous of her for a while but now he plays with her all the time.

In July of 2005, Peter had to file bankruptcy; I was very distraught. We put all of our things in storage and I started calling about places to rent. I called this one lady and she asked me why didn't I try and get a house through a special loan. So I told her I didn't know what my credit was because I hadn't checked it in a while.

She told me to fill out an application and let her find out. So I did.

In the meantime, Jason and Pasty said we could stay with them until I could find a place. We stayed with them for two and half months. During that time Uncle Billy Ray and White Feather had some problems and divorced. She moved back to Arizona. He moved to Indiana.

About this time in September, Peter's daughter had a baby boy; he decided to come in at six months, a "preemie." We went up to Indiana for a couple of weeks to help her, so now Peter was a grandfather.

We looked at different houses but none seemed right. I told God I would like a new house with a garage and hardwood floors, carpet in the bedrooms, and located in the country but in an area that was easy for people to find me. As we went down the road and over in this new subdivision, I saw a sign in front of this house and I told Peter to go over there.

"Those are probably over the limit they will loan you," he said.

"No, there is one that they will approve," I said.

And I found the one I ordered from the Universe and God. After a bunch of paper work and rigmarole, I finally signed all the paperwork to have a new house that no one had lived in before me. The guy that built it had just finished it several months before I found it.

So in November of 2005 we moved in. In a few months, Uncle Billy Ray moved in with us and signed up for a new house also. It took six months for him to find a new one.

After he moved out in 2006, I brought my brother Walter down. He came for a week and we went to the flea market and got talked in to visiting a resort place. So we went and the salesman there talked us into buying a vacation time share.

I was going back and forth to the herb shop when I met a woman that also had spiritual gifts. She was partially blind; her name was Penny; she wanted to know if she could call me from time to time. I told her that would be fine; I gave her my phone number. She wound up calling me several times. Once, she called me while Walter was visiting and at a time when I was very busy with another person. I told her to talk to Walter because he was also psychic and could give her some answers. So they began talking and, after several conversations, we took him to meet her for dinner. They hit it off as friends.

In September, 2006, Walter became sick with bedsores and died *five* times. We, that is, Peter, Penny and I, went to Indiana to see him. Our sister Sandra kept talking to him to stay with us. My brother Ronald said this was one time Sandra's talking so much came in handy. We kind of chuckled.

I took my eagle staff and went in. I started my prayers and I saw his spirit trying to leave.

So I said to him, "You said you always wanted to go to Las Vegas before you died. If you leave now you will miss your trip, and we brought Penny to see you too."

And Penny started talking to him. He had to have a respirator to help him breathe. He could barely open his eyes. He relied on the respirator for three days but he eventually pulled through. Walter had to go to another hospital so a new machine could be attached to his hip to pull the infection out. We stayed in Indiana until he was stable. I made the reservations for Las Vegas for the end of April.

We went back to Indiana to take some Christmas presents to the family, Peter's and mine. But, Peter's mom became sick. She moved to Alabama to be with her older son; but she kept growing weaker and weaker. She passed away in February of 2007.

In April, Peter's brother distributed some money to the other three siblings.

Keeping my promise to Walter in mind, Peter said, "We need a vehicle to take Walt on this trip."

"Well, Tom's spirit has been coming to me and showing me this white bus," I said.

We were driving in Knoxville at the time and I looked over and saw it. I told Peter that was the type of bus I saw in the vision. So we went to look at it. Then down the road we saw another that looked like the first one but it had a better body and interior. And that's the one we bought, even though we did have to replace the transmission.

Peter started having more pain in his body and problems with his arms and legs going numb. He was finally sent to a specialist. They said he had to have neck surgery right away.

I asked my nephew Brandon to go with us to help me with driving and lifting things. And so he, Walter, Peter, Penny, Mattie, Bear and I went on the adventure. On the way we stopped at truck stops to park and sleep because the interior benches were fixed so we could lie down and rest. Brandon had a mat to put on the floor.

We drove to Santa Fe and saw the Loreto Chapel and the spiral staircase. We had to find a parking place because the chapel was closed when we arrived there. We cooked on this little stove device that Terri loaned us. She and Barbara had come to one of my channeling sessions and we met and became friends. She gave me a little notebook computer, and loaned us a cooler and gave us some homemade canned food to take with us. So we were cooking that using a hot plate when it blew the van's power converter.

We managed to get through it even though we all were tired and frustrated. Brandon went down the street to have a couple of beers.

The next morning we went to see the staircase and Walter said he saw two angels go through him. He said they must have taken something because he felt better.

We took some pictures and then left. I did most of the driving because of Peter's surgery. We were going to go to the Four Corners area but the road we took was extremely snaky. I somehow missed our turn and drove many miles out of the way; so we didn't go reach the Four Corners area. But we all were okay so we decided to drive on to the Grand Canyon.

On the way there, Brandon and I were the only ones awake and he was watching out for elk and other animals. He had really good eyes, probably because he was a hunter. But he sure spotted the elk in the dark. There were herds of them. I was exhausted and didn't see everything that he saw; but that was probably a good thing. I drove five miles an hour along the road that led to the Grand Canyon. We got there about five in the morning and then we parked and laid down for a short rest.

When it was about eight we all woke up and got ready for the day. We drove to many of the sights the tour busses visited. We were allowed to follow them in so it would be easier for Walter to see the sights. We got him out and took pictures and he wheeled around for a while. Then we got back in our bus and went to the next place and did the same thing. He had a great time.

We left there and headed to the white buffalo farm. We all enjoyed that too. We drove on to Arizona and saw White Feather for a few hours.

Then we were to be in Las Vegas at a certain time and although we got there about three hours late, Spirit said it was still okay. But they didn't have the handicap room for us so we had to use our own ramps to get Walter in and out of the room.

We slept and waited around the resort for the first two days. Then on the third day we went to the casinos. I only had one hundred dollars to split between Walter and Brandon. They won a little bit back so they played on it for a couple of days. We won tickets to see the show 'Stomp Out Loud'. And then we got to see the show 'The Rat Pack' for free.

On the fifth day we chilled out. Penny wanted to get a shower so I started moving towels away from the shower door when I looked down and saw what looked like a piece of dirt moving and Spirit said it was a scorpion. At first I thought I was just hearing things but sure enough, it raised its tail and I saw that it was a scorpion.

I just screamed and yelled for Peter. He and Brandon came running and they killed it. It happened so fast. Since we killed it, I said we had to pray it over to the light, and we did.

"We should have caught it in a cup and put it outside," I said.

Peter said it was a poisonous one and, sure enough, we found out the next day through the resort that it had been. I didn't sleep too well after that.

We finally left and drove on to California. I had written to the television network to get tickets for a well-known long-running game show. Some of the people there were rude to us and didn't want us to park anywhere. But finally it came time to go to the show; it was disappointing to me because you had to stand in line for most of the night and some people came there and stayed on the sidewalk all day and night and got in first and that is how they ended up getting in first. They picked their contestants from the first forty or so that were there. But we did get to see the host of the show, before he retired.

After the show, we headed toward the State of Washington, to see Penny's aunt. On the way there we stopped in Mount Shasta to re-fuel. While we were there, we began to smell this extremely strong perfume scent.

"What did you do Penny; take a bath in that stuff?" I asked.

"I thought it was you," she said.

Then it smelled like someone blew cigar smoke in my face and kept blowing it.

"Okay, we have to get rid of this," I said.

So I started calling in the light to anchor in the Angel to help these spirits over. I looked out the window and we all saw what looked like a bunch of zombies. It took a couple of hours to get them crossed over. I don't know where they all came from.

The one perfumed woman kept repeating, "My body is in the woods."

"God will have to get a park ranger to find your body," I said, "because it's dark and I'm not familiar with the terrain."

She acknowledged this and went on.

God said, "I will allow a couple of hikers to find her."

I don't know what happened after that. It was dark and what looked like a blizzard came, then our brakes went out. I let the bus coast down the hill and into the small town where I saw I could pull into a shopping center parking lot. When daylight came, I told a lady what had happened and that I needed a phone book to find a parts store. She said she would take me to one. So Peter and I got in her car and she took us to the store.

They had to order the part, but they finally brought it.

Later, we came upon a man whose vehicle had also broken down, so Peter went and helped him. I guess the Universe wanted us to help him for the woman helping us.

We finally got back on the road and took Penny to meet her aunt and her family. We found an RV park to stay in.

The next morning our battery was dead; so then we had to recharge it before we could finally get the van started. Once we had it running, we went to pick Penny up and started back.

We traveled a different route so we could see different scenery, stopping for a little while in Montana; the scenery there was beautiful. We stayed the night in South Dakota. The next day we went up a mountain to see some sights. We drove through a huge rock with a hole in it. We barely fit in it, but it was the only way to get to the top. We took pictures and then went to see Crazy Horse Monument, and then later Mount Rushmore.

After that we traveled to Sioux Falls. We finally found it, although it became dark about eight but we could still see the falls because of their street lights.

"Are you going to say a prayer or ceremony to help shift the earth bounds over?" Brandon asked.

"Oh heck, I left my tobacco in the bus," I said. "Give me a cigarette."

He handed me one and I said the prayers and threw tobacco and my aventurine bracelet in the water from the falls. Penny was taking picture after picture and then she had me take her camera and take some more. We all walked around and I could see and feel some spirits that were leaving. One grabbed my ankle and asked for help so I stopped and asked the Angels to come and help this one up to go to the light. They came and drew him up and out of the ground and took him on up.

After we left there, Peter said he was okay to drive so Brandon sat up with him while I laid down for a while. We kept trading out the driver's position until we reached Illinois. But once we made it to Illinois, we experienced two front tire blowouts. We finally made it to a store and bought some tires before they closed. Then we drove on to Indiana.

We rested for awhile then took Walter to his doctor for a check up. Walter explained to the doctor how he enjoyed the trip and how the mountains looked like a painted picture that you could just jump in. The doctor was glad Walter had been able to go on the trip.

The next day I left Peter at his daughter's house while Penny and I went to give a reading to a lady I knew named Janice, who lived near the river.

Well I did the reading but on the way back the bus broke down again. Just as Peter finally got it to run, the wrench dropped on the radiator and put a hole in it. So I had to beg the auto club and offer to pay more money to have us towed to Peter's daughter's house. We finally got it fixed and drove home.

June of 2007 arrived and I was being more and more encouraged to write about some of my stories so that maybe some of my experiences might help some people with their gifts, or at least give them hope.

CHAPTER 21
∞
THE CLEARING

Using the example of someone I will call Jeannie, the following is general example of a "clearing." She was a singer, but felt she couldn't accomplish moving further along in her career. She also had a twin. Her twin was outgoing and everyone gravitated to her; but Jeannie was not quite the extrovert and did not have quite the charisma of her twin.

Jeannie's clearing process began when she came in and I asked her questions about any existing health problems. I also asked if she had any metal in her body. I asked this because when I look into a body I see different energies and metal appears as a black blob; so do negative energies and entities. Of course, I don't want to take out something that is supposed to stay.

I also asked her if she had ever attempted suicide. I needed to know that in case her spirit had fragmented and moved to another dimension. If it did then we had to go and retrieve it.

I explained that her hands would then be checked to see if one finger appeared to be longer than another, indicating an attached spirit. If one was then we would ask that the attached spirit be escorted to the Light, especially if they were family, friend, or pet. For other spirits or entities that may be attached, we say a prayer that is a little different.

Then Jeannie laid on the massage table and I asked for the Light of God to come over her through the assistance of Jesus, the angels and the guides that work with me on this endeavor. I also asked Mother Earth (Singing Fawn) to release the gravitational pull for the unseen, then we proceeded with the clearing prayer.

I started with her feet and had Jeannie say an affirmation for that. This prayer would state something such as:

"I release all laws and judgments over me from the beginning of time. I forgive myself. I love myself. I am worthy and deserving of the finest and the best."

Then I pulled both of her feet toward me. I do this provided she doesn't have an artificial leg or hasn't had major surgery, or any metal implanted in the legs or thighs. If the legs are uneven then they should move back in place.

When a person is down on themselves or accepting negativity from others, the body tells me, "Well, the mouth is saying we are not perfect," so the hip goes out. When you say the affirmation then the hip can move back in place.

I worked up along her body; having her repeat a different affirmation for each part. When I got to her head, Spirit had me place both hands over her face because her face was misaligned.

I heard, "Have her release all laws and judgments over her twin and to state that she is safe and beautiful and can successfully accomplish whatever she wants."

And as she repeated that, her face moved back into alignment.

I asked her, "Did you feel anything?"

"Yes, my whole face moved," she confirmed.

After she recited more affirmations, she said she felt lighter and better. She later reported to me that she had the courage to travel and to stand up before people and sing; that people truly enjoyed her presence. Now she is invited to many places and other countries to sing.

So clearings can help people in many ways. The blockages that some people carry could be past lives or other dimensional debris that I see. The angels tell me which particular affirmation a person is to repeat to help them release emotional issues or karmic baggage so they can move on to a healthier, more productive life.

Illustration by Samantha Robbins.

My Friend Jesus

The following is a song I wrote about my friend, Jesus the Christ.

I was walking in the valley when I saw an old friend. He said come and sit down beside me; let's reminisce again. – He gave me hope and laughter instead of despair. We talked and laughed, and He said you will now understand – .

I love you, I need you, for all the world's sake. You will bring hope and joy to those who will remain. I will be there beside you all of the way. For I love you and need you for all the worlds sake.

I will bring you joy and laughter, hope instead of despair. I will lift you up and forgive you if no one remains. I am your friend always to the bitter end.

We will now work together until there's an end to all of the chaos in the world today.
I will stand beside you, walk with you and be your best friend. Jesus.

Printed in the United States
99661LV00003B/148-192/A